MADE IN CHINA

Women Factory Workers

in a Global Workplace

PUN NGAI

Duke University Press

Durham and London

2005

Hong Kong University Press

Hong Kong

2005

2nd printing, 2005

© 2005 DUKE UNIVERSITY PRESS

All rights reserved

Printed in the United States

of America on acid-free paper ∞

Designed by Amy Ruth Buchanan

Typeset in Minion and Meta by Keystone

Typesetting, Inc. Library of Congress Cataloging-

in-Publication Data appear on the last printed

page of this book.

This book is among a series of titles
co-published by Duke University Press and
Hong Kong University Press, a collaboration
designed to make possible new circuits of
circulation for scholarship. This title is available
in Asia, Australia, and New Zealand from Hong
Kong University Press; in the Americas and
Europe from Duke University Press; and from
either publisher in the rest of the world.

DUKE UNIVERSITY PRESS

Box 90660

Durham, North Carolina

27708-0660

www.dukepress.edu

HONG KONG UNIVERSITY PRESS

14/F Hing Wai Centre

7 Tin Wan Praya Rd

Aberdeen, Hong Kong

www.hkupress.org

To my mother,

Wong Wai Leung

and the

Chinese women

workers

CONTENTS

ACKNOWLEDGMENTS

Starting and finishing this book on Chinese women workers has taken me on a long journey with many detours. In retrospect, the book would never have been accomplished if I had not received consistent support from so many people. It is, first of all, a dedication to the Chinese *dagongmei* whose lives and struggles moved me and helped to weave together each and every thread of this ethnographic study. I am especially grateful to Yu Qin who assisted me in gaining access to the field site and in setting up the Shenzhen Nanshan Women Workers Center immediately after my fieldwork in 1996. Needless to say, it has been an immense challenge to create a home for the working daughters and it would have been impossible without the generous help of the dignified local people who deserve my greatest acknowledgment.

This book evolved from my doctoral dissertation, and I am most indebted to my supervisors and colleagues in the School of Oriental and African Studies at the University of London. I would like to express my special gratitude to Elisabeth Croll, who provided me with invaluable intellectual insights and guidance. Her pioneering achievements in women studies in China and her firm belief in solid ethnography inspired and directed me to the field in China. I am also very grateful to Nancy Lindisfarne, who has been a constant source of critical and reflective ideas and who shared many of my intellectual puzzles throughout the process of thinking and writing. I would also like to thank Mark Hobart, Kevin Latham, Jos Gamble,

Ku Hok-bun, Jens Franz, and the many others who provided stimulating discussions on the practices of anthropology and on postmodern challenges—my memory often draws me back to those days at the School of Oriental and African Studies.

I must also thank Lau Kin Chi, Yip Hon Ming, Ng Chun Hung, Thomas Wong, Lee Ching Kwan, Choi Po King, Stephen Chiu, Lui Tak Lok, Law Wing Seng, Hui Po Keung, Luk Tak Chuen, Leung Hon Chu, and all of my teachers in Hong Kong who introduced me to gender, labor, and China studies when I was first thinking about which direction to pursue intellectually. Special thanks should be given to Wong Tak Hing and Fred Chiu, who gave me invaluable inspiration in formulating this study initially.

This volume could not have been transformed into a book without the encouragement of Tani Barlow, who read the whole manuscript in its early stages. Valuable suggestions from two anonymous reviewers also helped to refine and sharpen my thinking throughout the revision process. Anita Chan and Jonathan Unger were the first to bring this ethnography to the public and have given me unlimited encouragement. Thanks also to Tan Shen and Shen Yuan for their help in introducing this study to a Chinese audience by publishing part of chapter 6 in Chinese. Special gratitude should be extended to Ann Anagnost, Li Zhang, Lisa Hoffman, Yan Hairong, Helen Siu, Bob Jessop, Sum Ngai Lin, and Chris Smith, who provided many insightful and critical comments in the later stages of revising the manuscript. I am deeply thankful to them.

I am very grateful to Alvin So, Bian Yanjie, Ding Xueliang, David Zweig, James Kung, Lin Yimin, Agnes Ku, and many other colleagues at the Hong Kong University of Science and Technology who inspired, read, and commented on chapters of this book and, most important, provided me with friendship and a warm intellectual learning community. Many thanks should also be given to Wong Siu Lun and Elizabeth Sinn, who at the University of Hong Kong Center of Asian Studies provided me with an amiable environment where I could continue my academic interests and studies.

Over the years I have also received meticulous support, concern, and encouragement from many good friends in the course of writing this book. Many thanks to Eva Hung, Anita Chan, Lee Kim Ming, Ng Siang Ping, Ng Kin Wing, Chan Yu, Puk Wing-kin, Rebecca Lai, and Merina Fung. William Chiu, Yu Xiaomin, and Caren Wong's final support in editing and assisting with computer graphics helped to realize this book project. Many thanks should also be given to Ryan Conlon who devoted care and patience in helping me to polish my English.

I owe my greatest thanks to my mother and my two brothers, who have always supported me in times of difficulty during the long process of research and writing. Without their love, patience, and understanding, this book would not exist.

Earlier versions of some of the chapters have been published elsewhere. Parts of chapters 4 and 5 appear in "Becoming *Dagongmei*: the Politics of Identity and Difference in Reform China," *China Journal* 42 (July 1999). Chapter 6 appears in "Opening a Minor Genre of Resistance in Reform China: Scream, Dream, and Transgression in a Workplace," *positions* 8.2 (fall 2000). Parts of chapters 1 and 7 appear in "Global Capital, Local Gaze, and Social Trauma in China," *Public Culture* 14.2 (2002). I am grateful for permission to include these materials here.

I don't know how I survived, but I am the only one who can be alive. All the women
from my village died in the fire. I still can't believe that I'm lucky enough to have
escaped the gates of hell.
—A survivor of a factory fire in China

On 19 November 1993, a fire engulfed a factory in Shenzhen, China, run by a
Hong Kong subcontractor to a European toy maker, a brand famous in both
U.S. and European markets. The blaze killed over eighty workers, all but two
of them female. Fifty others were seriously burned and another twenty were
injured. The tragedy shocked Chinese society as well as the international
community, as if it were the first trauma inflicted by global capital in reform-
era China and as if the mass media had suddenly awakened to acknowledge
the great costs to rural migrant workers that had been paid as the price of
rapid economic development.[1] However, the dream of modernity in Chinese
society—the great belief in capital and the market, especially after the illusory
promises of the Chinese state and the Communist Party—is permanently
inscribed with factory fires, which burn with the hopes and desires, as well as
the evils of postsocialist development, and in which the sacrifice of ordinary
people and subaltern classes are seen as a must for development. Chance had
brought me to meet one of the factory's workers, Xiaoming, who of all the
migrant women workers from her village was the only one to survive the fire.

It was both the survivor, Xiaoming, and the blaze, which caused the collapse of the factory building but never dashed the dreams of the young Chinese dagongmei, the migrant working daughters that drove me to write this volume. I am still not sure, however, whether it is those survivors who lived on with dreams and desires, or the fire and the deaths that most moved me toward the present book.

In assembling this inescapable social violence on women's lives, I started the long journey in search of a Chinese worker-subject within the trajectory of China's state socialist system's incorporation into global capitalism. I also wanted to articulate a possible minor genre of social resistance in contemporary China, a country that is rapidly transforming itself into a "world factory" for global production by providing to investors a great quantity of cheap labor and natural resources. Fire, pain, and memory flash across Xiaoming's life story, highlighting an epochal trauma and the social resistance that runs through the lives of dagongmei in this time of restructuring Chinese society.

More than ten years have passed since the blaze. Xiaoming's life still shimmers in my mind, offering both shadow and light as I try to glimpse the birth and struggle of a new social body—the dagongmei in a rapidly globalizing China. I met Xiaoming in a hospital. Her body was completely burned—all of her skin was seared and charred—but left behind was a pretty face with glinting, innocent eyes. She looked weak but very calm. During my visits, she told me about herself and her life in her village at home:

> Kids liked to fight, to jump, to sing. But I liked to dance, so I figured I could be a dancer someday. . . .
>
> It's not easy to get to my village. It's in a mountainous area that no train or bus can reach. You have to walk about an hour to reach my home. . . .
>
> I have no idea of how to go back home now. . . .
>
> People there are poor, but very simple . . . there is almost no trust in the city. I don't like city people.
>
> For a couple of years, I helped my parents by doing farm work and housework. Young people nowadays no longer like tilling the fields. I didn't either. Everybody said working "on the outside" was fun and I could earn a lot more money that way.
>
> In 1990, I left with some fellow villagers and took a job in a garment plant in Shenzhen. That was my first time looking for a job. I was very scared when I was given an interview and tested by the management. Many people competed for jobs in the factory, and I felt I was alone fighting for it.

I told myself to be grown-up, as I had to take care of myself with or without fellow villagers in the same plant. I was placed in a tiny bunk in the factory dorm and I knew nobody. At that time, I understood the often-said *ziwei* (feeling) of leaving home that means you have nobody to depend on but yourself.

But getting out for the first time was still exciting—the big city, the skyscrapers, the shops, and so many people. . . . It was like watching a film, and I was there. Everything was interesting to me, and I found myself to be very rustic and innocent. . . .

But I wasn't happy with my first job. The factory, which was owned by a Taiwanese boss, often put off paying our wages. We were supposed to get paid on the first day of each month, but they were often late, sometimes a month, sometimes two months. . . . At least the pay wasn't lower than in the other factories. I could make about 300 yuan [US$38] each month.

I left the factory in May 1991 and was introduced by my cousin to the toy company. It was a big plant. . . . We worked very hard, from sunrise to midnight, twelve hours a day. Every day I would be worn out, all my energy gone. . . . But I felt happy there. I had dozens of relatives and friends; we chatted a lot and helped each other.

From that point on, I never thought of working in another factory. . . . Every three months I could send about 600 yuan back to my hometown to my father as well as keep a few hundred for myself. I thought I could work there for at least another few years.

But then the fire happened, the fire.[2]

I never expected to meet Xiaoming, a twenty-one-year-old migrant worker fresh from a village in Hubei, a relatively poor region of China. Because I was worried that recalling memories of the fire would be too difficult for her, we chatted about her childhood, her family, and her work experience in Shenzhen. Many years later, after I had returned to the field site in Shenzhen, I still could not forget Xiaoming's face and voice:

> I was satisfied with my job in the toy plant. It was terribly hard work, but we had fun too.
>
> We had a plan. Before we went back home for marriage, we were going to save money to go to Beijing. It was such a big dream.

———

Social traumas such as factory fires adumbrate social violence in general, as well as the specific triple oppressions of the Chinese dagongmei by global capitalism, state socialism, and familial patriarchy that work hand in hand to produce particular labor exploitations along lines of class, gender, and rural-urban disparity. These triple oppressions—political, economic, and sociocultural—reinforce one another as they present new configurations specific to Chinese society at the opening of the socialist system to global production. While these oppressions are still attached to their own cultural and social conditions, they are rapidly shifting and being remade, eagerly looking for new matrices of power and practices to regulate society. The repositioning of China as a "world factory" in the new international division of labor is without doubt a project of global capital, which provides the bedrock for nurturing a new Chinese working class in general, and a new worker-subject, the Chinese dagongmei, in particular (Lee 1995, 1998; Jacka 1998; Pun 1999; Xu 2000). Cheap labor and low prices for land are not the only reasons for the current relocation of transnational capital to China. Diligent, well-educated Chinese women workers who are willing to toil for twelve hours each day, who are suitable for just-in-time global production, and who are potential consumers for global products are all factors that contribute to tempting transnational capital to relocate to China (Croll 1995; Davis 2000; Chen et al. 2001; Pun 2003; Yan 2003).

The lives of Chinese dagongmei have to be understood against this larger development, which consists of two reactionary forces in China. The first force is comprised of the changing modes of social regulation and political engineering of society by the party-state, and the second is the increasing capitalization or marketization of socialist society, embroidered with the hegemonic eulogy of the "search for modernity" or "quest for globality" and branded with the slogan *yu quanqiu jiegui* ("setting China on the track of globalization"). At one time the central component in understanding Chinese society was the party-state planning nexus. Now it is the party-state market complex—with its enlarged power blocs and blurred boundaries among political and business elites—that drives ongoing conflicts and tensions in Chinese society, inevitably generating new social forces and social resistances. The rapid changes in China in the past two decades—the opening of the country to global capital and the introduction of market mechanisms to rescue the declining legitimacy of the party-state, and thus the contractual engineering of society by both market and state—inflict double wounds and triple oppressions on Chinese society. The hybrid marriage of state power and global capital generates new forms of control on both the societal and individual levels. This time, land and labor, nature and human life, are all marketed as commodities for sale, not merely by the "capitalist" market but by the "socialist" party-state. However, the decentering of central power and the weakening of the ideological apparatus are far from representing a "retreat of the state" in regulating social life in reform China (Shue 1988). Rather, the worn-out yet still-existing *hukou* system (the population registry system); the parochial nature of urban governments with expanding administrative power; the strict control of the population and economic development; and repressive measures against independent labor organizations all dictate a specific process of proletarianization and struggle in contemporary China.

Transience is the dominant characteristic of the lives of Chinese dagongmei. Their stay in the urban factories is often short term—four to five years on average. This transient working life is not the choice of the women migrant workers but rather is a consequence of the legacy of socialist control and the residue of the Chinese patriarchal family. Structurally bound by the state, the hukou registry system ties the fate of the dagongmei to their rural place of birth. Thus Chinese migrant workers, often called *mingong* (peasant workers), are deprived of the basic right to stay in the cities, to establish families, and to enjoy proper education, medical care, and other social welfare systems to which urban residents are entitled.[3] This results in the widespread utilization of dormitory labor in the industrial or developing zones in Chinese urban areas, by which both foreign and local enterprises maximize working time and extract labor power without worrying about the reproduction of labor in the long run. Hence the temporary use of Chinese labor is institutionally legitimated by the Chinese state, whose hukou system, albeit changing, provides population and labor control that favors global and private capital.

The exploitative features of the system are further inscribed with local social and cultural configurations that perpetuate the temporary use of labor in global workplaces in Shenzhen as well as in other economic development zones. The Chinese patriarchal family, although rapidly changing in the reform period,[4] still seriously constrains the life course of Chinese rural women, especially in terms of education, household division of labor, wage labor, and the timing of marriage. The majority of the women migrant workers, who most often are young and single, still have to struggle to make their own decisions about wage work and marriage. A woman's mid- to late twenties is typically the point at which the family decides whether to allow a woman to work in the urban areas (Pun 2000). Beyond this age the delay in "marrying out" will be considered too high a cost to pay. Short-term wage work thus is expected in the premarital life cycle for most village girls. Quitting work for marriage and then returning to village life is still the shared feature of most migrant working daughters, although this common fate is not without resistance. The golden period of youth, between the ages of eighteen and twenty-five, is thus subsumed by the expropriation of global capitalism and the state socialist system, which is continuously in favor of urban and industrial development.

Taking a path different from Western proletarianization, the Chinese migrant workers did not launch open confrontations with capitalist management, nor were they able to become a significant political force, because any formal attempt to organize or form an independent trade union would have been vigorously suppressed by the Chinese government (Chan 2001; Lau 2001). However, although the formation of an organized working-class force was curtailed, if opportunities emerged the migrant workers did not hesitate to initiate short-lived, spontaneous strikes and collective actions that were generally unrecorded. Transience and liminality as the dominant characteristics of migrant working life also raised barriers to nurturing over time a collective class force in the cities. However, in a situation in which confrontational collective actions were severely contained and politically suppressed, a motley collection of transgressive actions, ranging from common workplace defiance to everyday tactics of resistance, sprouted and spread (see Liu 1996; Lee 1998b; Blecher 2002; Perry 2002).

Individual migrant workers like Xiaoming, the survivor of the fire, seemed to understand well their situation. Xiaoming knew that she would encounter the same impasse as other working daughters: a choice between a single life as a worker in the city and married life in the village. Nevertheless, she and her friends had other thoughts. They knew that after marriage they would be forced to stay in the village of their husband for the rest of their lives probably without another chance to work in the city.[5] Therefore, around the time of the 1992 New Year holiday, their wish became a plan: save money for a tour of Beijing, the capital, before they were married out. The everyday tactics of dagongmei, always lively, situational, and collective, composed a new symphony of migrant workers' transgression in contemporary China (Certeau 1984; Scott 1990). And thus Xiaoming began to save money for herself. By late autumn 1993, after sending money to her family, she had 500 yuan. One chilly day, however, the fire burned the money and the dream.

Social Actor or Class Subject?

Xiaoming's passage to becoming a dagongmei coincided with the social transformation that began in the early 1980s, as the state socialist regime of contemporary China launched the shift from a rigid planned economy to a market economy. The quest for modernity (or "globality," to use the new language) in China's postsocialist period opened Chinese society to private and global capital and allowed the capitalist apparatus and relations to regulate not only economic life but also social and cultural life. The first broad issue that runs through this book is that of the change in individual lives in the wake of China's search for modernity and globality in the reform period. In a society in transition, what does the hybrid mixture of state socialist and capitalist relations ask individual bodies to live up to? What sort of new subjects, new identities, and new relationships of power and resistance emerge?

In *Critique to Modernity,* Alain Touraine remarks: "We are all embarked on the adventure of modernity; the question is whether we are galley slaves or passengers with luggage who travel in hope, as well as being aware of the breaks we will have to make" (1995, 201). Alain Touraine highlights the paradox of the hegemonic project of globality by arguing that "the contemporary world accepts modernity by an overwhelming majority"; "almost all societies have been penetrated by new forms of production, consumption and communication"; and in some cases, "even when leaders denounce their country's penetration by the market economy, the people welcome it," especially among the poor or unemployed workers (1995, 201–202). An eagerness to articulate a modern imagination is demonstrated as much by the Chinese state as by the Chinese migrant workers. This process of globalizing modernity is by no means a simple process of universalizing new forms of production, consumption, and communication, and no doubt it requires more sophisticated studies that should seriously take into consideration the force of universalization on the one hand and of disjunction and cultural differences on the other (Appadurai 1996). Theorizing these two forces not as oppositional but as multilayered, criss-crossing, and overlapping, sometimes cooperating, sometimes confrontational, and sometimes retreating, is more helpful in trying to disentangle the competing forces in this process of globalizing China. And if "modernity at large" is a project too big for any single national or individual imagination to contain, then the argument for an "alternative version of Chinese modernity" based on a conventional nation-state or a political agenda of the state as a unit of analysis is also very problematic (Ong and Nonini 1997; Rofel 1999).

Becoming dagongmei, a journey of subject making in this project of modernity at large (Appadurai 1996), conjures up a new dialogic space where the force of universalism and the force of historical specificity and cultural difference can meet and collude in new configurations. The genealogy of the new subject, the dagongmei, derives insights from Foucault's "techniques of the self," in which he clearly argues for attending to "the procedures, which no doubt exist in every single society, suggested or prescribed to individuals in order to determine their identity, maintain it, or transform it in terms of a certain number of ends, through relations of self-mastery or self-knowledge" (1997, 87). Foucault suggests a kind of project that can articulate the intersection of two themes: a history of subjectivity and an analysis of forms of "governmentality" (87–88). On the issue of subjectivity, we have to ask how the subject was established at different moments and in different institutional contexts as a possible, desirable, or even indispensable object of knowledge (87). For the analysis of governmentality, what is at stake is not only performing the necessary critique of common conceptions of "power," or analyzing these as a domain of strategic relations focusing on the behavior of the other(s), but also as "the government of the self by oneself in its articulation with relations with others" (88). Nevertheless, Foucault's genealogical projects on the technologies of the self are inclined to highlight the detailed techniques of individualizing the subject, which somehow overshadow what he has argued concerning the "articulation of relations with others." If individuation is indeed the central "technique" of making a modern self, as many would like us to believe, it is high time to review this process not in dichotomized Western or Eastern contexts but rather so as to show how this process of subjectivization involves a project of both atomized individuation and relational subject making.

I do not intend here to suggest that the Chinese subject is more relational and therefore that the Western-oriented model of the individualized self is irrelevent to understanding Chinese modernity and its subject. On the issue of constituting the modern Chinese self as part of the project of modernity in general, and of turning Chinese rural migrant bodies into industrial workers in particular, there is always a complex dual process: an intensity of market forces geared toward an increasing atomization of Chinese individual lives, and a recurrence of social forces entangled in the meshes of *guanxi* (social network), *tongxiang* (native-place relationship), kinship, family, gender, age, marital status, and so on (Honig 1986; Hershatter 1986; Perry 1993;

Yang 1994). When Xiaoming was placed on the production line in the garment plant, facing multiple examinations and controls by management, she was no doubt displaced—separated from her family and tongxiang, who were also striving for jobs, and alone in facing the imperative of capital, whose techniques were oriented to individuation. The process of entering the factory at the beginning was a process of individuating the self, letting the individual realize that it had recourse to nobody but itself. This struggle was a social one, a struggle to become dagongmei, but its passage was that of a loner. Xiaoming highlighted that learning to be grown-up was to take care of herself with or without fellow villagers in the workplace. Indeed, aloneness was an overwhelming theme repeatedly articulated by the dagongmei in their diaries, letters, and various genres of literature.

While individuating the subject is a project of capital, practicing forms of collectivity embedded in social relations or enacted from cultural resources are also persistent "everyday tactics" of women working against market forces, both in early modern China and in the contemporary period. In early-twentieth-century China the formation of tongxiang enclaves in the Shanghai or Tianjin workplaces was an important means of generating social identities (albeit fragmented, fluid, and changing), and thus overt or covert social actions (Honig 1986; Hershatter 1986; Perry 1993).[6] In contemporary China, women in the foreign-owned workplaces and elsewhere are still very much encircled by tongxiang and kin networks that, although reimagined and reconstructed, often provide the most intimate and trustful supports. The distinctions between Cantonese, Chaozhou, and Hakka workers, or the outside workers of provinces like Sichuan, Hunan, or Hubei, still mattered most among the women workers themselves (Tam 1992; Lee 1998a; Pun 1999). The articulation of tongxiang identity is very much a project of cultural performance used by Chinese migrant workers as a counter tactic to the individuation project of capital in the process of Chinese proletarianization. The process of subjectivization—the making of dagongmei—thus involves the multiple elements of atomized individuation and certain forms of collectivity specific to Chinese society.

Embedded in specific familial relations, the lives of dagongmei in the reform period remain very much constrained while also supported by the rapidly changing Chinese patriarchal family. These patriarchal relations, as Stacey (1983), Andors (1983), and Wolf (1985) have argued, were never undermined by the socialist revolution in China. The patriarchal family was maintained throughout Mao's period by patrilocal marriage practices and the unequal sexual division of labor in the realm of work and household.

The post-Mao family, especially in rural areas, repeated and reenacted patriarchal relations by openly discriminating against female babies as the inferior sex and by continuing to pressure daughters to marry out in their mid-twenties (Davis and Harrell 1993; Croll 1995). For Chinese women, their fates as daughters and wives of men were extensively renegotiated, and although little collective resistance to the Chinese patriarchal family was recorded (Sheridan and Salaff 1984; Judd 1994), painful individual acts challenging family decisions about work and marriage were numerous in the workplace. Touching stories of escape, either from a father's or a husband's home, to work in the factory were often shared among the women workers.[7] Vacillating between industrial work and rural family, most of the dagongmei nevertheless opted for the former and dreamed of staying in the city as long as possible. However, when conflicts between these two realms were not overt, family and kin supports were still the last resort for the Chinese rural migrant workers who had nowhere to turn when problems or difficulties arose in their urban industrial work. Nevertheless, these familial relations and their cultural practices provisionally helped to keep the individuation process of capital in check and espoused a cultural difference in the process of subjectivization and modernity in China.

In addition to drawing on Foucault's insights on techniques of self, the Marxian analysis of class struggle, and women's studies of gender and labor, I turn to the work of Alain Touraine and his concept of "social actors" as I embark on this dagongmei project. Dagongmei like Xiaoming, working in foreign-invested factories, are pioneers in experiencing the deep and rapid social transformation of Chinese society—the change from an agricultural and state socialist mode of production to an industrial and capitalist mode of production. As women, as peasants, and as migrant workers, dagongmei are liminal subjects living in a shifting society. They can never be easily co-opted by any dominant language, whether intellectually or politically. As Ann Anagnost (1997, 17–44) puts it succinctly, "making the subaltern speak" as a revolutionary project in Chinese literary realism in the early twentieth century was paradoxically subsumed into a party-state parlance making use of an alienated category of Marxist class analysis. While the category of class no longer seems alien in reformed China, the making of the new worker-subject is still far more complicated than a conventional, or worse reified, Marxist notion of "class" can discern.

Maoism, in contrast, placed great emphasis on human agency and creativity and thus was antithetical to the orthodox Marxist analysis of class and society. The notion of class was no doubt alien to the Chinese peasantry who formed the base of the Chinese Communist revolution, and yet the Communist Party persistently proclaimed itself the vanguard of the Chinese proletariat. The arbitrary relationships between political symbolism and class subjects were too conspicuous, making the Chinese Communist revolution look like a postmodern project long before postmodernism came into play in the field of social analysis. There was too great a gap between the signified and the signifier, and the discrepancy sustained and yet at the same time defeated the language of "class" as a meaningful signification, while the language persistently and seriously affected the configuration of the Chinese subject status. It is no wonder that the political signification of socialist China required mass mobilization from time to time to cover up this discrepancy. The Chinese subject in terms of class identity thus was not understood as a distortion, but the interpellation of subject positions demanded a force if anything greater than the economic or material. The dialectics of class relations, Mao believed, required a cultural revolution.

The formation of the new social body, Chinese dagongmei, with all of their struggles—rich, heterogeneous, and multisited—can no longer be described or politicized as mere class struggles as the subjects experience, make sense, react, and project their life trajectories in contemporary China. It does not mean that class analysis is simply outdated as the language of class is now diluted by the hegemonic discourses of state and capital in the search for a global China. Indeed, it is not that simple. Restructuring class structures and relationships is a contemporary project for capital and the newly emerged elites in Chinese society. And yet the subsumption of class analysis in order to hide class positions and social privileges is their political strategy. The language of class is subsumed so as to clear the way for a neoliberal economic discourse that emphasizes individualism, professionalism, equal opportunities, and the open market. Thus the history of class in China is doubly displaced, first by the Chinese state-party and second by the market. The double displacement of class is very political in the sense that it helps to truncate the signification of class experience in rapidly shifting contemporary Chinese society.

As a weapon of social struggle class analysis, if useful, can only be reactivated by rooting it in class experience from below—that is, in the everyday infrapolitics of the Chinese workers themselves in confrontation with capital and the market.[8] Chinese dagongmei, caught in the impasse of triple oppressions, have to live out their own class experience as part of their life struggles. And if the Chinese subject has been traumatically interpellated by an alien language of class from above, then dagongmei, as one of the new subjects to emerge at the intersection of global capitalism and the Chinese modernity project, invokes a desire for a return to class analysis, which paradoxically became a dead language because of its hegemonic nature. I take care here to note that it was not class analysis as such that grafted onto the Chinese subject the effects of a hegemonic discourse, but instead the very nature of its political arbitrariness from above. If class analysis is already a dead language in today's China, the rearticulation of the new subjectivity, which I will describe below as *dagong,* in postsocialist China is nevertheless a timely project.

Becoming the Dagong Subject

Dagong denotes a process of turning individuals into working subjects, particularly for a capitalist "boss." The term *mei* further registers the working subjects with a gendered identity in a specific context. Imported from the Cantonese in Hong Kong, where labor relations are mainly regulated by the market, dagong simply means "working for the boss," a term that powerfully connotes the commodification of labor, or the exchange of labor for a wage (Lee 1998a). The terms dagongmei (working girls) and *dagongzai* (working boys), used extensively over the past two decades, contrast with the term *gongren,* the proletariat, a far more popular usage in Mao's period, and one that denoted a highly privileged class status in Chinese society that was out of the reach of the Chinese peasantry. The state propaganda stated that gongren, the proletariat class, were the masters of the country; they were not the alienated labor that Marx said existed in capitalist societies. The gongren as an ideal type was a new kind of subject produced by the Chinese socialist state to liberate labor from alienation and to fully actualize itself in the process of production. In reality, in the past three decades of state socialist experience the Chinese gongren worked virtually for the state, with the state as a "socialist boss" providing not only wages but permanent employment, housing, medical care, and education for the younger generation (Walder 1986). It was nevertheless a special type of state socialist labor relations that struggled to change capitalist labor relations.

Dagong means not just a departure from the socialist boss but also the coming of new bosses from global capitalist societies. No longer under the protection of the state, dagong also refers to casual labor—labor that can be dismissed at will, that can be replaced by anyone who is willing to sell his or her labor for a lower price. The value of dagong, if any, is determined by market forces and its surplus value is extracted as a component of capitalist profit. In other words, the term dagong signifies the change to capitalist labor relations and the dagongzai/mei is a new configuration imbued with an awareness of labor exploitation and class consciousness.

How can this new *dagong* subject develop its subjectivities and identities in a way that can be completely differentiated from its previous class subject—the gongren of the state socialist period? And how can the making of this new Chinese worker-subject derive dynamics and "life tactics" from below that cannot readily be subsumed into any single political agenda? Further, what modalities of transgression, individually or collectively, can be formulated without anchoring them in any "teleological vision" of proletarianization? These are the primary questions that form the core of this book.

Stripped of any essentialized connotation of class, dagongmei is a specific worker-subject not only embodied with production relations but also social and cultural discourses, consumption relations, social networks, familial relations, gender tropes, and social resistances. If the class subject is a project of othering, with an inclination to externalize onto others an abstraction that renders access to political maneuvers, then the dagong subject is a "return to the actor" who, as Alain Touraine argues, is "a call to transform the self into a social actor" (1995, 207), and as such strives to resist both state power and market forces.[9] It is a return to individual experience and the realization of the individual's position in relation to others. From that realization the individual decides to take action, either as an individual or as a collective. It is the firm return to oneself, and the mastery of the subject's right, that can be safeguarded against political arbitrariness. And if dagongmei is a female worker-subject, the social resistance generated by the subject should not be reduced to class struggle only, for it is not a workers' struggle as defined in the traditional sense, where the workers' autonomy and dignity against state and capital, and women's rights against patriarchal culture, are defended. As such, this collective resistance is at once a social conflict and a cultural project.

Subject, Desire, and Transgression

The episode of the factory blaze that I describe at the opening of this book contains nearly all of the crucial story lines that need to be disentangled in the chapters following. First, the great force of rural-to-urban migration meets with the advent of global production in contemporary China. Industrial capitalism simultaneously manipulates wants, lacks, and desires and enshrines them among the Chinese peasantry, who not only dream of becoming industrial producers but also modern consumers. The creation of desire and lack is an art of the market economy that, in the words of Gilles Deleuze and Félix Guattari, "involves deliberately organizing wants and needs (*manque*) amid an abundance of production; making all of desire teeter and fall victim to the great fear of not having one's needs satisfied" (1984, 28). The desire to be dagongmei, shown by the great flux of mobility to the urban industrial zones, traces the politics of capitalist production in manipulating social lack and generating the desire of Chinese rural workers to fill the void. This void, nevertheless, as the genealogy of the rural-urban disparities, regional and gender inequalities, shows, is historically and institutionally fixed by the Chinese socialist system (Perry and Wong 1985; Selden 1993; Solinger 1993, 1999; Stacey 1983; Wolf 1985; Croll 1985, 1994). The urge and eagerness of the young women to leave their rural hometowns, forms a picture far more complicated than the simple explanation that current migration flows in reform China are dictated by the logic of poverty or surplus rural labor (West and Zhao 2000; Zhang 2001c). Poverty, or on the other hand abundance (surplus labor), as crystallized forms of social lack, are produced and organized by the power of state and capital. Poverty, especially the huge gap between urban and rural societies, is artificially and historically made and, most important, is something that needs to be consumed and refilled.

The depreciation of agricultural work and its contrast with industrial production hinted that the politics of difference, hierarchy, and othering are involved in the process of producing the new industrial subjects of dagongmei (Pun 1999). Rural bodies, often imagined as rough, dirty, rustic, or lazy, are contrasted with the sharpness and dextrousness of industrial bodies who are often said to be young, female, single, and particularly suited to the new international division of labor, as illustrated by many studies on women workers and industrial capitalism (Nash and Fernandez-Kelly 1983; Kung 1983; Leacock and Safa 1986; Ong 1987; Lamphere 1987; Rosen 1987; Hsiung 1996). The constitution of new selves and identities is an act of power (Laclau 1990) and a process of self-subjectivization, exclusion, and displacement (Foucault 1988) that involves the deployment of institutional controls, disciplinary techniques, the art of naming, and the power of language (Kondo 1990). To construct new industrial subjects in the workplace, old socialist and rural beings are constantly devalued, downgraded, and forsaken. Rural bodies, especially non-Cantonese speakers, are imagined as abject subjects—that is, the dark flip side of the new, modern, and desirable identity. Existing social differences such as those between rural and urban, north and south, male and female, and married and single are all manipulated to maintain, extend, or modify the new power of domination and hierarchies. Dagongmei, as a new identity and as a cultural artifact, is produced at the particular moment when the global capitalist machine comes to fruition in post-Mao China; it marks the beginning of a new phase of proletarianization regulated by market, state, and social forces.

If Karl Marx has already pointed out that the division between town and country is the basis of the accumulation of capital, I add that sexual difference is another requirement, especially in the age of global manufacturing (Nash and Safa 1976; Ong 1987; Stitcher and Parpart 1990; Ward 1990). Mao's China highlighted class while negating sexual differentiation; reform China, on the other hand, is marked by the proliferation of sexual discourses and female bodily images (Croll 1995; Evans 1997). Capitalist production and consumption rely on a sexual discourse as the basis of the system of difference and hierarchy. Xiaoming was recruited not only because she was a rural migrant worker but also because she was a female who was imagined relative to males to be easier to regulate and control. Foreign-owned electronic manufacturing compounds in China are metaphorically depicted as peach orchards, where female adolescents wait for men to pursue them. The biopower of the production machine has no interest in a general body; it is interested only in a particular body, a feminine body, that is imagined as more obedient, tolerant, and conforming to the factory machine.

But dagongmei is far from a simple cultural artifact, an effect of power and discourse, or a gender construct. As a worker-subject dagongmei is a subject over which the process of subjectivation fights with the process of subject making and the struggle for a return to the actor. The political techniques of control over rural bodies meet with the tremendous desire of Chinese peasants to liberate themselves from their long-segregated lives, and hence act as agents in changing their lives. Dagongmei, as a specifically Chinese subaltern, embodies the dual process of domination and resistance and is marked by various forms of collaboration, transgression, and defiance that together come to make up its complex, dissident, and heterogeneous subjects (Certeau 1984; Guha and Spivak 1988; Scott 1990; Willis 1981). Dagongmei is formed of complex, dissenting, and tactical subjects who are up against a system of inherently incomplete domination, and who know how to locate fissures for transgression within the grids of discipline and power (Ong 1987; Kondo 1990). Before the disciplinary regime, no matter how powerless they are, dagongmei are more than simply docile bodies. Rather, they are also tactical and resistant bodies, confronting domination, sometimes covertly, sometimes overtly, and sometimes successfully subverting or breaking down disciplinary power. I do not want here to romanticize these "everyday life practices" (Certeau 1984) or "cultural struggles" (Ong 1991), but the stories and the experiences, the pains and the suffering, the screams and the dreams of the women workers on the shop floor reveal an intriguing portrait of "the politics and poetics of transgression" (Pun 2000).

Field Site and Field Worker

The field is a labyrinth for most ethnographers, and the attraction of the labyrinth comes from temptations that are often culturally and spatially specific. My urge to work in a factory and to act as a dagongmei is definitely subjective and loaded with ideological burdens. The search for identification with the female workers helps to prop up my intellectual and "radical" fantasy of resisting the irresistible advent of global capitalism. The work-place, I believe, is the "right" space in which the female bodies of dagongmei, this project, and myself will be properly situated. The mushrooming of global factories in the Shenzhen special economic zone demonstrates the rapid transformation of Chinese society over the last decade. These factories provide the best places to see how the microphysics of capitalist forces and state socialist relations produced the new subjects of dagongmei. I decided to intrude into one of them and start my nomadic ethnographic journey. The failure of Mayfair Yang's (1994) attempt to get into a factory in China by using introductions from state bureaucratic agents warned me against con-tacting any state organs. My identity as a Hong Kong person, rather, helped me to make connections with these factories, because more than 80 percent of factories in Shenzhen are owned by Hong Kong capital. The factory where I worked in Shenzhen during 1995 and 1996 was an electronics company owned by a group of Hong Kong businessmen. For anonymity and aesthetic reasons I named it Meteor Electronics Company, in response to a popular nickname that for me evoked the rapid changes and epic shifts in contempo-rary Chinese society. A good friend of my family, Mr. Zhou, was the major shareholder and the company director, and he approved of my research project.

My enthusiasm for working in a factory was somewhat cooled not as a result of the difficulty of getting access to the field but by the postmodern critique of the fieldwork experience and later by the daily negotiations in the field site. The postmodern critique as expressed, for example, by Paul Ra-binow (1986), says that there is no "field" as such, and thus that there should be no "reality" of Chinese society "out there" waiting for me to know and understand it. The knowing subject is not value free but is complicitous in creating known objects. Foucauldian insights tell me that the making of "truth" and knowledge is about power, resistance, and social practices. For me, it is clear that the "field" in China is neither "out there" nor freely and arbitrarily constructed by one's own will; rather, it is always historically, politically, and locally embedded and located. The field, for me in China, as a living text, as an orchestration of moving signs, is definitely not an arbitrary construct but rather is instantaneously negotiated and enacted by the political situation in China; the agency of the field informants; and my experiences and representations as a novice ethnographer.

My access to the field was made possible, nevertheless, by China's open-door policy, which was adopted in 1978. Ethnographers from the outside were in 1978 for the first time allowed to stay in China to do intensive fieldwork, albeit under official supervision most of the time. My research proposal, written for the factory management in early summer 1995, emphasized understanding labor relations and workers' psychology, and thus required that I work on the shop floor and sleep in the workers' dormitory. I received a response from management in August 1995, confirming that I could start my fieldwork in two months' time.

Although my proposal was accepted, a number of modifications were suggested by the company director, Mr. Zhou, who did so for health and safety reasons rather than because of political or other sensitive issues. He suggested that I work in the general office as a clerk rather than as a worker on the assembly line. For working hours, he suggested that I leave work at 5:00 P.M. and do no overtime work at night. Regarding accommodation and food arrangements, he suggested that I eat and stay with the Hong Kong staff in a shared apartment rather than with the local workers in the dormitory. Needless to say, it took me a long time to convince him that his good intentions would spoil my research if I could not work and live directly with the production-line workers. He simply took me for an idealistic student who had no experience of working and thus did not understand the hardships of factory life. In the end he allowed me to try it out for the first month and readjust my demands afterward if necessary.

When I finally became a full-time worker in November 1995, however, my ambition to go directly to the heart of workers' lives did me little good. I tried to present myself as a "student trainee" who came to learn the operation of the factory system and the lives of women workers, but still most of the line workers did not trust me during the first month. Instead, I was encircled by the supervisory ranks, such as department managers, foremen, and line leaders, who showed much curiosity and interest in me. These people were much more educated than the women workers and could imagine what research meant. Indeed, they often directed and delineated my research interests with their own imaginations. Surprisingly, I was heartily helped by these people, as they enthusiastically showed me their work and explained to me in detail what they were doing. At first I found myself too exhausted to cope with the long working hours because I was not yet used to them. Moreover, I was forced to develop too many "friendships" that I did not know how to handle. The relationships that I developed with the supervisory staff hindered my communication with the shop floor workers. I was always treated as a "special guest" in the workplace, which spoiled my dream of becoming a "real" dagongmei.

Fortunately, after the first month or two the managerial staff's curiosity about me began to wane, and as days went by I became "normal." Women on the line started to talk to me. They shared their hardships and feelings, hoping that I could understand them because I was working on the line and was willing to listen to them. My merging into the workplace community was significantly aided by staying in the workers' dormitory, where all private spaces were shared and little could be kept hidden. Trust was built as every day we chatted, ate, read, and listened to popular music together. While most of my coworkers or roommates could never make sense of what social research meant, they nevertheless had their own understanding and imagination. Writing fiction about "real" workers' lives and about poor people was the role they imagined and inscribed on me as an ethnographer. Thus "bitter" stories and female grievances, somewhat exaggerated or invented, started to bombard me, the never-failing good listener. On many occasions several women from the Hakka ethnic region talked to me with great passion in their local dialects for a long time, murmuring about their hard experiences of life while the entire time I understood nothing. I am fluent in Mandarin, Cantonese, and Chaozhou dialects, and therefore with the exception of those who could speak Cantonese, most of the workers talked to me in Mandarin, although with strong local accents. Cantonese was the official company language, while in daily life Mandarin was the most common language that workers of different origins used to communicate with each other.

My fieldwork in the factory ended in June 1996, at a time when I already had a lot of good friends and when I had started to grasp a few dialects that could help me to communicate with my coworkers with less difficulty. The nightmare-induced scream of a woman worker in the dormitory finally brought my fieldwork to a standstill as I became aware of the pain of ethnographic practice. In a situation where I had little time to write down field notes and, most important, to make sense of the shifting daily experiences in the workplace, I found myself lost. The eleven or twelve hours of work each day sapped all of my energy, and in the moments where there was still something left I preferred to use it chatting with my coworkers before we went to sleep. If there were a rest day on Sunday, everybody "slept like pigs" until midday and then went out shopping in the afternoon. Most of the time I struggled to get up early in the morning to write down what I thought was particularly important and what should not be forgotten; however, failure to do so was the normal case. Thus, I was forced to write field notes based on memory and afterthought, which gave me an acute sense that ethnography, after all, is a written construct. Ethnographic reconstruction is a never-fulfilled attempt to make sense: to order and reorder rich yet chaotic lived experiences that are inherently resistant to patterning and conceptualizing.

───────

The formation of the new worker-subject, dagongmei, is the central theme of this book. Dagongmei is a specific cultural-symbolic artifact as well as a worker-subject, constituted at the particular moment when transnational capital came to China in the postsocialist period. Dagongmei thus is a newly embodied social identity emerging in contemporary China to meet and resist the changing socioeconomic relations of the country and the needs of capital. As a condensed identity, it tells the story of how a state socialist system gave way to the capitalist world economy and of how capitalist practices depended on the regulation of class and sexual relations. As a worker-subject, it foretells the new configurations of social resistance and the coming of a silent "social revolution" from below.

In chapter 1, after a brief introduction to local changes in an industrial village in the Shenzhen special economic zone, I illustrate the making of the new Chinese worker-subject emerging in the contemporary period. In doing so I argue that making and unmaking are aspects of the same process, as the new Chinese worker-subject struggles to emerge in a rapidly changing economy in the postsocialist period. I try to elucidate how the newly formed "working class," born under the light of the Chinese socialist economy integrating into the world economy, is subjected to the workings of both market and state forces, and is specific to the form and process of its historical making. The specificity of the "new working class" lies in the paradoxical processes by which it is often deformed, or even killed, at the moment of its birth.

In chapter 2 I deal with the production of social desire, specifically the desire of the young rural women to leave home that drives them into industrial work. The puzzle in this chapter is that there is no violence, no coercive force, no misrecognition involved in the process of moving labor into the industrial world. Young Chinese village girls are well informed about life in the sweatshops and the hardships of factory life. Yet they are still eager to leave the village to sell their labor in urban areas. In light of this I reevaluate Marx's concept of the "alienation of labor," as further elaborated by the workers' subjective experiences and processes through which they actualize themselves as laborers. The huge waves of migrants moving from the rural areas to the cities portray the great hopes and desires of an entire society reorienting toward a market economy. Relating to this I look into how the workers' desires are articulated and produced, and why individual desires are so in harmony with the demands of industrial capitalism. I will also discuss how the women's desires are negotiated and reenacted between wage labor and family as these Chinese dagongmei's lives are embodied with a changing patriarchal culture.

Situating myself in the electronics factory, I discuss in chapter 3 the imperatives and techniques of the production machine in producing a social body: docile, disciplined yet productive, dagongmei. I show how the techniques of disciplinary power over the body (Foucault 1979) are deployed in the workplace of the Meteor factory. The study of the body, especially the female body, is particularly crucial in this chapter, as I show vividly how the production machine can work arbitrarily and violently on the lived body and how the body then reacts and resists. My interest in chapter 3 is in the modalities of power specific to Chinese society in the contemporary period. In addition to unveiling the microphysics of power over the Chinese female body, I look at resistance and practices of transgression in the workplace. Dagongmei is never the "docile body" but rather is the "tactical body" of agents who strive to survive, who can transgress in order to live in a newly oppressive industrial world. In this chapter I show the creative attempts of women to develop everyday life tactics to confront disciplinary power, such as forming kin and ethnic networks to assert control over work processes, manipulating hegemonic language to challenge factory regulations, or formulating innumerable informal codes of workplace defiance.

In chapter 4 I ask how dagongmei, as a new social identity, is crafted and then inscribed on rural female bodies when the young women enter into a particular set of production relations, when they experience the process of proletarianization and alienation. As a process of subjectivation, I probe the process and analyze the regulatory and identificatory practices inside and outside of the workplace. I then discuss how the production of identity deploys the art of metaphor, the power of language, and the politics of othering and differentiating. I also study how regional, kin, and ethnic differences are imagined to shape identities in the workplace. The central argument in this chapter is that the process of subject making, according to the principle of locality or ethnicity, is political and embodies rural-urban disparity and spatial inequality. Rural-urban inequality, as the major social difference in China, is manipulated, invented, and reinvented to create abject subjects in the urban industrial space. Local and kin-ethnic identities are seen as performative cultural artifacts and practical relationships that are produced at particular moments in specific situations. The politics of dialects, as a system of social differences, hierarchies, and distinctions, is also examined to disclose the struggle over power, resources, and identities in the workplace.

In chapter 5 I discuss the power, discourses, and processes of sexualizing bodies in the workplace. Sexed subjects will be seen as the effects of power and as constituted through a process of signification and resignification, differentiation and exclusion, in specific times and places. For Foucault (1978), the body is "sexed" within a discourse of sex that is itself an effect of a specific organization of power, discourses, and pleasures. In this chapter I try to link the process of discipline controlling the body in the workplace to the process of registering a feminine identity (gendering) at its nodal point: daily language, local practices, social discourse, and institutionalized regulations. I focus particular attention on conflicts embedded in the process of gendering, and the perversity not the homogeneity of the workings of disciplinary control on bodies. My contention in this chapter is that sexualizing laboring bodies is another necessary project of capital in contemporary China. Dagongmei as a sexual working subject stands in great contrast to the asexual subject of gongren in Mao's era. Dagongmei highlights the sexual reorientation in industrial work that is crucial to industrial capitalism. In light of this I discuss how the regulation of a sexed body is fundamental to the disciplinary techniques in the workplace and how individuals cope, negotiate, and transgress hegemonic control.

Finally, in chapter 6 I arrive at the scene of bodily pain: the notion of the scream and dream of workplace life. I trace how individuals are torn by the tensions between capitalist forces, state socialist power, and the local patriarchal culture; I show how individuals meet social violence and how bodily pain develops in the workplace. The painful body, I argue, is not the defeated body but rather the resistant body. Chronic pains, such as headaches, backaches, and menstrual pain, are pervasive in the factory and provide an index of social alienation and the domination of the female body. But as Arthur Kleinman (1995) has observed, chronic pain as the embodiment of human suffering could be viewed as the same process of embodiment of resistance to the lived flow of daily experience. Menstrual pain, the specific feminine experience, unravels the inevitable conflict between women's bodily time and industrial time. Julia Kristeva's (1986) insight is that women's time is periodical and cyclical in nature and thereby inherently contradictory to linear and progressive industrial time. Thus no matter how overwhelming the disciplinary power, the female body resists it through various chronic pains, dysmenorrhea, or fainting in the workplace. Scream and dream are the extreme limits of human experience (Bataille 1985), crying out the impossibility of human suffering and the possibility of human freedom. In this chapter I argue, following Foucault's (1985) reading of dreams, that struggling in the borderland between consciousness and unconsciousness the dagongmei's scream and dream is an attempt to achieve human freedom.

In chapter 7 I reflect on this volume as a political project and as the practice of a minor genre of resistance in China. The scream of dagongmei is an outcry in the present epoch in which state, capital, and patriarchal relations simultaneously inflict violence on society and individuals. It is also a scream directed at the age of reform and globalization in which the formation of a new working class has been given no space to articulate itself, as if the language of class were sentenced to death by the hegemonic project of the market. The nature of social violence in a globalizing China is highlighted so as to open up a call for a new theorizing of resistance that can go beyond individual and collective actions, nonpolitical and political engagements, local and global struggles, and the like. In chapter 7 I also foretell that a silent social revolution in China is underway and its members will be these new worker-subjects of dagongmei. The act of turning China into a world factory, with all products "made in China" by women workers, will certainly be met with a great force of resistance and social change. In my brief concluding section I mark the (in)conclusiveness of the project and I ask for an open and participatory reading.

1
_____

We are a mass of dagongzai
Coming from the north, coming from the west
At first we didn't know what dagongzai meant
Now we know, toiling from the sunrise to the sunset
Toiling with drops of blood and sweat
Selling our labor to the boss, selling our bodies to the factory
Do what they dictate to you, no negotiation, no bargaining, but obey
Money is the magic, and what the capitalists bestow on you
A commodity, a commodity
—A worker's poem found in the factory dormitory

I found the above verse, written with a ballpoint pen, on the wall of a men's dorm room at the Meteor plant when I stayed in the factory dormitory in late 1995. I was attracted by the verse at first glance, and I made numerous inquiries to locate its author, but to no avail. No one staying in the room would admit that they had written it, but rather suggested to me that the writer might already have left or that somebody might have copied the verse from a magazine. But the workers all said they loved the graffiti, emphasizing that the poem helped to "speak to their real situation and their life as underdogs." Indeed, during one such inquiry, four workers in the room circled around me and complained persistently: "We are not treated as human beings, you don't get it lady. We work like dogs and never stop. When the superior asks you to work, you have to work no matter when and where. . . . Who cares who you are? We are nobody, we are stuff." Although I was struck by the articulateness of their class positions, I protested and did not hesitate to argue: "You are dagongzai, you are certainly not nobody." Surprised by my seriousness, the workers fell into laughter and said, "What is dagongzai? Dagongzai is worth nothing. Dagongzai is only disposable stuff (*feiwu*)."

It is this painful confusion of Chinese migrant workers regarding their class positions and class consciousness that compelled me to try to make sense of the class struggles in contemporary China. A language of class paradoxically was emptied out, like a phantom of the past yearning to be alive even though it was dead. I was perplexed trying to understand the strange but cruel lived experience of class that was very acute for the Chinese workers and yet not discussed. The discourse of class was not only displaced by the hegemonic project of Chinese modernity but also widely abhorred by the common people, not only in the newly emerged urban middle class but sometimes in the working class itself. In this chapter, my first task is to figure out a geneaology of class, from Mao's China to the postsocialist period, contrasting the daily struggles of the workers in urban industrialized areas in order to make sense of the trope of "making and unmaking" of the Chinese working class in the reform age. My contention here is that this discursive dyslexia of class has a tremendous effect on policy and institutional controls on population and labor issues in China, and may not only constrain labor mobility, work opportunities, and settlement patterns but also the formation of the working class itself. We see a new Chinese working class struggling to be born at the very moment that the language of class has been sentenced to death. Indeed, the formation of a new working class in contemporary China has been checked structurally by these discursive and institutional effects.

The second focus of this chapter is to highlight the fact that the notions of class, class consciousness, and class struggle are highly contested, requiring sophisticated theorizing based on in-depth historical and ethnographic studies. In postsocialist China, we still cannot observe systematic and collective class struggles with formal political agendas working against state and capital, but this does not mean that there is no class consciousness germinating in this rapidly shifting society. As I demonstrate below, in China's first special economic zone, Shenzhen, a new generation of migrant workers has rapidly developed a range of examples of class awareness and understanding in the workplace. To situate this concrete daily struggle of class, and the processes of making and unmaking of class in contemporary urban China, I will in the pages following probe the change from a village commune into an industrialized zone in Shenzhen, where changing state-society relations; new forms of urban governance, market discourses and mechanisms; and the new social structures of the industrial village have generated particular power effects on the lives of Chinese migrant workers (i.e., peasant workers, or mingong) and their struggles. A new Chinese working class, struggling to be born alongside the Chinese socialist economy's transformation into part of the global capitalist economy, subjected to both the workings of the invisible hand of the market and the governmentality of the state, again is specific in the form and process of its historical making in contemporary China.[1]

Revisiting the Class Subject

E. P. Thompson, in his classic, *The Making of the English Working Class* argues that class formation is "an active process, which owes as much to agency as to conditioning. The working class did not rise like the sun at an appointed time. It was present at its own making. . . . More than this, the notion of class entails the notion of historical relationship. Like any other relationship, it is a fluency which evades analysis if we attempt to stop it dead at any given moment and anatomize its structure. . . . The relationship must always be embodied in real people and in a real context" (1963, 9).The subtitle of this chapter, "The Making and Unmaking of a New Chinese Working Class," is a trope or an irony more than a statement. Insights from E. P. Thompson (1963) have alerted me to the need to avoid turning the real lives of Chinese workers into dead data, patterns, or structures by the enunciation of a class language. Thompson's work makes two contributions. First, he argues against empiricist historiography, which ignores both the cultural and qualitative changes of "industrialization" and the political presence and agency of the working class. Second, he challenges the conventional materialist Marxists who would give greater priority to material determinations than to social or cultural initiatives, thus evading the complexities of agency and consciousness. Thompson offers the argument that class, far from being a structural determination, entails historical relationships, and that the making of the class was its own doing. According to Gregor McLennan (1982, 109), Thompson's volume is history from "below" not only because culture and popular mentalities are emphasized but also because of its moral and theoretical sense. The agency and varied experiences of the work-ing class itself provide clues for us to understand its making. Nobody except the working class itself is the agent of history.

While the agency of the working class is restored to the center, the neces-sary mediation between culture, agency, and the representation of the class is still seriously undertheorized by the Marxist tradition of class analysis.[2] Thus it has been subjected to criticism from poststructuralist studies that highlight both the politics of articulation and a project of decentering the subject that work against any unified or teleologized notion of class. Here I would like to stress two points: first, the politics of articulation is always historically sited, spatially situated, and culturally mediated in a particular time and space. The field of articulation is exactly the arena where all kinds of forces—state, capital, intellectual, media related, and last but not least, the workers themselves—will intervene and strive to interpellate the nature and forms of the working class. Maoism serves as the best example to illustrate how the politics of articulation forcefully "announced" and then shaped the Chinese proletariat in the socialist period. In Maoist China, class was formed without its corresponding subjects; the interpelling power was taken over by the party machine in order to create class actors.

My second point is that inscribing class with a telos is definitely problem-atic but, as Thompson has shown, class is as much a concept of culture and lived experience as of historical and structural conditioning. Like the con-cepts of gender and ethnicity, class speaks to a set of particular human relationships that cannot be declared by a unified category or subject to be the embodiment of an essence. As Don Kalb rightly puts it, Thompson, Raymond Williams, Eric Wolf, and many others all work with a relational reading of class to evoke the "dynamic, and sometimes even contradictory intersections of culture, society, and production," and address "their mutual determinations and conflictual interdependencies in reproducing a whole way of life" (1997, 5). Kalb holds that such a historical and relational class concept "offers the best possibilities for escaping the intellectual errors of reductionism, reification, and essentialism" as well as implying "a more open and contingent form of social class analysis" (6–7).

Accompanying a relational reading of class, there is another strong ten-dency to replace class as such by class struggle. McLennan (1982, 112) sharply points out that Thompson, in *The Making of the English Working Class*, has shifted from constituting the working class to the period of "class struggle without classes," for he holds the general view that abstract "class interests" are not fought over by classes as classes. McLennan further comments that in both *The Making of the English Working Class* and in Thompson's later work, there is an affirmation of the superiority of "struggle" over "class." Thompson is acutely aware that there were great discrepancies between the language of class and, in McLennan's words, the "popular mentalities of subordination" that were more inclined to a traditional "moral economy" (113). Studies of labor strikes tend to draw the conclusion that there is no class without class struggle and it is always in the process of struggling that workers acquire class consciousness and are thus constituted as a class. Fred Chiu clearly articulates this position: " 'Class' exists only while individual workers are intepellated and involved in a process of forming a collective identity—a particular historical moment when individuals consciously formulate moral-political positions and carry them into the battlefield of concrete struggle. At such moments—not earlier and not later—one can conceive of 'class' " (2003, 220).

While I agree that agency, along with active participation in labor strikes or labor movements, is an indispensable part of the production of "right" moments for constituting class consciousness, it is still not justified to posit class issues as class struggle, especially reified in the form of a collective movement. In my ethnographic study of the workplace, class consciousness is also constituted through everyday practices that may be performed anytime and anywhere and as such could hardly be reduced to moments of collective class struggle. The politics of articulation, from both the dominating and the dominated sides, involve techniques of condensation, displacement, and representation that are flexibly diffused and dispersed everywhere on the shop floor, and often simultaneously entangled with the language of gender, ethnicity, and urban-rural status (Perry 1996). No class struggle does not mean that there is no class consciousness and thus no class. There is obviously no direct correspondence among these three subjects, not even in an inverse order. A distinction between class in itself and class for itself is still useful for understanding the structural constraints and historical conditioning that always work upon agency.

The problematic of class analysis in China is not simply a canonical or disciplinary issue but rather is far more political. Subjected to reductionism, reification, and essentialism, the language of class was for more than half a century strongly linked to waves of socialist movements. If we say that it was Mao's revolutionary ideas that engendered a class struggle language in China, then it was Deng Xiaoping's reform that announced its death by replacing a modernity discourse with a promise to allow "a proportion of people to get rich first." "Speaking trauma" in the early 1980s, as an intellec-

tual project to disclose the "evils" of the Cultural Revolution, helped denounce Mao and his belief in class struggle in making history. A farewell
to Mao (and thus farewell to Marx) rapidly became the consensus. There is
no doubt that the postsocialist party machine turned its hegemony upside
down by targeting class language when the society itself was undergoing a
rapid process of capitalization and when class, no longer an empty signifier,
was going through a rapid process of making and remaking. The historical
paradox is obvious: the Chinese Communist Party, once proclaimed as the
avant-garde party of the working class, now turns the sword against its
constituency. The party machine now openly and sincerely invites capitalists, businessmen, and managers—the new social classes that emerged in the
reform period—to join its membership at the turn of the century.

New hegemonic blocs are forming—self-consciously pitted against the
language of Marx in general and class struggle in particular—that may still
shape the popular memory and history of Chinese socialism. Fashioned
with a neoliberal discourse of modernity, the new hegemonic machine is
geared up to denounce class as a relevant social discourse and refute Maoism, especially its tenet of perpetuating class struggle, as an obsolete and
harmful mode of thought. However, it is against this paradoxical historical
moment that the specters of Marx, in Jacques Derrida's words, are returning.
They have to come: as Derrida puts it, "The objection seems irrefutable. But
the irrefutable itself supposes that this justice carries life beyond present life
or its actual being-there, its empirical or ontological actuality: not toward
death but toward a *living-on*" (1994, xx). This had the "*visor effect*: we do not
see who looks at us," but "this spectral *someone other looks at us*" (7). A new
Chinese working class is struggling to be born at the moment when the
language of class is curtailed and becomes inarticulate. The new working
class is this spectral other, gazing at itself but expecting no one else to see it.
An orphan's fate is its misery as well as its luck. It is not only a matter of
making its own, but also a struggle of life and death, a chance of incarnating
this specter into life.

Making and Unmaking of Class in China

The worker's verse on the dormitory wall denotes this class struggle for life
and death—a journey of taking back its own agency and politics of articulation for making its own class. In this chapter I regard class not only as fluid
historical relationships but also as specific relationships that contain many
human tensions, multiple structural contradictions, and sometimes even

self-defeating elements. From the start this was a difficult journey because the process of making the new working class from the bottom was countered by techniques of unmaking it from above. The technology of unmaking is as complex as the politics of making, and we must pay sufficient attention to it in the form of the historical conditions and the art of governmentality in China. Making and unmaking are two faces of the same coin as a new Chinese working class struggles to emerge in contemporary China's rapidly globalizing society.[3]

The process of "proletarianization" in Maoist China, as Andrew Walder (1986) puts it, was unique in that political forces rather market forces dictated the entire process. Maoism provides a reinterpretation of Marx's class analysis in Chinese society by highlighting class struggles. As early as 1926 Mao, in his famous article "Analysis of the Classes in Chinese Society," argued that the reason for offering an analysis of classes in Chinese society was to identify enemies and friends for the Communist revolution: "Who are our enemies? Who are our friends? This is a question of the first importance for the revolution." He further states that "the leading force in our revolution is the industrial proletariat" (1965, 13). However, in early-twentieth-century China, the modern industrial proletariat only numbered about two million, and "these two million industrial workers are mainly employed in five industries—railways, mining, maritime transport, textiles and ship-building—and a great number are enslaved in enterprises owned by foreign capitalists" (18–19).

Mao understood that the numbers of industrial proletariat were still small in pre-war China, even though he had high expectations about the participation of this class in the revolution.[4] The subsequent revolution and the wars against Japan and the Guomingdang actually relied on the vast peasantry in the rural areas, who nevertheless were classified by Mao as semiproletariat, the surest allies of the proletariat (Schram 1969). However, after liberation it was the urban subjects not the rural masses who were proclaimed as the avant-garde of the Chinese proletariat, and thus the owners of the new China. One of the revolutionary goals of this new Chinese proletariat was to keep class struggles alive in order to safeguard the socialist revolution. The Chinese working class in the Maoist period, unlike its embryonic form in the 1920s, was formed within a short period—a few years under a command state economy in contrast to the English or other European working classes whose formation, dictated by a market economy, took at least half a century. Chinese subjects were interpellated to a "class position" or "status" by the Maoist ideology of class. The politics of articulation was so forceful that it had no difficulty overshadowing the obvious "misrecognition" of class in itself as class for itself.

In reform China, the class structure of the society, constructed by Mao, was rapidly shattered when Deng launched the reform and open-door policies at the end of the 1970s. The Chinese working class, previously protected by state enterprises or collective enterprises, was forced to smash its "iron bowl" when urban reform started in the mid-1980s (Leung 1988; Walder 1989; Sargeson 1999). Together with state bureaucrats, the newly emerged bourgeoisie and urban middle class looked to a neoliberal discourse of modernity to justify these rapid changes. The Maoist language of class struggle was permanently abandoned, and the privileged position of the Chinese working class was denounced. A new workforce was quickly filled with rural migrant workers who poured into the newly industrialized or development zones that constituted the base for global capital seeking to tap into the huge quantities of cheap labor in China. Thus a new working class—comprised of vast numbers of peasant workers from rural China—striving to be born as China entered the global economy, was manipulated by both the workings of capital and the state. Its fate was unclear and by no means a cause for optimism.

My contention here is straightforward: this newly formed Chinese working class, consisting mainly of migrant workers in south China, as in other economic developing zones in the north was structurally obstructed at the very moment of its birth as a class force. The hegemonic blocs had no mercy for this working class and attempted to contain it by various techniques of power. In what follows I try to establish the details of these hegemonic modalities of power—spatial transformation, state mechanisms, and state-capital nexus—in unmaking this newly born working class. This detour into the life-and-death struggle of the Chinese working class will be opened up in a specific locale in order to provide a close-up view of its history and spatial development.

Mapping the Factory in a Changing Community

"Shooting Star" was a nickname the workers gave to the factory where I worked, so I decided (for anonymity) to give it the pseudonym Meteor Electronics Company. On a normal day, everyone rushed to breakfast in the canteen at 7:00 A.M., and work would start at 8:00. It was a ten-minute walk from our dormitory to the factory, and the air was fresh and chilly on mid-autumn mornings. Dagongmei and dagongzai flocked together like

Figure 1. A workers' dormitory at a factory in Shenzhen. (photo by author)

Figure 2. The view from a factory in Shenzhen. (photo by author)

morning birds from the factory dormitory, talking and laughing along the way, passing the workers' dormitory zone, market streets, shops, clinics, and a large playground in order to reach our factory premises. There was a great contrast between the old and new buildings and our modern factory premises, which had been built in the early 1990s. Like the homes of other big companies in Shenzhen, the five-story building was furnished with large glass windows and air conditioners and was surrounded by a wall guarded by a huge iron-barred gate. The premises looked modern, elegant, and outstanding, signifying the coming of a new industrial world into the socialist land (Lee 1998a). Inside the gate of the Meteor plant there were over five hundred workers—the total ranged from 520 to 580 during my stay. Most of the workers were from rural areas all over the country and nearly 75 percent were female. The average age of all workers in the factory was above twenty, although most of the production line women were younger, usually only sixteen to eighteen years of age.

The Meteor factory is located in one of the industrial villages in the Nanshan district in Shenzhen, within the confines of the special economic zone. To preserve its anonymity, I call the village "Blue River." It is in the eastern part of Nanshan district, connecting the Shekou industrial zone and the main highway of Shenzhen to Guangzhou, the provincial capital of Guangdong. Nanshan is the former official administrative name given to it in 1985 when the Shenzhen special economic zone rearranged itself into three administrative districts, the Luo Wu, Fu Tian, and Nan Shan districts.[5] The local people call the district Nantou in daily conversation, and as an old town Nantou is famous for its ancient castle. After twenty years of rapid development, however, the sense of antiquity has been lost, and everywhere there is a mixture of new and old buildings. The commune era is also gone. In the center of the town is a marketplace where numerous fashion boutiques, department stores, hairdressers, bookshops, restaurants, and hotels are clustered. The "prosperity" of the town center evokes a rapidly changing society with all kinds of cultural symbols foretelling the coming of capital. High skyscrapers, a luxurious five-star hotel, and gated communities have sprouted among the shabby buildings of the 1960s. This hybridity, or in Foucault's (1986) term, "heterotopia," creates a telling example of socialist society meeting global capitalism, the result of which is a sense of anachronism. At night the place is crowded with factory workers who can only afford window shopping. Indeed, shopping, and most of the time not buying, was the favorite pastime of my coworkers. Production and consumption were the two aspects of city life that provided dreams and promises for the Chinese workers to live up to an age of modernity.

The arrival of the Meteor plant in Shenzhen highlights the advent of global capital in Chinese society. It also helps to bring out the hybrid sense of this development and the changing social relations of a local community. Meteor was set up in 1985, a year after Blue River village, formerly a rural production brigade, had undergone a dramatic change. Shenzhen was chosen to establish a special economic zone by the central state and the Guangdong provincial government in 1981, as a stepping stone for introducing foreign capital and as an experimental model to stimulate such growth in other mainland cities. Encouraged by the open-door policies and economic reforms, the local government of the village, supported by the Nanshan district government, decided to form a company in 1984. In the reform period it was not at all unusual for all local governments to set up companies. What is interesting here is that the local government of Blue River not only formed a company but completely turned itself into a collective enterprise in 1992: a production brigade formed in the 1960s in Mao's era became an industrial company in the reform period. The formerly named Blue River People's Commune became Blue River Manufacturers' Chief Company, under which it owned over thirteen companies.

The former government office building remained, but it was expanded to include a new wing of four stories connected to the old one. The "bureaucratic" structure of the Chief Company was changed and expanded as well, and now there was a general office, an external trade department, a finance department, an administrative department, a population and birth control department, a labor regulation department, and a mass organization division that included a youth committee and a women's federation and trade union. The company itself was a mixture of preexisting socialist "politics" and reform market "economics," a hybrid (if not absurd) reflection of the ongoing development of the socialist market economy. By turning itself into a company, the Blue River government gained complete independence in regulating foreign investment and local trade without any intervention from the upper governmental levels like the district government or city government. The local people believed that more freedom, more efficiency, and then more development would come if they could avoid possible "administrative intervention" from higher political forces. Blue River was not an exceptional case but rather represented a common practice throughout Shenzhen, as many rural towns rapidly transformed themselves into modern industrial enterprises during the 1980s and 1990s (Lyons and Nee 1994; Lin 1995; Christiansen and Zhang 1998; Oi 1995, 1999). In this process of transformation from a socialist production brigade to an increasingly privatized company, it was the local state rather than capital that acted as the force for capitalizing its own society. More than most, Blue River, as a local government and as a company, fully disclosed the essence of political economy. This mode of rural development in China's transitional economy, as Jean Oi (1995, 1999) might argue, is an exemplar of "local state corporatism," which highlights the power of the local state to incorporate rural society and peasant life into a state-society contract oriented to market-driven growth.

Blue River is also a complex cultural-political economy. As a Hakka ethnic village it is composed of a neatly woven kinship network that provides a foothold for the local power structure. The former village elites or cadres, now the managers, all came from the same kin lines if not from direct father and son relationships. Nan Lin (1995) rightly argues that village corporations in China are informally private because the governance structure is notoriously entwined with family and kinship networks. These networks often constitute the "trinity" of the local power structure: the party, the government, and the industrial corporation. Under this corporatist governance structure, Blue River village had a relatively homogenous local population of two thousand in the 1980s, which held a Shenzhen hukou, the household residence registration. Previously the local residents held a rural agricultural hukou and were officially categorized as peasants. Shenzhen urban hukou were granted when the Shenzhen government set out on a course of rapid change in this "backward" area. Land was distributed for less than two years in Blue River and requisitioned again in 1984 for industrial development. It was not confiscated at once as happened in the 1950s and 1960s but rather step by step, although in a speedy way.

In a casual meeting in a small restaurant, Mr. Zhou, director of the Meteor plant, described the area to me as follows: "It was really a backward place when I came here in 1985. Where we sit now was a paddy field; everywhere there were paddy fields and lychee trees. The people were farmers and very poor. But now none of them farm; they own shops or restaurants, do business, or work in the factory." Land was requisitioned with compensation; every household, according to the number of household members, was to be allocated a share each year of the yearly profits made by the Chief Company, formerly their village government. Time and time again villagers complained about the corruption of the Chief Company and how it was owned by father and son. Yet their grievances never ended up as direct confrontations, which elsewhere have been frequent in the Pearl River Delta zone villages in the past two decades.

One local shop owner talked openly to me when I was having tea in his shop: "I know there is serious corruption; the leaders of our village drive expensive, famous-brand cars and live in luxurious houses. But what can we do? It is they who make us rich." Every year, each household member obtained share dividends ranging from renminbi (RMB) 15,000 to 20,000 (US $1,800 to $2,400); the variations were seen as following the ups and downs of the company's earning capabilities.

A local cadre proudly told me that the money was "almost ten times what a family could earn before. Nowadays people don't need to do anything but just wait for their share dividend at the end of the year. What's more, the families are no longer obligated to farm, and they can choose to do business."

The local residents suddenly became rich, with their official identity changed from rural people to urban citizens. More strikingly, their economic status or class position was totally altered. They were no longer part of the agricultural population lying at the bottom of society in socialist China but rather a privileged class of urban people who held a valuable Shenzhen hukou living in the special economic zone. The living standard of the village was rising and was comparatively higher than other cities in China. Every family was well furnished with electric appliances, a color TV set, stereo, and air conditioners. But life was not without concern. Starting from the mid-1990s onward, increasingly more foreign capital moved out of the special economic zone to the much cheaper areas of the internal mainland. Foods, goods, and daily necessities there were relatively expensive. Indeed, prices were generally one-third higher than in Guangzhou and Shanghai and probably double those in other northern cities like Beijing and Tianjin. Yet as long as a family could afford it, they still preferred to buy imported foreign-label goods, even if they knew these products in fact were made in China.

The local residents of the area considered themselves as Shenzhen *ren*, or the people of Shenzhen, a broad cultural identity inscribing a modern cosmopolitanism onto the space and the people who lived there. Few would identify themselves in class terms, despite the fact that the local people enjoyed a middle-class or upper-middle-class lifestyle. The houses of the richest not only were large but were styled as modern, glamorous villas, their appearance mingling with a vulgar European architectural style. Anachronism colludes with heterotopias (Foucault 1986, 22–27), mirroring a sense of otherness not only of economic power but also of cultural superiority whose hegemonic meaning in China lies somewhere other than in anything "authentic." Some of the families even owned more than one or two houses and rented out empty houses or rooms to outsiders, most of them migrant workers. Wealth in the community was less determined by the ratio of working labor in the household than by the possession of political and cultural capital that could generate socioeconomic status (Oi and Walder 1999).

On the other hand, the majority of economic producers or the working class in the village were not local residents. They were temporary migrant workers who had moved in from outside the village. Besides the thirteen big factories affiliated with the Chief Company, all of the other small-sized companies owned by locals employed workers from other areas, especially from rural areas, both inside and outside of Guangdong Province. As in the Meteor factory, apart from three staff who held Shenzhen hukou, all of the Mainland Chinese staff and workers were hired as temporary labor and held a temporary hukou. Except for most of the engineers, technicians, managers, supervisors, and some office clerks who came from urban areas, more than 80 percent of the workforce formerly held a rural hukou, and thus were "agricultural producers" in the official categorization.

The workforce in Meteor, and in the manufacturing industry as a whole both in the village and in Shenzhen, was mainly made up of the rural population, who were only allowed a temporary hukou when they were employed by the factories in Shenzhen. A hukou is attached to employment, and once a migrant worker is dismissed or otherwise leaves the job, he or she is not granted the right to stay in Shenzhen. The socioeconomic structure of Blue River village was thus conditioned mainly by a two-tiered system. One tier comprised local urban residents who not only possessed the means of production but also the space, the right of abode. The other tier consisted of rural migrants who had to sell their labor to the factories in which they worked, while having no right to stay permanently where they worked. These migrant temporary laborers were almost ten times the number of the local working population, and they formed the lowest social stratum in the community.

In the case of Blue River, the question of whether economic reform in a state socialist system produces a genuinely autonomous civil society or rather a more symbiotic relationship between society and the state, posed by many political scientists concerned with changing state-society relationships, no longer seems relevant (Harding 1994; Pery 1994). Nor need we ask whether economic reform produces a supportive democratic and political culture in transitional China (Harding 1994). Elizabeth Perry (1994) is right to say that when we look at the changing state-society relationship in China, there are spatial and sectoral variations across time and space. Yet no matter how large the variations are, we can hardly find a case of autonomous civil society becoming established. For example, in Blue River village notions of people's power, rights of association, and civic culture are seriously disarticulated if not intentionally suppressed. This is not to say that the local state is not changing but rather that it is reconfiguring in a way of co-opting economic power as the presentation of civil power. The institutional shape of the Chief Company, previously the village government, is no doubt altered, and to an extent it looks like a hybrid form. But the inherent power structure based on a kinship network remains intact. The same kin in the positions of power, shifting from political capital to economic assets, still maintained dominance over the local society. During my time in the village I hardly saw a meaningful popular election or an act of collective decision making over the development of the Chief Company. The villagers, as the de jure shareholders, were often mobilized to support the changes of land use for industrial development and public infrastructure or the mergers between private and collective enterprises, but seldom could they oppose any major decision taken by the upper levels of the Chief Company, even when those decisions did not benefit the villagers.

In reform China the newly born bourgeoisie closely overlaps with the bureaucrats and intertwines with Chinese kinship networks (Bian 1994; Lin 1995). The complicity between the bourgeoisie and bureaucrats to form a state corporatist form of governance is perhaps the major force suppressing or disarticulating a new class language. The legitimacy of this corporatist governance is based entirely on the economic growth of the village and the general improvement of the living standards of the villagers. This implies, however, that market forces are often used to justify the social inequalities or disadvantages of certain individuals and families. In Blue River village the mounting wealth of the local villagers in recent years is often exaggerated and shown off to the nearby villagers or to outside visitors like me. However, increasing disparities in the community are often downplayed or denied, as is the expropriation of rural migrants as the cheap labor for local industrial development. In the eyes of the local elites, there is no such thing as class division. Rather, in an argument approved by the central state leaders, the situation is such that only a certain proportion of people who depend on their own abilities can get rich first, and the others lag behind at the moment. The hegemonic interest in displacing a possible class society with an open society, at least in Blue River village, is very clear. The subsumption of a class society into an open society is "imagineered" and highly regulated by dominant discourses, and thus should be taken as a political process that is often legitimated by reference to irresistible and invisible market forces.

Shenzhen as an Immigrant City

Shenzhen is an immigrant city that has been built quickly with a borrowed population. In 1979, after the Eleventh Plenum of the Third Plenary Session of the Central Committee of the Communist Party, the central government and the Guangdong government decided to upgrade a small town, Bao'an, to the status of a city named Shenzhen. Then in May 1980 the special economic zone was set up. Shenzhen thus became the first reformed city, erected as a test-case economic development zone open to global capital. Indeed, I chose Shenzhen for my study because it was the place where global capital and the socialist state first encountered each other and worked hand in hand (although not always in harmony) in forming and deforming a new Chinese working class.

Shenzhen is on the east side of the Pearl River Delta. In the north it is connected to Dongguan, in the south to Hong Kong, and in the east it faces Daya Bay, for a total area of about 2,020 square miles. The Shenzhen special economic zone (SEZ), with an area of 327.5 square miles, occupies only one-sixth of Shenzhen city. The SEZ is shaped like a triangle, and one can travel by bus across the zone in less than two hours. The SEZ is special not only in its economic aspects but also politically and socially. There is a long fence running east to west that separates the SEZ from the rest of the city. The "customer gate" is set up at the western end of Nantou district, and those who want to enter the SEZ require special permission from the public security branch of their local regions.

Before the establishment of the SEZ, Shenzhen was only a small town with 310,000 residents and less than 30,000 workers. In 1995, the total population was 3.45 million and the total labor force 2.45 million. Five years later, at the end of 2000, the total population had climbed to 4.33 million and its labor force to 3.09 million. Around 30 percent of its population composition is categorized as permanent residents who have come from major cities and become state officials, entrepreneurs, technicians, and skilled workers.

About 70 percent of the total is made of temporary residents, which means those who lack the official household registration entitling them to recognized citizenship in Shenzhen. In 2000, the total number of temporary residents was 3.08 million, which is equal to the total labor force in Shenzhen (*Shenzhen Statistical Yearbook* 2001).

It is clear that the expansion of Shenzhen and its special economic zone is based on the mobility of migrants as temporary residents (Andors 1988). Temporary residents from rural areas undertake most of the manual labor in the SEZ. In Shenzhen, when one becomes a legal temporary worker then one is entitled to be a temporary resident. All workers and staff members are placed into one of three categories: *guding zhigong*, regular workers and staff members; *hetong zhigong*, contract workers and staff members; and *linshi zhigong*, temporary workers and staff members. Guding zhigong refers to those employed by state-owned enterprises or government organs and they enjoy state welfare such as housing and food provision. Hetong zhigong refers to those employed on a contract basis by all kinds of enterprises; the contracts may last for three or five years. Most contract workers in Shenzhen are university graduates who are employed as technicians, skilled workers, or management staff. Linshi zhigong, temporary workers, are the most disadvantaged in Shenzhen, and it was not until 1988 that they were officially given temporary contracts on a yearly basis. In the second half of the 1980s the number of temporary workers increased rapidly and began to surpass the total number of regular workers and contract workers. Most of the temporary workers are employed in either collectively owned or privately owned enterprises, and especially in foreign-owned enterprises.[6]

Labor appropriation in Shenzhen as well as in other economic development zones is unique in its use of temporary labor from the rural areas. The mobilization of migrant labor or casual labor, which in China is termed temporary labor, is one of the most distinctive elements of capitalist development in both developed countries in the last century and in newly developing countries in the 1960s and 1970s (Burawoy 1976; Cheng and Bonacich 1984; Sassen 1988). Reform China, like other developing countries, depends on the mobilization of rural labor as the cheapest labor supply as part of the process of primitive accumulation in economic development. The use of temporary labor nevertheless was not common in Mao's socialist period but rather is a specific phenomenon in the SEZs and a significant developmental strategy in the reform period.[7]

The rapid economic rise of Shenzhen and the advancement of its position in the global economy is dependent not simply on the extraction of labor from the rural areas but more specifically on female labor. The process of "globalizing" Shenzhen depends on this female labor, which is the cheapest and most compliant, in the development of export-processing industries (Andors 1988; Tam 1992; Smart and Smart 1992; Lee 1998a). However, the official statistical data fail to show estimates of the sex ratio of temporary laborers as a whole as well as in different economic sectors.[8] Phyllis Andors (1988, 31–32) estimated that over 70 percent of the temporary labor force in Shenzhen was female. Josephine Smart (1993, 10) believes that about 90 percent (in 1989) of the total labor force in the light manufacturing industries run by Hong Kong capital was comprised of young female workers under twenty-five years of age. In my study of the Meteor plant, I found that all women workers except one were classified as temporary workers. No matter how long they had worked in Shenzhen, they could never become a gongren (worker), in the official categorization of status.

Techniques of Labor Appropriation

China as a state socialist regime is not unique in taking the initiative and bringing in global capitalist elements in the course of national development and promoting the capitalization of society (Frydman, Murphy, and Rapaczynski 1998). Like the reform programs in Eastern Europe, China, after the failure of totalitarian state planning, tried to usher in market mechanisms to solve social crises such as low levels of development, massive unemployment and underemployment, and declining living standards, especially at the end of the Cultural Revolution (Dirlik and Meisner 1989; Nee, Stark, and Seldon 1989). Shenzhen then became the point of intersection between a socialist state and international capital. As noted by Vivienne Shue (1988), the retreat of the state-planned economy in the Shenzhen sez does not mean that the socialist state gave over all of its power to market mechanisms or global capital. In Shenzhen, power was handed over to the local government, which tried to develop the city as a "world factory" site. The local government had no hesitation in imposing strict social controls for the purpose of purely economic development, even at the expense of "socialist" goals. It is in the gap between the dream of a big modern city and the desire to impose greater bureaucratization on the people that the complex, exploitative mechanisms of labor appropriation and labor control in Shenzhen were precipitated.[9]

In setting up *laowu shichang*, the labor service market in Shenzhen, the local state intervened politically on behalf of foreign capital in the extraction of labor. The state intervened not only in its administrative regulation of labor but also in its changing control of population migration and labor recruitment. The labor service market represents the reorganization of labor by the state to help it cope with the new international division of labor in its transition to a market economy. The labor service market can be divided into two parts—one organized and one unorganized. The organized labor service market shows the strategy of the state in regulating labor appropriation under its administration; the unorganized sector reveals the failure of labor control in the course of rapid development.

When the SEZ was formally set up in 1980, the Shenzhen Labor Service Company (LSC) was founded. The company is an official organ for labor supply under the control of the Shenzhen Labor Bureau. The purpose of the company is to regulate the transfer of labor from inland China, especially from rural areas to the newly established enterprises in Shenzhen. In the early reform years, migrants were not officially permitted to find themselves jobs without the mediation of the LSC and the regulation of the Labor Bureau in Shenzhen. At the beginning of the 1980s the LSC had the power to transfer labor legally from all provinces as required by foreign enterprises. In Shenzhen, each administrative district has its own LSC and Labor Bureau. These agencies formed a network for regulating the transfer of labor as well as the control of labor recruitment in Shenzhen. In the first half of the 1980s, about 250,000 laborers were transferred by the LSCs each year (Shenzhen Labor Bureau 1991). In the second half of the 1980s, the number of laborers increased by 350,000 yearly. The labor service market network was further developed with over sixty labor service stations formed in Shenzhen by cities and counties of Guangdong Province. These stations assisted with sending out laborers from their local regions and also helped to manage and control labor migration. Although the local state is active in allocating laborers, it is nevertheless dangerous to overestimate the capability of the state in shaping the labor force. The actual number of laborers supplied by the organized labor service market is still unknown.

The unorganized labor service market is far closer to the actual practice of labor appropriation in the Shenzhen SEZ. It is impossible for the local government to control the rapid increase of temporary workers every year through its administrative network (Andors 1988). It is well known that general labor recruitment is done privately without the regulation of the LSCs. Job seekers from the rural areas go from one factory to another to find opportunities by themselves, and employers simply select suitable workers from those seeking jobs. The labor recruitment history of the Meteor plant showed that at the early set-up stage, the company depended mainly on the local labor bureau to help them recruit laborers in large numbers. But after 1990, the need for labor grew constantly and the company started to hire workers privately. The practice is convenient and cheaper because the company does not need to pay service fees. The Shenzhen government does not and cannot prohibit such practices, but it has established new mechanisms to control labor appropriation.

With the rapid increase in labor migration beyond the control of the organized labor service market, in late 1988 the Shenzhen Labor Bureau created new regulations whereby private labor recruitment by enterprises would be recognized, if not formally accepted. The regulations state that all temporary laborers in Shenzhen shall sign a one-year temporary contract, and at the beginning of the year all enterprises in Shenzhen are required to submit their estimates for new recruitment, which then has to be approved by the district Labor Bureau. Thus enterprises are allowed to employ laborers throughout the year by themselves if the number is kept within a quota. In the case of Meteor, the employer was required to inform the Labor Bureau whenever they hired laborers and a sum was paid to the bureau to buy a temporary labor contract. When the contract was signed by both the employer and the employee, the Labor Bureau checked the quota then provided a temporary labor handbook for the worker employed, charging 50 yuan each. The handbook is a register of the background information on the worker, including name, sex, and date of birth, as well as education level, marital status, original place of residence, and duration of employment. The handbook is kept by the employer and when the temporary worker leaves the enterprise the handbook is sent back to the Labor Bureau. The government hopes that the regulation through the system of the temporary labor handbooks will enable it to control the migration of rural labor, including numbers and mobility, and thereby retain its macroplanning capability.[10]

Enterprises are supposed to renew these application procedures for every worker each year, which means that the enterprises pay the Labor Bureau every year. Moreover, enterprises are supposed to decide how many temporary workers they intend to use in the next year and then go to the district LSC to renew the certification. If the original place of residence of the temporary workers is within the Guangdong Province, at the beginning of the year the enterprises must go to the labor service stations, set up by different cities and counties of Guangdong Province in Shenzhen, in order to extend the use of labor (Shenzhen Labor Bureau 1995). Another lump sum of 20 to 60 yuan per laborer must be paid to obtain a card called the "registration of employment for out-going person card." The justification for collecting this money is that in sending out labor (although most of the rural laborers come out by themselves) to help Shenzhen's economic development, their original counties will lose productive labor. It is therefore reasoned that they should receive some compensation. If the temporary workers come from other provinces, the enterprises need not pay any money because labor service stations from other provinces are not allowed in Shenzhen. The Shenzhen government does not welcome labor from other provinces and tries to give priority of employment to labor from Guangdong Province.

However, no matter whether the laborer comes from within the province or from outside, after the application for a temporary labor certification, the enterprises must pay another 300 to 400 yuan for each worker they hire each year. Laborers coming from outside Guangdong Province have to pay a higher fee. This payment, known as *chengshi zengrong fei* (city increased capacity fee), is justified by the argument that the migration of labor increases the workload of management and the burden of urbanization. In order to prevent evasion of payment, the Shenzhen Labor Bureau every year sets up an inspection team to check use of labor by enterprises. If the enterprises do not follow the procedures and apply for the correct number of laborers used, and do not pay the city increased capacity fee, they are punished with a fine. There are, however, ways around these regulations; for example, at Meteor they applied for a quota of four hundred laborers each year and ignored registration for more than one hundred unregistered workers.

It is clear that the regulation of labor by the state is not only for the sake of pooling labor for foreign investments but, by appropriating labor for enterprises, to make a profit from it. Making money from labor control is not a secret. As a staff member in Meteor's personnel department explained to me: "These are only formal procedures. Actually, we can hire as many laborers as we like and whenever we consider necessary. In the past five years, we have hired all our laborers by ourselves. To inform the Labor Bureau, to apply for the temporary hukou and temporary labor permit is only a waste of time. Sure the bureaucrats of the local government depend on these to make money. We loathe these procedures because they do not do anything for us and our workers."

Thus for every worker that Meteor hired, the company needed to pay a total of RMB 400 to the district government each year. This was a seldom-noted invisible production cost, but the company paid for four hundred workers and therefore the amount was considerable: an additional labor cost of RMB 160,000 annually. Of course, this cost would be reclaimed from the workers they employed. In addition to the payment to the district government, the money paid to the local government of Blue River village is even more significant. The local government draws 30 percent of the total wage bill of the enterprises, leaving only seventy percent to go to the workers. In the case of the Meteor plant, every month the company paid HK$750 (US$96) per worker employed to the Blue River Chief Company, to which the Meteor was affiliated as a *sanlai yibu* enterprise, that is, a production-processing enterprise. The Chief Company then exchanged the Hong Kong dollars into renminbi at the official rate and returned 70 percent of the amount to Meteor as workers' wages. Thus, at the 1996 rate, for every worker the Meteor employed, the local government could earn about RMB 240. This kind of labor payment to an affiliated company, often set up by the local government, is common practice in Shenzhen. The rationale for it is that because the local government allows foreign capital to invest in their administrative domain, they need management fees to regulate labor and to provide land for factory premises and workers' dormitories. However, the labor payment is negotiable. Some companies have to pay more, some less, depending on the number of workers the companies employ and the guanxi, the relationship with the local government. It is quite clear that the local government makes a profit on migrant workers from outside the community, especially those from rural areas. By appropriating rural labor, controlling and selling it to global and private capital, the local Shenzhen state collected revenue and built a dual society.

Ambiguous Identity: Uprooting Class Force

Besides labor control, population control is another specific strategy of the Chinese socialist state in appropriating labor into global capitalism. Population control in China is effected by the hukou system of household registration, which was formally set up in 1958 when the central state promulgated the Regulations of Household Registration (see Zhang 1988). As Dorothy Solinger (1991, 8) points out, the hukou system in China determined not simply where a person could live but rather a person's entire life chances—his or her social rank, wage, welfare, food rations, and housing. In the prereform era, there was only one strict system of hukou: the registered urban permanent residence and the rural permanent residence.[11] Peasants, with their fate sealed by the rural hukou, were banned from leaving the land for over three decades. Although some managed to evade the system, in terms of numbers illegal migration was never able to challenge the bifurcated social order between the rural peasantry and the urban working class.

Shenzhen was in the early 1980s the first city to change its hukou system dramatically when it introduced provisional measures of control on the moving population. Besides the permanent household registration, a temporary household registration was established so as to hire temporary laborers. In Shenzhen the hukou system is well connected with labor control. When rural migrants are hired by enterprises and approved by the Labor Bureau as temporary laborers, after the payment of the Increased City Capacity Fee, the enterprises are to apply to the Public Security Bureau for a certificate of temporary residence registration and then to the local police station for registering a temporary hukou. Finally, the enterprise is to apply to the District Public Security Bureau for a temporary residence certificate so that their workers can become legal temporary workers in Shenzhen.[12] The temporary residence permit is for one year only, after which annual renewal fees need to be paid. Local government strategy is to change the use of rural labor regularly; officials have openly declared that if work exists, rural laborers will be allowed in and given a temporary residence. However, if the availability of work were to decline, such migrants would have to leave so that the local government would not have to bear the burdens of proletarianization and urbanization.

These techniques of mingling labor control and population control are also visible in the system of inspecting temporary residents. The inspection is carried out in the middle of the year with a search of all of the enterprises, including both foreign invested and locally owned. The purpose of the inspection is to ascertain whether the enterprises have applied for the quota of use of labor, completed the procedure of use of temporary labor, and applied for the certificate of temporary residence for all of their workers. If any enterprise were found not to have followed all of the labor regulations and not to have applied for the certificate of temporary residence for its workers, it could be punished with a fine of RMB 300 per month for a worker from another province and RMB 100 per month for a worker from Guangdong Province. Inspections were also carried out on major festival days to expel illegal temporary workers from the city. At such times of inspection, the Meteor workers were often very worried because they were never sure whether their legal status to stay in Shenzhen had been applied for and granted. And those workers who did not hold proper legal documents were advised by the personnel of the company not to search for work elsewhere in the city because they would be arrested by the police. Workers not holding legal documents were identified as "three withouts persons" (*sanwu renshi*)—that is, persons having no identity card, no temporary residence certificate, and no temporary labor handbook. These "three withouts persons" were targets of arrest in Shenzhen.

The existing hukou system helps to create exploitative mechanisms of labor appropriation in Shenzhen as well as in other cities in China. The maintenance of the distinction between permanent and temporary residents by the hukou system facilitates avoidance by the state of its obligation to provide housing, job security, and welfare to rural migrant workers (Solinger 1999; Mallee 2000; Zhang 2001c). The labor of the rural population is needed, but not their survival in the city once their labor power ceases to be necessary. Indeed, this newly forming working class is permitted to form no roots in the city. Worse still, the hukou system, mixed with labor control, is the specific modality of power that makes up the ambiguous identity of the rural migrant labor and deepens, but at the same time obscures, their exploitation. Are the temporary residents treated as urban residents or not? Are the temporary laborers regarded as workers or peasants? The answers to these questions are always ambiguous (Andors 1988, 40–41). The ambiguity of their status helps appropriate labor from rural areas without giving them the Chinese state's full recognition as laborers. As Solinger (1999) further argues, this has created a contested, if not deformed, citizenship, which has disadvantaged Chinese migrant workers attempting to transform themselves into urban workers. The term mingong—"peasant workers" or temporary workers—blurs the lines of identity between peasant and worker.

The contention here is that this process of proletarianization was launched by the Chinese socialist state when it allowed rural migration to meet the needs of global capital and national development at the same time that it constrained and contained the formation of this new working class. The developmentalist state contrived to impose capitalist mechanisms onto the socialist system while at the same time refusing, or unable, to undertake the costs of proletarianization and its generational reproduction. The blurring of the peasant/worker identity, or the subalternity of the newly born working class, is a strange outgrowth of the Chinese socialist state in its extraction of labor from rural areas. This modality of power is clearly shown by the Shenzhen Labor Bureau itself, as follows: "The major component of the labor service market is the temporary workers. Their characteristic is that they are active and flexible in the market. They are assiduous, hardworking, easily manageable, and economically productive. What's more they do not transfer their hukou [actually they are not permitted to do so]. If there is work, they come; if not, they go. This lessens the burden of enterprises, solves the problem of labor use, and at the same time does not result in urban overpopulation" (Shenzhen Labor Bureau 1992, 80).

Furthermore, education, housing, and other elements of infrastructure are not provided to the temporary residents by the Shenzhen government. Migrant workers themselves are not rightful citizens and, moreover, their family members are not allowed to live in Shenzhen unless they too can find a job and acquire the status of temporary worker. Marriage and childbirth cannot be registered in Shenzhen. Officially, these workers are still regarded as peasants and are supposed to rely on support from their families in the rural areas. Thus local government and foreign enterprises are able to reduce their burdens while at the same time make use of the rural labor for their own profit. The cost of labor reproduction is borne by the rural society. Migrant labor is distinguished by its transient nature; normally a worker, especially a female worker, will spend three to five years working as a wage laborer in an industrial city before getting married. The long-term planning of life activities such as marriage, procreation, and family were all expected in rural communities. As in other developing countries, the process of proletarianization in contemporary China relies heavily on the subsistence mode of agricultural production. China is an extreme case in that the process of proletarianization has been strongly dictated by political-administrative rather than market forces, and it was the political-administrative forces that helped to co-opt existing social relationships and economic structures into capitalist development. Given that there is a great labor surplus in rural China, it is almost unnecessary for the urban government to consider the long-term reproduction of labor.

Because this newly formed proletariat is not allowed to built slums in the urban areas, the burden of the daily reproduction of labor is left to the factory. Most workers are housed in factory dormitory buildings, with about fifty workers in one flat or house built of wood and iron sheeting provided by their employers. Even Mr. Zhou, director of Meteor, complained that "the Shenzhen government does not provide any housing and basic infrastructure for the workers but demands money for every worker we hire. The money is claimed for the so-called Increased City Capacity Fee. However, the city does not provide any facilities for them. Our factory still needs to provide food and housing on our own." Yet Mr. Zhou admitted that the company also benefitted from the status of the workers. Because the temporary laborers were not officially recognized as gongren, the factory did not recognize them as such either. Mr. Zhou said that the workers the company previously employed in Hong Kong were still under the protection of the labor law in Hong Kong, and thus they could not dismiss the workers arbitrarily without compensation. In Shenzhen, however, they could dismiss workers at any time; according to Mr. Zhou, "The labor regulations simply are not working here, nobody cares to enforce them, not even the trade union and labor bureau." This situation thus creates a space for global capital to extract labor surplus in China at extremely low cost.

In sum, the dream of developing the Shenzhen SEZ as a modern industrial city is dependent on the use of mingong, the rural migrant workers, from all over the country, while consciously or unconsciously the hegemonic discourse works to denounce their class status. The blurring of identity is a strange blending of exploitative mechanisms of population control and labor control, which helps to maintain the availability of a massive cheap and flexible labor force in the course of incorporating China into the global economy. A neoliberal discourse of modernity and development that justifies exploitative controls simultaneously contributes to the subalternality of this newly emerged Chinese working class, which is not even given an enunciative space to speak of its existence. What is at stake for this new working class is that the basis of its formation is uprooted because the right of abode of migrant workers in urban industrial centers is denied. Urban slums, places for migrant workers to organize themselves as a class force, are wiped out, despite the rapid growth of slums in some big cities like Guangzhou and Beijing (Zhang 2001c). Rural proletarianization in contemporary China is unique in that life as an industrial worker for every rural migrant is transient, and few have hope of changing their social status from peasant to worker. The growing roots of an enduring and substantial working-class force are dispersed when migrant workers are sent back to their rural hometowns. Administrative/political forces, (albeit in a chaotic way), together with the abandonment of class language, make and unmake this newly formed working class in contemporary China.

2

It was 4 March 1996, a week after the Chinese New Year holiday, and thus the day looked forward to by rural migrant workers hoping for the chance to be hired by a factory in the Shenzhen special economic zone. At 1 P.M. the gate at the Meteor electronics plant was surrounded by more than two hundred people, most of them women, hoping to get in for an interview. It was not hard to tell by their appearance that they were the mingong (peasant workers), members of the first wave of rural migrants who came annually, immediately after the Chinese New Year, to hunt for jobs in the city. In launching its economic reform, the Chinese state had decided to open not only the national door to foreign capital but also the urban door to its rural people. Thus Chinese society began to ride on top of a great movement—of economic systems, of political ideologies, of practices of everyday life, and of people.

The crowd stood fast at the factory gate. Three uniformed guards, tall and strong, each holding an electric baton and standing beside the gate, tried to maintain a seemingly impossible order. Two women from the personnel department, Ying and Jun, stood at the entrance examining the documents held by each job seeker. As they worked busily, they tried to explain the situation to me as I stood behind them. Ying stated: "We didn't put ads in the newspaper or on the notice boards on the street. We simply spread the news on the shop floor that we were going to recruit labor this afternoon. Now so many people come here, we can't handle them. Every year is like this." When I asked her where the job seekers came from, she replied, "Oh, provinces all over the country. But anyway, I'm sure they're people who have some relationship with our factory—maybe they are sisters, relatives, or fellow villagers of our factory workers."

Ying and Jun checked four kinds of papers: identity cards, secondary-school graduation certificates, certifications of unmarried status, and entry permits for the Shenzhen SEZ. As Ying told me, "Priority goes to the workers from Guangdong, who are at least sixteen but preferably eighteen to twenty-three, and who are single and have a high middle school education." Jun added: Nowadays, people can easily buy a school certificate at a low price. So it's difficult for us to tell the real from the fake. We need to judge not only from their certificates, but also from their appearances." Following Jun's eyes, I looked at the crowd, focusing on their faces and bodies. They were so varied: some tall, some short, some thin, some fat, and some with a more urban look than others. Whatever their appearance as individuals, the entire crowd had set their gaze in my direction. The only direction, the face of the factory, where gaze and gate met, absorbed all kinds of expectations into a single flow of desire—the desire for factory life. That day twenty people were hired. Then the gate was pulled down, leaving the crowd outside disappointed. With the new hires Meteor's total number of workers was up to 526, and they planned to hire fifty more workers later in the year. The previous year they lost about forty workers who had returned to their hometowns during the Chinese New Year holidays and never came back.

The twenty new hires were directed to a huge dining room on the second floor of the factory compound. Ying and Jun asked them to sit at the table, after which they distributed application forms for them to fill in. No guidance was given. After ten minutes, Ying and Jun collected all the completed forms and started the first round of interviews. Liu Siu Hua was the first one to be called. A young girl with a round face stood up among the group and came to the table. She looked firm but also a little nervous. Jun looked over her documents again, this time more deliberately in order to make sure that the information on age, place of residence, marital status, and education level corresponded in each paper. If Jun had any suspicions, she would not ask for any explanations but rather would simply send her off. The basic information was correct, so Ying started asking questions.

> *Ying* (in Cantonese): Can you speak Cantonese? You are a Hakka?
> *Siu Hua* (replying in Cantonese): Yes, at least I can understand almost all.

Ying: Our department heads all come from Hong Kong. You need to
understand them well.

Ying continued by asking about Siu Hua's past work history: the wages,
working hours, accommodations, and other fringe benefits that the factory
she worked for previously had provided.

Siu Hua: I did quality control jobs. I worked in X electronics plant for
more than two years. They paid me a basic wage of RMB 375 and
overtime of RMB 200 to 300.

Ying: What were the working hours?

Siu Hua: 7:30 A.M. to 11:30 A.M.; 12:30 P.M. to 5:00 P.M.; and 6:30 P.M. to
10:00 P.M.

Ying: Did they provide meals and accommodation?

Siu Hua: Yes.

Ying: They why did you leave?

Siu Hua: The factory moved to Guangzhou and we all lost our jobs.

Ying: Did you find a job elsewhere?

Siu Hua: No.

Ying: No? Really? You are so lazy then?

Siu Hua: I did try . . . but . . . but I got no interviews.

Ying: Hmm, go back to your seat and wait.

Siu Hua left the table looking uneasy. Ying put remarks on the application form, suggesting that Siu Hua meet with the quality control department
staff. Jun soon arranged for Ah Biao, the department foreman, to come to
the interview room. In his early thirties, Biao, holding an internal mobile
phone in his hand, looked confident and talented. He walked straight to
another table to read through the application form and the remarks. I
moved my seat to his table; he nodded, but gave me a look of surprise that I
was there. I was supposed to be working on the line in the production
department, but I had been granted leave in order to observe the process on
this first day of annual labor recruiting.

"Liu Siu Hua," Biao shouted. Siu Hua looked more nervous this time and
walked quickly to the table.

Biao: You are aged twenty, with two years of working experience. What did
you do in the factory?

Siu Hua: I did . . . I did quality control.

Biao: I know, but what tasks did you do?

Siu Hua: I checked the functions, the defects, and . . .

> *Biao*: Okay, okay, if I give you this mobile phone to check, what will you do?
>
> *Siu Hua* (more hesitantly, with her hand shaking while holding the phone): I will, I will look over the appearance, and check the function. I will follow the steps carefully.
>
> *Biao* (showing a little bit of impatience but laughing when he saw the shaking hand): What's the problem with your hand? You haven't eaten enough to hold the phone? Let me look at your hand.

Siu Hua stretched out her palm, small and soft. Biao held her fingers and Siu Hua wanted to draw back but controlled herself. She flushed.

> *Biao*: Oh, not too bad. I guess you didn't do farming work at home. I hope you didn't.
>
> *Siu Hua*: No, I did not do farming at home.
>
> *Biao*: So you are the lucky one. What is your schooling?
>
> *Siu Hua*: Middle high school.
>
> *Biao*: Completed?
>
> *Siu Hua*: Yes.
>
> *Biao*: Really? Then you should have the talent to recognize the English word "open." (Biao wrote down the English word on a paper, passed it to her and smiled at me.)
>
> *Siu Hua*: *bi*, "pen," isn't it *bi*?
>
> *Biao* (laughing): You said you have completed secondary school, and you can't distinguish between the word "pen" and "open."
>
> *Biao* (passing the paper to Siu Hua): Well, if you really have secondary schooling, write me ten English letters of the alphabet, starting from the thirteenth letter.

Siu Hua hesitated for a while, and immediately wrote down all twenty-six letters and simply crossed out the first twelve and the last three. We all smiled, and I thought she was clever, but Biao said that was always the way the silly workers did it. Siu Hua was told to sit back down and wait.

Ying and Jun finished the first round of interviewing and asked two people to leave immediately after looking at their certificates. Among the remaining eighteen people, sixteen female and two male, twelve were assigned to the production department, while six were sent to the quality control department for further interviewing. After the second round of interviewing, seven were asked to leave and the remainder were sent to see various department heads or assistants. Criteria for selection were set, although the guidelines were flexible and specific to the demands of the different departments and work positions. A command of Cantonese, a certain education level, previous work experience, nimble fingers, and a good attitude were all basic requirements.

Ms. Tang, the quality control department manager, a Hong Kong citizen, showed up at 4:00 P.M. Dressed in casual wear, she looked stout, energetic, and quite handsome. "Any perfect candidates? I want perfect!" she remarked. Biao did not give her a direct answer but said, "It's like finding needles in the sea." Five people were waiting to be interviewed by Ms. Tang. The interviews were to take place at the far end of the large common dining room, in a canteen reserved for the Hong Kong staff who worked in the factory. Biao and I sat beside Ms. Tang. Biao tried to provide Ms. Tang with as much information as he could.

Liu Siu Hua's name was called again, for a third time. She looked tired, fraught, and nerve-wracked as she walked to the table and sat down. Ms. Tang then said, "Sit Straight. Don't bend your back. You're not farming now, are you?" Siu Hua showed fear when Ms. Tang spoke. She instantly stretched her back straight and looked at Ms. Tang, whose voice turned soft when she was satisfied with Siu Hua's posture.

> *Tang*: You've got experience working in an electronics plant. How many models have you seen?
> *Siu Hua* (hesitated): Perhaps ten models, or more.
> *Tang*: Were the checking processes similar or different?
> *Siu Hua*: Quite similar.
> *Tang*: Did you do the bookkeeping yourself? Could you recognize those model names?
> *Siu Hua*: Yes, I did. And I seldom made mistakes.
> *Tang*: Hmm. I will give you a three-month probation period. During this period, the basic wage is RMB 320 per month and the overtime work is RMB 2.5 per hour. Do the rates sound reasonable to you?
> *Siu Hua*: Yes, Madam.
> *Tang*: Hmm. Then start working tomorrow. And if you are hardworking and skillful, I will shorten your probation period and adjust your wage. All right?
> *Siu Hua*: Yes, thank you.

Ms. Tang turned to me and said, "I won't waste time asking questions. I judge them more on attitude. It is politeness, honesty, and obedience that I value most, and it is their readiness to be a dagongmei that matters."

On the second day after entering the factory gate, Siu Hua fulfilled her dream of becoming a dagongmei in a modern industrial world.[1] She also made me want to understand the wishes and dreams that cause female migrant workers to leave their hometowns and enter the factories, and it is this desire to understand that forms the primary concern of this chapter. I am particularly interested in women's struggles between work and family, in particular their personal desires and struggles for dagong, together with society at large and the rural-urban migration of the past two decades. I also provide a close-up view of the extensive renegotiation by women of their gender role and performance in the Chinese patriarchal family, which provides support for their rural-urban migration as well as hindering their ability to leave. This suggests a complicated relationship between dominance and resistance that hardly can be dichotomized when examining the tensions and the struggles between marriage and family life in the village and waged work in the urban areas. As I will show, the daily struggles of both single and married women workers, contesting the gender performance in rural China, are recorded in the workplace.

Rural-Urban Migration and Familial Networks

Despite the structural conditioning of the formation of the new Chinese working class described in chapter 1, rural migrants continue to flow to the cities at a pace far greater than the state can contain.[2] According to the population census of 2000, as reported by *People's Daily* (27 January 2001) the total floating population is estimated at 120 million. Loraine West and Zhou Yaohui (2000, 4) report that during the period from 1982 to 1997 on a net basis nearly 112 million rural residents migrated to urban areas, an average of 7.5 million annually. Sarah Cook and Margaret Maurer-Fazio (1999, 1) estimate that in 1996 there were about 45 million migrant workers seeking jobs in cities and the floating population ranged between 70 million and 120 million. A study by Zhou Daming (1996, 75), which focuses on the Pearl River Delta, provides an estimate that the migrant labor population in the delta was 5 million in 1991 but reached 10 million in 1993, thus almost doubling within two years. Shen Tan (2000, 292) also based her study in the delta region and reports that among the total number of migrant workers working in foreign enterprises, about 74.7 percent were female. At the turn of the century a common estimate holds that between 80 million and 120 million rural laborers were searching for jobs in cities or in urban economic development zones, and among them over 10 million or more had found jobs in foreign enterprises in the Pearl River Delta area. There is thus little doubt that rural labor flows over the past fifteen years have launched a silent "social revolution" in Chinese society that is challenging the existing rural-urban divide, reconfiguring the state-society relationships, restructuring the patriarchal family, and remaking class and gender relations in particular.

Great efforts have been made by many scholars, both Chinese and Western, to help us understand the rural-urban migration phenomenon in reform China and thus the desires and dreams of dagongmei like Siu Hua (Wu 1994; Mallee 1996a; Croll and Huang 1987; Huang 1997; West and Zhao 2000; Sun 2001; Zhang 2001c; Sudy Group 2000). Nevertheless, migration studies in the early 1990s tended to look at macrolevel and structural factors, such as rural-urban disparity, the hukou system, the household responsibility system, and the surplus labor issue within the context of economic reform and rural development and their contribution to the number, characteristics, and destinations of rural labor flows.[3] Supplementary to the structural factors and the logic of rural surplus labor, middle-range studies in the late 1990s, based on county, township, or village-level surveys, contributed to highlighting the huge variations in rural-urban migration flows in China and called for more sophisticated studies to take factors of household dynamics and community development into consideration (Mallee 1996a, 2000; Huang 1997; Hare and Zhao 2000). Despite various contributions to the study of rural labor flows, however, these studies seldom look into the lives of dagongmei to examine their personal struggles over the experience of migrating to the urban industrial world.[4] This is not to say that familial and community factors are not important considerations when women make their decisions to leave their villages and look for jobs in the factories. Factors such as job opportunities in nonfarm activities in the village; specific family economic situations in terms of household income, assets, and the amount and quality of land holdings; the development cycle of the family; and the patriarchal culture of the rural community in general all contribute to negotiations for labor migration in general (Mallee 2000; Hare and Zhao 2000). But it would be wrong to assume that female migrant workers were the passive objects of the Chinese patriarchal family, sent out by their households based on pure economic factors and deliberate family calculations, without individual anticipation and struggle between work and family and without women's negotiations over when, where, and with whom to migrate and for how long. In the Meteor workplace, what often surprised me was that most of the dagongmei could not inform me of how much land their families owned or even sometimes provide a rough idea of the annual income of their households.[5] Because they were either kept detached or had attempted to subvert the familial grip of power, I found a few women who had escaped their natal families or husband's families to work in the factory without their father's or husband's agreement. Nevertheless, familial and community factors, acting as a complicated relationship of dominance and subversion, should be taken as major cultural conditionings and possibilities that produce chances as well as pitfalls for rural women to undertake factory work as part of the fulfillment of their life goals.

One of the most important, although paradoxical, dimensions of family and community that facilitated rural-urban migration and job-hopping for rural women was the configuration of familial and kin networks. As a consequence of social and cultural gaps between rural and urban areas, as well as serious discrimination in industrial areas, rural migrant workers showed their power and creativity in making and remaking their familial and kin networks in the village. As performative and cultural resources that migrant workers had to actively produce, these familial and kin networks with their open-ended and negotiable boundaries helped to facilitate movement and were especially significant in determining when and where to go. These networks, often nuanced, proved to be particularly useful not only in providing information about job opportunities but in introducing family members to jobs in the workplace (Honig 1986; Hershatter 1986; Perry 1993; Lee 1998a). Acting counter to the derogatory images of *mangliu*, migrants of blind flows,[6] these kin relations and networks provided clear migration routes and destinations before most rural migrants had finally made their decision to leave their villages.

An interesting phenomenon I discovered in my 1992 study of a garment factory in Shenzhen was that kin-ethnic enclaves were developed rapidly in the workplace and occasionally would be articulated in a honeycomb pattern (Pun 2001; see figure 3). For example, the honeycomb could start with two or three women coming from the same village, thus forming a core. Then, step by step, the core kin would help their family members and relatives from the same or related villages to find jobs at their workplace. These family members and relatives then form the periphery and continue to help distant kin and fellow villagers to migrate and thus enlarge the layers of the enclaves. Kinship and ethnicity often intersected in cementing group formation. Sometimes a kin enclave would be clustered with relatives from more than three or four villages in the same place of origin. Kin obligations were mutual and equal, but in a time of scarce resources they skewed toward the core members. Nevertheless, the boundary between core and periphery

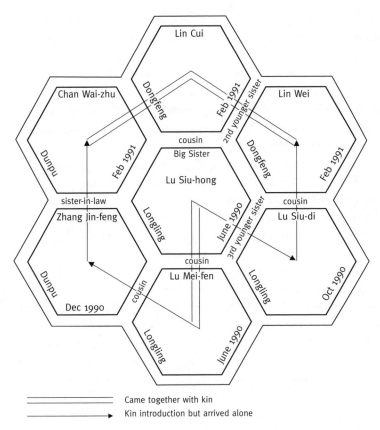

Came together with kin
Kin introduction but arrived alone

Figure 3. An example of the honeycomb pattern of Jieyang kin in the workplace, including names, villages, and dates of entry into the factory. (Pun 2001)

was not fixed but rather changed in response to the frequent movement to and from the factory. Indeed, the boundary would be changed, created, and re-created as time went on. The honeycomb shape could easily be destroyed, but it also could be rebuilt overnight when other kin filled vacancies.

The formation of kin enclaves and chain migration in the Shenzhen workplace is well illustrated by an example provided by the Jieyang group (a Chaozhou community). In this Jieyang group the position of eldest sister was held by Lu Siu-hong, which meant she held the highest status and was the most authoritative person in the kin enclave. This position was not exclusively about age but rather indicated who came to the factory first and who developed the network to help other kin into the workplace. Siu-hong and her younger cousin, Lu Mei-fen, the daughter of her second uncle, came to work in the garment factory in June 1990. According to them, the job-hunting experience was extremely difficult because none of their village kin worked in Shenzhen. There was only one distant relative, living in a different village, who worked in a bonnet factory, and when they went to look for her they found that she had already left and had left no forwarding address. After wandering for three days in the streets of the industrial zone and making inquiries at more than ten companies, they finally found work at Lung Garment in the Nanshan industrial district. Siu-hong said they were just lucky, but the others considered her a capable person because she was not intimidated by the situation and was daring enough to knock at every personnel office door in order to find a job.

After working at the garment plant for four months and getting used to the factory regime, Sui-hong started to arrange for her family members to come to Shenzhen. In October 1990 her third youngest sister, Lu Siu-di, who had graduated from junior secondary school in the summer of that year, arrived at the Lung factory to join her sister. In December, Siu-hong and Mei-fen introduced another cousin, Zhang Jin-feng (their aunt's first daughter), who lived in a village about five miles away from Lu's village. At Chinese New Year, Siu-hong and Mei-fen went back to their home village where they were welcomed by their family and the rest of the village folk. Besides bringing back 1,500 yuan, representing seven months of work, they offered many exciting stories of their experiences in Shenzhen. Their stories quickly spread to other nearby villages, and after the Chinese New Year two cousins from Dongfeng village came to find them and asked to be taken to find jobs. Siu-hong agreed and the two cousins, along with Jin-feng's sister-in-law, Chan Wai-zhu, went to Shenzhen. In this kin enclave it was clear that Lu Siu-hong and Lu Mei-fen formed the core, surrounding which was the periphery of Lu Siu-di, Zhang Jin-feng, Chan Wai-zhu, and the cousins Lin Wei and Lin Cui. Mutual obligation and the principle of reciprocity were presumed in the kin circle, and Siu-hong, as the head figure, was obliged to take care of all her kin at the expense of her own interests (Pun 2001).

My view of the epistemological problem of the concepts of kinship and ethnicity is that they are not fixed, inclusive categories in a structural-functional sense, but rather are performative cultural artifacts and practical relationships. These relationships are produced at particular moments in specific situations, and they are fluid, changeable, invented, and reinvented (Fardon 1987). In the Meteor workplace, the boundaries of kin-ethnic groups were resilient and ever changing and not strictly attached to reified cultural or geopolitical definitions. Individuals negotiated or identified themselves with a group of fellow workers according to situational needs in determinate settings.[7] Thus a term like *Sichuan mei* or *Chaozhou mei* could be expanded to include people from very different backgrounds, or narrowed to exclude quite similar individuals. Kin-ethnic boundaries were situational and shifting (Fardon 1987, 176). Geographical, genealogical, and cultural elements all worked together to weave a group identity and signify individuals.

Not all of the kin networks found in the workplace were shaped in a honeycomb pattern, however. At the Meteor plant there were many that were loosely linked and could be formed or reformed when different family members moved in or out of the workplace. Some groups grew stronger and better developed than others over time. But, as usual, the Meteor workers were brought in by their sisters or relatives for the job interview process immediately after the Chinese New Year. Siu Hua, the interviewee described at the beginning of this chapter, had three relatives working in the Meteor workplace, and one of them, her cousin, brought her to the factory. The cousin, who was three years older than Siu Hua, had already been working at Meteor for more than two years. She provided Siu Hua with temporary accommodation in her dormitory during Siu Hua's job search in Shenzhen. Providing a place to stay was considered one of the best types of assistance and one that Siu Hua often emphasized because she could never have afforded to stay in a Shenzhen hostel, even at the cheapest rate, which in the mid-1990s was 100 yuan per night. In this way, the bigger the gap between rural and urban areas, the greater the need for the dagongmei to manipulate informal ties and strategies to cope with everyday pressures. These ties of assistance in the urban area, often tied to familial, kin, and ethnic relations that were rapidly reconfiguring, silently rendered support to the social revolution from below by migrant workers in the city.

Rearticulating Women's Fate between Family and Work

The active rearticulation and reconfiguration of familial and kin relations among women in the workplace speaks against a large body of literature on Chinese women and the family. The literature tends to reify the Chinese family as a rigid system under which women's agency and subjectivities are thwarted. Since the literature posits a homogenous pattern of effects on women, it creates a fatalistic image of Chinese women, as if their low status were permanently rooted in the Chinese family system. Inescapably, Chinese women's lives, and hence their fates, are said to be confined within the patriarchal family, which is organized along male kinship lines and is patrilineal and patrilocal in nature (Johnson 1983; Kung 1983; Andors 1983; Stacey 1983; Wolf 1972, 1985). Women in traditional China were thus deprived of the means of production and the right to land, and their personal autonomy was entirely submerged under male authority, whether that of their father or their husband. As Kay Ann Johnson puts it, "The patriarchal-patrilineal-patrilocal configuration, in China, as elsewhere, made women marginal members of the entire family system. They were temporary members or future deserters of their natal families and stranger-intruders in their new husbands' families" (1983, 9). Women, then, were born into a system that structurally placed them in a vulnerable position where they were essentially powerless (Johnson 1983; Kung 1983). These interpellations of Chinese women as abject subjects, occasionally backed up by empirical studies, are exaggerated and stereotyped, however, and suggest an orientalist image of Chinese women who are always submissive, repressed, and even pitiful.

Ironically, the orientalist image of Chinese women was further construed by a number of critical studies on Chinese socialism and gender. Studies of modern Chinese women work to convince us that forty years of experience in socialism in China did not fulfill its promise of women's liberation, which was one of the major revolutionary goals in the course of socialist development. The Chinese road to socialism was nevertheless paved with patriarchy and male authority, whether intentionally or not (Johnson 1983; Andors 1983; Stacey 1983; Wolf 1985). Both the revolutionary strategies of the pre-liberation period and the development policies of the socialist construction era perpetuated and reinforced rather than destroyed the traditional family system and ideology. The reluctance of the Chinese state-party to vigorously pursue family reform goals and the failure to perceive and act on the patrilocal and patriarchal marriage system, these studies argue, maintained traditional male-centered family structures (Johnson 1983; Stacey 1983). The priorities of economic and political development overshadowed the goals of social change, even at the cost of sacrificing the promise of women's emancipation as understood as part of the Chinese socialist project.

A depressing tale of macrohistory was thus enacted and reenacted in its short-lived socialist construction: socialism and patriarchy could actually exist hand in hand in stable harmony, as imaginary and as real. A lesser hope in the reform period that never aimed at challenging the traditional culture, the patrilocal-patrilineal-patriarchal family system would only result in further consolidation, perpetuating an outmoded yet existing social relation. When land was restored to the household; when the household head, who was male, represented all female interests; when the men again controlled all the resources and means of production, women's rights and situation further deteriorated (Croll 1985, 1994; Davis and Harrell 1993). Worse still, women's fortunes were further denied by the one-child policy, which controls not only women's fertility but also their bodies, sexuality, and personal autonomy, thereby perpetually trapping women in the so-called patriarchal system. Consequently, neither socialist revolution nor reformist transformation liberated more space and power for Chinese women.

It seems difficult to deny that women in China are the victims of structural configurations, especially the seemingly never-fading Chinese family system championed by most scholars. Yet Chinese women are still far from being "family puppets," rendering their fates for someone to decide. Although powerless, they have been tactical agents in negotiating their own lives and in manipulating those exploitative forces for their own ends in the daily struggles. Put in specific moments and situations, like dagongmei in the workplace, Chinese women's lives were acted and re-acted in multiple and shifting ways, weaving a grip of social relationships embedded in various regional cultural forms, in differences in family economic status, in individual life cycle, and in the changing identity of women overall.[8] To manipulate an alienated living space, women could be active in organizing their own community—which Margery Wolf (1972, 9) called the women's community—once they married into a new village.

Women in the workplace also actively rendered familial and sisterhood networks to protect themselves by providing new connotations and significance to family and community. As woman, in the singular form, the female population was probably the structural victims of Chinese history; but as women, in plural and nuanced lives, their everyday struggles demonstrated their creativity and strength to reverse male control in certain situations. Moreover, the common view that holds that women in traditional Chinese society were restricted to the home and were never allowed to participate in productive labor is actually an exaggeration (Johnson 1983, 15). The record never shows a lack of Chinese women participating vigorously in the production sphere. Among poor peasant families, keeping girls at home was only an ideal that could rarely be achieved. A history of women as active players in productive work can be rearticulated when we examine some valuable historical studies that show that Chinese women engaged frequently in productive work and contributed a considerable share in meeting the needs for family survival. John Buck, in his research on China's land utilization in the 1930s, estimated that women comprised more than 16 percent of labor used in farmwork (1937, 303). Hsiao-tung Fei and Chih-I Chang (1945), in their study of Chinese villages in Yunnan Province in the same period, also reported that women played an active role in the family economy and sometimes even did more farming work than men.

Women not only undertook farming work but also a variety of other jobs. In the late 1920s Hakka women in southern China, some of whom were over forty years old, performed a range of transport work such as carrying coal, charcoal, steel, and cement for construction (Johnson 1984). Women were successful at peddling because women peddlers were allowed to enter the houses of affluent families, according to Ida Pruitt's (1967, 175) story of a Han daughter. Women were also active in home industries such as weaving and spinning, and in doing so they could contribute income equal to men's share from farming. Evelyn Rawski's (1972, 47) study shows that a skilled home weaver could weave a bolt of cotton cloth every four or five days, the value of which was equal to one sixth of the annual production from one acre of fertile land. Rawski goes on to point out that in Suzhou a woman weaver could earn twenty silver liang a year, while a hired laborer for farming would be paid only 13 liang a year (1972, 55).

Since the early twentieth century, women in the Pearl River Delta were famous for participating in silk production, where many earned a considerable wage from harvesting mulberry leaves, raising silkworms, and reeling silk (Topley 1975; Stockard 1989). This income provided not only the economic base but also the power for women to develop many marriage-resistance strategies, and it contributed to the rise of the famous compensation marriage in the delta, especially in the Sunde region. While women in the Canton area were active in the silk industries, those in Shanghai in the pre-1949 period were already predominant in the early development of the textile industry. Emily Honig, in her study of Shanghai women workers, states: "In Shanghai, China's largest industrial center prior to 1949, cotton was king and the majority of mill workers were women. Including those employed in the silk and tobacco factories, women accounted for almost two-thirds of the total industrial work force in Shanghai" (1986, 1). These early working daughters presaged women's active role in a great diversity of productive work, challenging the common assumption that held Chinese women to be passive and economically dependent.

Although far from an abrupt reversal of the patriarchal structure, this active participation in economic roles did provide room for renegotiating women's power in the family. Honig's findings refuted the belief that women's status would be increased greatly simply because their wages contributed to the family (170). The findings in early Shanghai were echoed by Janet Salaff's (1981) and Lydia Kung's (1983) studies of their counterparts in Hong Kong and in Taiwan in the 1960s and 1970s. These studies also argue that women's participation in industrial work and wage labor did not contribute much to a significant increase in women's power and status within the family. Further, recent studies on modern and contemporary Chinese women workers also show no trace of a breakthrough in enhancing women's power at home or in society through contributions to their family income (Lee 1998; Rofel 1999). However, the fact that women workers, especially those from rural areas, were still under the control or support of the family, did not mean that patriarchal relations and culture were not under attack, or at least undergoing rapid renegotiation and remaking. The workers in the Meteor workplace often were proud of their earning capacities, their work skills, and their dagong identities. Attempts at transgression, such as escape to work in the city or refusal to go back home for marriage, worked to challenge the patriarchal power of the family and submissive images of Chinese women. The women workers were, at least, active agents in living their own lives, and their wage-earning experiences in the factory granted them new power and freedom to balance their lives between work and family. In the following section I show the strength of the desire of rural women to leave their village for industrial work—a desire that helps to reconfigure both women's identities and the Chinese familial relations, to which dagongmei attached as well as attempted to subvert.

Struggles in the Midst of Alienated Labor
and Rural Family Life

The following quote by Karl Marx sheds light on the contemporary scene in China, in particular the strong desire to leave home to do industrial work that represents a fundamental challenge to the patriarchal culture:

> What, then, constitutes the alienation of labour?
>
> First, the fact that labour is *external* to the worker, i.e. it does not belong to his essential being; that in his work, therefore, he does not affirm himself but denies himself, does not feel content but unhappy, does not develop freely his physical and mental energy but mortifies his body and ruins his mind. The worker therefore only feels himself outside his work, and in his work feels outside himself. He is at home when he is not working, and when he is working he is not at home. His labour is therefore not voluntary, but coerced; it is *forced labour*. (1964 [1844], 110)

Marx's statement that when the worker is at home he is not working, and when the worker is working he is not at home is of particular interest here. For Marx, "at home" means more than a geographical location—it is also an existential mode of being by which a man or woman actualizes his or her being in the world.

The puzzle here is that Chinese migrant workers did not feel "at home" in the village, when they actually were at home. Rather, they desired to leave home by choosing to sell their labor to capitalists in the economic development zones. For Marx, this act was to lead to a fatal process of self-estrangement and the self-objectification of the true self through participation in the activity of wage labor. Immediately following the quotation cited above, Marx wrote:

> It is therefore not the satisfaction of a need; it is merely a *means* to satisfy needs external to it. Its alien character emerges clearly in the fact that as soon as no physical or other compulsion exists, labour is shunned like the plague. External labour, labour in which man alienates himself, is a labour of self-sacrifice, or mortification. Lastly, the external character of labour for the worker appears in the fact that it is not his own, but someone else's, that it does not belong to him, that in it he belongs, not to himself, but to another. (110–11)

But there was no violence and no coercive force involved when the Chinese dagongmei were determined to escape their home. They desired to do so in the hope of challenging the patriarchal family and changing their life situation in rural China, even if it meant "alienating" themselves through industrial labor. Moreover, for the dagongmei there was no misrecognition of the "I" as suggested by Althusser (1990), who argued that the domain of ideology was paramount in interpellating individuals, and fooling them into following the interests of the dominant class. Most of the factory women knew quite well before they left their village that they were going to be working in a sweatshop for twelve hours each day, earning about 500 or 600 renminbi each month. They all knew the factory boss would not be lenient and treat them as equal human beings. They knew there was a huge gap between industrial life and rural life. They knew they were going to sell their bodies. They knew almost everything. But by engaging in this basic struggle to work, there seemed to be a chance that women workers might be able to transgress their individual "fate" (a term they used often in the workplace) of rural family life.

Dong: "It's Not the First Time I've Gone Out Working"

Dong is a rural female migrant worker somewhat typical of her generation. At the age of twenty-three, she was an experienced dagongmei who had been working in Guangdong for more than four years when I met her at the Meteor plant. Each year she changed her workplace at least once. She had worked in garment and plastic plants before she went to Meteor, where she now worked in the quality control department. Staying in the room next to me she often invited me for supper, when we shared many valuable childhood, family, and work experiences. Compared with other women workers, Dong knew more about the functioning of her family economy back in the village. She was the eldest daughter in her family, which meant that she had taken on family burdens when she was still young.

Dong was born in a relatively poor village in Hunan, but over the past twenty years she had grown up alongside China's rapid economic reform. In 1981, when she was eight and of age to enter primary school, land reform was launched in her village. The family of five—Dong, her two siblings, and parents—had about three and a half acres of arable land and two acres of mountainous and forest land, and they depended on it for their everyday survival, which was limited to intensive farming. Because of the lack of resources and labor power, the family was not able to develop any type of sideline production, which in other families at the start of the 1980s helped them past a subsistence income.

Relative to some, life was not too hard for Dong, especially during her childhood in the mid-1980s when state taxes and the price of seed, fertilizers, and insecticides remained reasonable. However, the family hit hard times when all three children went to school. Besides dealing with the roaring inflation in China in the late 1980s and into the 1990s, the family had to cope with stagnant land resources and increasing education fees for their children. Rapid economic development in the coastal and urban areas and the boom in private trade accelerated price inflation, which had a direct effect on peasants' lives (World Bank 1992, 1997).[9] What was worse was that since the late 1980s land reform had began to manifest disadvantages rather than the advantages it was argued to have for peasants' lives in the previous period. Agricultural production on a local level stopped increasing, with limited land supplies in China and, after its division, its fragmentary nature and resistance to technological innovations (Wang and Hu 1999).

As the eldest daughter Dong was the first to take responsibility for alleviating the family's burden. Her father asked her to quit her junior secondary school at the age of sixteen, when her younger brother entered secondary school and the family did not have enough money for both educations (gender inequality is often experienced when a family lacks resources). Dong then remained at home, helping with farm work and domestic chores. The division of labor in the family was straightforward: the father and the mother shared all farm work such as irrigating, planting, fertilizing, and harvesting, and the mother spent additional time on poultry rearing and housekeeping while the father did more work in planning the household economy and making transactions in outside markets (Croll 1985; Judd 1994). In addition to grain, the family produced peanuts, cotton, beans, and several kinds of vegetables, which together with pigs, chickens, and eggs helped the family to earn about RMB 2,500 each year.

The family focused most of its hopes on Dong's younger brother—the only son. They dreamed that he would gain entry into higher education, find a job in town, and, finally, provide money for the family to build a new house for the son to bring his wife to when he married. Needless to say, saving money was the present concern. Dong shared her family's expectations, so when her cousin went out to work in Shenzhen Dong hoped to join the migration. As she describes it: "I thought I could earn more money in the special economic zone. I felt it was a waste of time to stay in the village because my parents could do all the farming work alone. My cousins and my friends who worked in Shenzhen often told me a lot of interesting stories. I knew quite well what the working conditions might be, and how much

I could earn before I went out for work. I knew it was not easy to work in a big city, which was a totally strange place to me. But I thought it was still worth it to try, and it was a chance for me to look at the outside world. We often thought we were *jing di zhi wa* [frogs living in a well, knowing nothing about the outside world], and we knew little about life outside the village." As Dong understood it, Shenzhen was a world full of struggles yet also an exciting place where one could make money in a short time. For Dong, to work in Shenzhen was not only a way to meet economic necessity and the expectations of her family but also a chance for self-exploration and self-growth in a modern city.

Dong returned home to visit almost every year. Each time she returned she brought back about 2,000 yuan to her father, which was more than her family's total annual income. The family was happy with Dong's contribution and she was satisfied too: "The first time I saw my father and mother smile so heartedly, I knew that there is big gap between urban life and rural life. My parents at first could not believe that I earned two thousand yuan within five months."

But for Dong, the life of the outside world became less and less interesting with each passing year. "I know there is a big difference. People in the city earn a lot and enjoy a different kind of life. I feel tired. The working hours are too long. It's too hard. What's worse, I could never have hoped to stay in the city. My hukou is in the village. . . . Last New Year, I went back home and thought that I would not come out again. I stayed home for two months and I slept, slept all the day." But later, with her energy and health restored, she felt bored at home and wanted to go out working again. Moreover, she had a boyfriend living in a nearby village and they had agreed to get married the following year. She knew that after marriage she might have limited chances to work in the city again. So despite the fact that industrial work was arduous and exploitative, Dong wanted to enjoy for a little more time her personal "freedom" outside the village. Saving some of the money for her future married life was another consideration: "Life will be happy if my husband and my parents-in-law treat me nice. But no one knows. It's better for me to have some money of my own." Thus the individual life cycle of the women's transitional life period between puberty and marriage meshed with social time—the transitional period of the socialist economy fusing with global capitalism—and crystallized in the everyday struggles of women workers.

Dong and many other women in the workplace all had stories, struggles, and expectations of their own about leaving their villages. Workers like Dong who shared most of her natal family's goals and expectations would be seen as filial daughters and good women (Salaff 1981). Marital life was still their foremost concern, and individual planning for work and migration to the cities was often related to this cultural conditioning. Many workers hoped to enjoy freedom and life in the cities before getting married, while at the same time saving "personal money" for protecting themselves. Although most of the women agreed that they had much more freedom than did previous generations in choosing their marriage partner, many still had great worries about life after marriage. As established by the patrilocal practices of family life, Chinese rural women still were expected to move to and settle down in their husband's village. However, as suggested by Margery Wolf (1972), women develop strategies to protect their situation in a stranger's community. Saving personal money and forming women's support networks are among the most common practices.

Overt resistance to the patriarchal Chinese family sometimes could be found in the workplace. For example, there were stories about single women who refused to return home for marriages arranged by their families or about married women who ran away to escape farm work. Runaway women in the workplace often helped each other at times of emotional or financial difficulty. While some women openly shared their stories and formed sisterhood networks across workplaces, some preferred to keep silent about their escapes. At Meteor, Dong's story sheds light on one prototype of rural women in negotiating her work and family life. However, there were others whose stories I heard whose transgressive acts were more subversive in rendering women's identity and role in Chinese family life.

Chun: "I Had to Live for Myself Sometime"

Chun was a married woman working as a cleaner in the production department. There were only a few women who were married and still working in Meteor, and most of them were cooks, cleaners, or packers who earned a little less then the single workers on the shop floor. Chun was a quiet person, and because of her low status in the workplace she seldom talked to people. She attracted my attention because there was a rumor that she was a "runaway woman." Chun, in her early forties, had been working at Meteor for nearly two years. While she was not a new worker, she was shy each time I tried to talk to her. After several attempts, however, she was finally willing to open herself up.

Chun was from a village in Sichuan, the most populated province in China and well known for its shortage of agricultural land. She was a mother of one son and one daughter, both of whom were in secondary school. Her husband was a farmer, who did all of the farm and domestic work at their home. As with all of the married women at Meteor, I asked Chun how she was able to leave her family and husband, and who now was responsible for caring for the children. She replied "I didn't have much conflict between my work and family. My children have already grown up, one is sixteen, and the other thirteen. They know how to cook for themselves, and my son studies at a boarding school in the county town." She said these words with a smile, trying to tone down the implications of the runaway issue.

I continued to ask: "Are there enough hands to till the land? Your husband does all the farm work, doesn't he?" To which she replied, "We don't have much land, we have four *kou* [heads], but only have three *mou* [acres of arable land] and the quality is no good. There was no more land to distribute in our village. You, lady from the city, don't understand our situation. Our village is a poor area, not worth going to." She then continued: "A few years ago, my husband had gone to work in a construction site in Xi'an for several months. But he was cheated and didn't get paid because the contractor ran away when the construction project was finished. After that, he disliked going out for dagong in the urban areas. . . . I had a big argument with my husband about my turn to go out and find a job in the city. He hated the idea and said it was very difficult for a married woman of my age to look for chances. . . . But we got into debt of a few thousand yuan for rebuilding our worn-out house, and I wanted to return that amount as soon as possible."

As Chun spoke she started to reveal her story: "I told my husband that land couldn't lay golden eggs. Our earnings on agricultural products are nothing, only a few hundred yuan each year. What use is a few hundred yuan? We would still have to wait a few years to repay the debts. But if I went out dagong, and was lucky to find a job in a foreign plant in Guangdong, I could earn ten times more than in the village!" She spoke with a self-confident tone. "Was your husband angry with you?" I was getting more and more interested in her story. "Oh, he lost his temper whenever I mentioned going out to dagong. . . . We argued over the issue several times. I complained that I had married a useless man and into a poor family. [She laughs.] I told my husband I had depended on his family for twenty years and now was high time that I supported myself. I wanted to contribute my share. I wanted to dagong and earn money for the family."

Chun married into her husband's village in the late 1970s at the time economic reform started in rural China. After her marriage, the production-team system was disbanded and the land was distributed back to households by the rural household responsibility system. As Chun recalled, the 1980s were the golden years of village life. Rural families got rich at a time when the state was still willing to buy their grain at a good price (Oi 1989).[10] In the 1990s, however, rural life stagnated and underemployment and unemployment became serious problems in rural areas. Out-migration then became a trend in Chun's village, and young women enthusiastically moved out of the village to explore a new life in the cities.

Chun, like other married women, was bound by her marriage; she gave birth to her son one year after marrying. Then her daughter came three years later, and for the years following she was completely tied down by family responsibilities. She had no opportunity to leave the village, but she did observe most of the young women moving in and out. She never enjoyed freedom, and she never earned money for herself and her family. In a retrospective mood, she stated: "I told myself to wait until my children grew up. I waited for more than fifteen years. One day, I made a decision to go out to dagong in Guangdong. I knew it was already late at my age, and if I didn't make it I'd have no chance anymore in my life. I left my son's father in silence with a letter."

Chun told her husband that she would return home at Spring Festival time and bring back money for the family. "I was so happy and frightened, it was the first time I had left the village." She then made her trip to Guangdong, and with the introduction of a fellow villager she finally got a job at the Meteor factory. Chun emphasized that as a married woman she was lucky to find a job: "You know, jobs here are all for young, single girls. Old women like me could hardly be given an offer. I was quite satisfied to work as a cleaner. Low status, but who cares? I can still earn five hundred each month, which is half a year's work in the village." At the time of our talk, Chun was struggling with whether or not to go back home. She had been working at Meteor for two years, and she missed her children, if not her husband, too much to continue her work in the factory. With a smile of self-esteem she told me: "I've saved a few thousand yuan in these two years, and now I can repay the family debt. I would also like to buy some new clothes for my son, daughter, and the children's father."

Chun's story articulates how a middle-aged Chinese married woman struggled to live for herself and not be tied to patriarchal family life in the village. By escaping to dagong in the city without her husband's permission, she openly challenged the patriarchal relations and gender imbalance at a time of rapidly changing family life in reform China. However, resistance and domination in family life is never a simple dichotomy in the lives of women in rural China. When we look deep into Chun's struggles, in addition to gaining independence and empowerment her dream was to repay the family's debt and contribute to the family's finances. As a married woman, her final desire from going out to work was to buy her husband and children new clothes for the Chinese New Year festival. Her desire of leaving home to dagong could be another alienation of her presumed attachment to her family, which provided the original placement for her identity. These intricate links between defiance and domination suggest a need to look at women's struggles and the dagong's desire within broader societal dynamics and as part of the structural factors of China's transformation.

Experiencing Antagonism

Dong and Chun's struggles illustrate the fact that they were not just fighting against the patriarchal family but also against an undesirable village life. A deep rural-urban divide existed in China and nurtured the soil for rural women's struggles between work and family and for rural-urban migration for the younger generation to live out their desires in the urban areas. There were at least two seductions—effectively a coin with two sides—for this strong dagong desire: one was the women's struggles between work and family; the other was the great disparity between the city and countryside, and between the working class and the peasantry.

In the following quote Marx expresses his view of the urban-rural divide: "The antagonism of town and country can only exist as a result of private property. It is the most crass expression of the individual under the division of labor, under a definite activity forced upon him—a subjection which makes one man into a restricted town-animal, the other into a restricted country-animal, and daily creates anew the conflict between their interests" (Marx and Engels 1976, 72). Here, however, Marx is wrong in saying that the antagonism of town and country could only exist in a society of private property. Chinese state socialism in the 1950s witnessed the confiscation of private property while at the same time a huge urban and rural chasm within Chinese society was created. Indeed it was neither feudalism nor the petty capitalism of past Chinese history that turned human beings into prohibited town or country animals but rather the socialist development dictated by the Chinese Communist Party that claimed to liberate all countrymen from oppression. It is surely not fair to say that the Chinese state specifically aimed at creating hierarchies among the people, especially the deep divide between the working class and the peasantry. However, it is correct to say that it was the by-product of the developmentalism and statism inherent in Chinese socialism (Seldon 1993; White 1993). In modern China, social and class divisions were not produced by the capitalist machine, based on market logic—that is, the "inequality but justice" of the distribution of private property among individuals through the exchange mechanism. Rather, divisions and hierarchies were created by a party-state that confiscated private property and turned it into "state property," and then arranged, distributed, and sanctioned different sectors of people according to the logic of its planned economy.

My concern in this chapter has been to understand the women's desire for dagong and women's struggles between work and family within a larger social dynamic, by which the present desire of a mobile society steered toward industrial capitalism by a "socialist" state and a mainly agrarian population. The existing social divisions that the state hoped to narrow by a hybrid "socialist market economy" were actually enlarged, especially between the city and the countryside and between the eastern coastal areas and the western interior. The great desire of labor flows, from the rural to the urban, from the west to the east, only signified the attempt from the bottom to challenge this seemingly unbridgeable social divide created from above.

The possibility of closing this social divide faded as the economic reforms continued. Indeed, as Wang Shaoguang (2000) has noted, the economic reforms turned from a win-win game to a zero-sum game in 1993 when Chinese reform entered the second phase, which was characterized by growing social inequality and worsening unemployment. Rural per capita income grew at an average annual rate of fifteen percent in real terms from 1978 to 1984, but then economic growth in terms of agricultural productivity and rural income stagnated in the second half of the 1980s and early 1990s. The gap between urban and rural income was further widened when rural income per capita increased less than 3 percent from 1985 to 1990 (World Bank 1992, 57–58). Unequal development, far more serious in reform China, further deepened the social lack, although opportunities given to the rural population to get rich seemed greater. Social polarization nevertheless became deeper and deeper from the mid-1990s onward. Wang states: "By 1999, the urban-rural divide was as deep as it had been in 1978. All the gains of earlier years had been lost. . . . While a typical urban resident earned about 200 Yuan more than his rural counterpart in 1978, by 1997, the difference amounted to more than 3000 Yuan. . . . Compared to other countries, China's rural-urban gap is unusually large. In other countries, the ratio of urban to rural incomes is normally below 1.5 and rarely exceeds 2.0, but in China, real urban incomes are as much as four times real rural incomes, if urban residents' welfare benefits of various kinds are to be included (2000, 386–88)."

China thus became one of the most unequal countries in terms of rural-urban disparity in its region of the world and among developing countries more generally in the 1980s and 1990s (Riskin, Zhao, and Li 2001, 3). The Gini coefficient of inequality in household income rose seven percentage points (18 percent) between 1988 and 1995, with a high inequality of rural households per capita income reaching an estimated 23 percent and urban inequality 42 percent over the same period. In terms of regional disparity, the World Bank (1997, 8) also indicated a sharply increased disparity since 1990 in per capital GDP between the eastern coastal provinces and western provinces. In 1997, nearly all of the coastal provinces had a per capita GDP higher than the national average. The per capita GDP of Shanghai, one of the richest cities in China, was 4.5 times the average, while Guizhou, a poor region, was only 37 percent of the national average (Wang 2000, 388). Carl Riskin, Zhao Renwei, and Li Shi comment, "Seldom has the world witnessed so sharp and fast a rise in inequality as has occurred in China" (2001, 3). With China's accession into the World Trade Organization, greater social polarization is expected. Huge social and political implications are expected as the already stringent life of Chinese peasants will be further adversely affected in the coming years. Thirteen to fifteen million more rural laborers will be driven off the agricultural land and become unemployed between 2000 and 2010 because of the expected large flows of foreign agricultural goods into the Chinese market (Wang 2000, 397). A still deeper chasm between urban and rural life is predicted.

The rapid and huge flow of rural population to the cities as a "social revolution" from below reflects the fusing and struggling of individual and collective desires to fill the social chasm as the only hope of escape. However, the struggles of rural migrants were neither appreciated nor accepted in the cities. Often called *mangliu* (people of "blind flows"), the rural migrants, while urgently needed for the growth of urban industrialism, were seriously discriminated against in official discourses, mass media, and urban daily life (Zhang 2001a). The term mangliu signified the aimless movement of the rural population and the potential disturbances that might affect urban stability and social order. Antagonism between the rural and urban population escalated when the urban governments stipulated restrictive measures and worked hand in hand with the mass media, which launched the propaganda machine against the rural migrants. For example, a regional newspaper, *Nanfang Ribao* (Southern daily), on 24 January 1994 provided a telling description of the rural-to-urban exodus: "A great mass of mingong [migrant workers] was pouring from the entrance of the railway station, nonstop. Mingong flux released from all coaches and buses ran to the square of the station. . . . Everywhere there was luggage lying on the ground, and mingong were eating bread and cakes. They were simply the mangliu who knew nowhere to go and so occupied the station, creating serious social problems for us."

Such news reporting was an everyday occurrence in both local and national newspapers in the 1990s. In July 1985, the Ministry of Public Security issued their temporary regulations on the management of the temporary population in cities and towns, which restated the methods for registering the urban temporary population. With regard to those age sixteen and over entering cities and staying temporarily for over three months, the regulations stipulated that they should apply for a temporary residence permit. People coming from elsewhere to run shops or factories, engage in construction, or work in the transport or services sector, with relatively longer periods of temporary residence, were to be registered as "attached" populations by the police substation at the place of actual residence (Shi 1996, 31).

However, throughout the 1980s and 1990s, nearly all urban governments lost control of the widespread rural-urban migration, and the 1985 regulations were only a remedy to deal with problems that were out of the control of the central administration. Local cities, on the other hand, developed regional measures or even used public security forces to drive out the influx of rural migrants. From time to time urban governments called for an "extermination" of the mangliu wave, especially during the Chinese New Year period. The following story was told by a male worker at the Meteor plant who experienced an "extermination" action against the migrant influx in the Guangzhou train station in December 1994:

> At about ten o'clock at night, my tongxiang [fellow villagers] and I just wanted to settle down in a place under the bridge near the train station. We had been looking for an empty place for ages before we could settle down. There were clusters of people wandering around the square in front of the train station, searching for places to pass the night and waiting for the next morning to hunt for jobs. Suddenly, a lot of government cars came and public security guards jumped down from the cars. They used sticks and water pipes to clear the people from the square. Masses were driven to one

of the corners of the square; some wanted to run away and were beaten. It was such a horrible scene; it seemed that we were all criminals and would be arrested. We were asked for, and separated by, our place of origin— people from Sichuan were grouped in one place, while people from Hunan and Hubei in others. Then we were sent on a large bus, people from different places were sent on different buses. The bus took us outside the city of Guangzhou and we were charged five yuan each person. Those who did not have money were scolded and beaten.

In short, the dreams and desires of going out to dagong, to help increase family income, explore individual life, resist family control, or escape poor village life, in the end had great costs. While the discourse of mangliu and the discriminations against migrant workers were, presumably, gender neutral, the experiences of rural-urban migration and the individual struggles were definitely gendered in nuance. Whether men's or women's struggles, Chinese family life entwined with the social divide between the rural and urban areas all came together to produce the great passion of the rural generation for moving out to dagong and the subsequent experiences of urban discrimination against them. Official discourses further depicted them in abject terms such as mangliu or mingong, which were repeatedly used in newspapers and on radio programs. Openly discriminated against by the urban population in their daily lives, the women workers in turn relied on themselves and their familial and kin networks, creatively twined and twisted, for survival in the urban industrial world. While they might run away from their home village to resist patriarchal controls either from their fathers or husbands, the rural women immediately reconstituted new familial or kin enclaves to protect themselves. Women's struggles between work and family were vividly interwoven with the Chinese patriarchal family, which simultaneously provided constraint and support to the migrant workers. Such tensions could hardly be resolved, especially when the rural-urban antagonism intensified the conflictual forces where rural women were not only fighting the patriarchal relations in particular but also the great rural-urban chasm and increasing rural poverty in general.

The desire of female migrant workers, challenging and transforming the Chinese family and rural society, meets squarely with the desire of global capital penetrating into Chinese socialist society and creating a world factory and a global market. It is these techniques of disciplinary power of global capital that I address in the next chapter.

3

THE SOCIAL BODY,

THE ART OF DISCIPLINE

AND RESISTANCE

This political investment of the body is bound up, in accordance with complex reciprocal relations, with its economic use; it is largely as a force of production that the body is invested with relations of power and domination; but, on the other hand, its constitution as labour power is possible only if it is caught up in a system of subjection (in which need is also a political instrument meticulously prepared, calculated, and used); the body becomes a useful force only if it is both a productive body and a subjected body.
—Michel Foucault, *Discipline and Punish*

The desire of dagongmei to pass through the factory gate meets the imperatives and techniques of global capital, and it is this intersection that forms the core of this chapter. Turning a young and rural body into an industrialized and productive laborer, a seemingly universal project of disciplining labor, is the primary task of transnational production when it meets migrant labor in urban China. Here, I am interested in understanding these disciplinary techniques over the body in the workplace, what Foucault (1979) termed the microphysics of power. The body, especially the female body, is of utmost importance to global capital in China because it is the means by which the production machine can extract labor power. Transnational capital's image of Chinese dagongmei, inscribed with China's reified patriarchal culture, is a homogeneous and orientalist construct: slim body, sharp eyes, nimble fingers, shy, and hardworking. Contrasting with this oriental imagination, women's experiences, practices, and forms of defiance were extremely diverse in the Meteor workplace.[1] In postsocialist China the production of dagongmei, new working bodies to serve the reimagining of China as a world factory, produced a spectacular "global explosion of labor" that is a hypermixture of the transnational and the local, and global capitalism and Chinese state socialism.

In this chapter I look into the specific practices of this Shenzhen workplace—the disciplinary techniques of the production regime and their discursive, spatial, and institutional practices. I focus on the extraction of labor power specifically from the female body—dagongmei—through a microphysics of power in the Meteor plant. My project here is also one of individuation through global disciplinary power. Individuating the body, as shown in the Meteor workplace, is the telos of the production economy. In addition to examining the usual workplace techniques and disciplines, I also explore the production machine's "imagineering" of a politics of discourse on the individuated body itself. Its specificity, its modality of power and language, can be readily discerned in the specific context of the postsocialist period in China. Moreover, I also attempt here to go beyond the dichotomy of relations of domination and resistance. These two extremes of a pendulum swing—one of oppression and the other of defiance—simplify if not overshadow the complexity of the everyday life politics of historical agents. The concept of "tactical bodies" highlights the richness and nuances of quotidian practices embedded in a multilayered relation of domination and resistance (Certeau 1984). Female working bodies, be they "docile bodies" or "tactical bodies" are always in a "structure of contest" to use situational opportunities and even hegemonic discourse to protect themselves. Their nuanced, although sometimes self-defeating, actions prevent disciplinary power from producing a reified, unitary image of their bodies.

Chinese Workers, Socialist Bodies

In the new millennium the project of transnational capital seeks to transform China into a world factory, a project that in turn has to be accompanied by the creation of a new army of transglobal labor fitted to global production. Nevertheless, this colonizing project of producing a universal global labor is by and large an imaginary that works to hide the hybridization characteristic of the new international division of labor and its very mixed and "located" labor practices (Rofel 1999, 257–58). The production of a new Chinese transglobal labor force is embedded in a very specific history of China, which provides not only the backdrop but also a language and a material base for global capital to enact a new labor force. Inside the Meteor workplace, I was intrigued by the intensive making of a hegemonic discourse about calibrating the value of dagongmei and dagongzai to meet the requirements of the modern production system.

An often-repeated story in the workplace, made up by Hong Kong businessmen, managers, and technical persons, was that mainland Chinese workers—socialist and rural bodies—were unfit for capitalist production. Making working bodies thus involved a delicate politics of value and assessment that made use of such reified images as the "socialist" worker and the urban-rural disparity in China. Because Hong Kong businessmen were very distrustful of mainland workers, rural migrant workers were portrayed as uneducated, "uncivilized," and thus undisciplined in the workplace. There was a general belief that these working bodies were ready to spit on the floor, to leave their work position at will, and even worse, to destroy the production machinery.

Together with fiery public discourses, visible in newspaper and magazine articles, the bodies of these migrant workers were inscribed with a blindness and unruliness threatening the order and stability of the city. Often called mangliu (literally "a blind flow") these workers made up the blind flow of deterritorization in the Chinese cities, and if this flood of blind migrants could not be properly regulated, they would tear down the "achievements" of economic reform (Zhang 2001c). Yet from the side of capital, it was exactly from these blind migrants, cheap but hard to control, that labor power would be extracted. Because they were so cheap, so abundant, it was worth spending time and energy to design a panoptic surveillance of these nomadic bodies. Thus the first task of capital was to transform individual undesirable migrants into useful workers, which involved projects of culture and power, both covertly and overtly, that worked on bodies and minds, behaviors and beliefs, gestures and habits, and attitudes and aptitudes.

If there is a universal rule that peasant life, indeed the human nature of "peasantness," has been commonly distrusted by industrial capital (Marx 1954 [1865]), transnational capital in China found itself caught up in another form of skepticism: it could not trust those who were raised within the socialist system in China. This double deficiency—unruly peasantness and impractical collectivism—could only nurture lazy and unproductive labor. Everywhere in the Meteor plant, there were complaints of suzhi, that the quality and nature of labor was unreasonably poor and unacceptable (Yan

2001). The legacy of the socialist system was therefore blamed for producing lazy and uncompetitive workers. I often heard managers from various departments fussing that the workers lacked *jingzheng yishi*, the sense of competition and struggle that was the basic principle of survival in a capitalist society. This deficient or incomplete body for capitalist production was often said to be inherently embedded in the "common rice bowl" practices of past socialist history. Indeed, the Hong Kong managers complained that they needed "ten times the effort" to control and educate the local workers.

If workers from Mao's era, ideologically if not in practice, were the avantgarde of the proletariat and the leadership of the revolution, now in the reform period the worker was the symbol of laziness, unable to conform to the rhythms of industrial capitalism, carrying with him or her the evils of past socialist history (Rofel 1999). In the eyes of the Hong Kong managers, Chinese workers were imprinted with their particular history and were therefore political and "red," not only in the past but in the contemporary period as well. Thus, even the most sophisticated microtechniques of disciplinary power would not be effective in regulating them. Socialist habitus was as solid as iron, so although the local managers' mentality could change, that of the workers could not. The younger generation, especially those from rural areas, were seen as historically endowed subversive subjects, and thus harder to incorporate into modern production.

The Chinese workers, as socialist bodies, were imagined and invented in contrast to the hidden but essentialized Hong Kong workers,[2] who as capitalist subjects were disciplined, productive, and profit minded, and who possessed rational economic sense rather than political consciousness. Socialist bodies, "red" and lazy, thus were inferior to capitalist beings born to be individualistic, competitive, hard working, and, most important of all, achievement oriented and therefore self-disciplined. This discursive politics worked to imagine a socialist body unfit for capitalist production, and thus further justified the imperatives and techniques of the production machine to transform these particular socialist bodies—the rural women workers—into modern and productive dagongmei. By looking at the specific capitalist/socialist trope and global/local practices, in this chapter I aim to show how Chinese female bodies were incorporated into this modern disciplinary power.

The Art of Spacing: Positioning on the Line

Once the dagongmei enters the factory gate of Meteor, she is immediately placed in a specific position and nailed down into a grid of power and discipline.[3] The techniques and power of the production machine thus wasted no time in starting its work on the working bodies. With twenty to twenty-five workers on assembly lines and fifteen to twenty on quality control (QC) lines, there was a total of ten production assembly lines and four QC lines on the shop floor. Placing a body on the line was the first technique of the disciplinary machine to work on the worker. A cog in a machine, the body was pinned down to its own specific position, functional and productive, and the disciplinary power started to demonstrate its art of spacing by positioning bodies on the production lines.

A coworker, Meifang, sat directly across from me on the production line. We had a particular relationship that would not have developed in another place or with other people. My presence as an ethnographer in that particular work position and the demands of production jointly shaped our relationship. Meifang was a fresh hand, hired two days after I arrived. With her rounded faced she still looked rustic, and she was timid in expressing herself. At age eighteen she was a fresh junior secondary school graduate from a village in Hunan Province. After keeping quiet on the line for a few days, she started to chat to me. Although talking was not permitted on the shop floor, it often spontaneously sparked up in the afternoon and at night when the workers felt that disciplinary control had been lessened.

"Why do you work here?" Meifang uttered in a small voice. Guessing that she knew me as a student from Hong Kong, I replied, "I want to learn the work process, the factory system, and the lives of women workers here." Then she asked me "Do you like to work here?" "Yes, because I can make a lot of friends here," I responded, without being prepared for her question. "Hmm," she answered and was silent again. I wondered if my reply made any sense to her.

We were both placed on the screwing positions on a production line of twenty-two workers. We had one foreman, one line leader, and one line assistant. The model produced on the line was an MB201 route-finder, a kind of electronic road map for drivers, produced for a big-name car company in Europe. The product came to our line at nearly the final stage of the production process. We assembled the main board, the liquid crystal display (LCD), and the plastic case around the whole product. With work divided into twelve processes, normally there were two or three people with responsibility for one process. My process was performed by three people: myself, Meifang, and Chinghua. To this day I still believe that Meifang was hired to accelerate the pace on the line because of my slow speed.

Figure 4. Women workers in the functional test section at the Meteor plant. (photo by author)

Each work position on the line was a procedure of knowledge and power. It was stated clearly in minute detail what position the body should take in each process (see table 1).[4] Workers were trained as specialists in just one process; only the workers who had been working on the line for more than a year had the opportunity to learn more than one work process. The work process was seldom changed unless a new model required a new arrangement of work positions. In front of every seat there was a layout hung on the shelf that demonstrated meticulously with pictures and graphics each step the worker should follow. The work was minute, specified, and systematic: what the individual could and should do was to follow it with precision, and if one were attentive and disciplined enough, one needed only to mechanically repeat specific bodily movements.

Each step of each work process at Meteor was meticulously demonstrated. The QC job for the route-finder products was divided into five work processes, each of which was further dissected into five to seven steps. Each individual occupied only one work position and was adept at only one work process. Moreover, most workers knew nothing about the product they worked on nor the meaning of the English words that appeared on the product itself. But that did not matter. They simply followed the instructions of the layout and forced themselves to recognize the English letters along with the arrows, graphics, and alphabets. Then, once they saw them, they could react instinctively without hesitation and press the right keys and buttons. I noticed one worker, Damei, whose memory, eyes, and hands were so well coordinated that she seemed incapable of failure. One day I asked her if she thought the layout was useful. She replied, "It was useful at the very beginning. You know the line leader will only show you one time how to do it and you never dare to ask a second time. The first time I saw those English letters as 'worms' I was scared to death. I couldn't recognize them, so I copied them down and recited them at night. On the second morning, they were all in my mind and I didn't need to see the layout anymore."

But what the disciplinary machine actually wanted was to produce a body without mind, a mindless body. "I don't need to use my mind anymore. I've been doing the same thing for two years. Things come and go, repeating every second and minute. I can do it with my eyes closed," Damei told me. And because the body was mindless, it was replaceable. Thus the strategy of the production machine, in order to safeguard its power and prevent any possibility of the producing body taking charge, was to ensure that every body be trained to be a mindless body. The Chinese migrant workers, as stated earlier, were always seen as untrustworthy workers who would leave the factory any time they liked. This situation was often exaggerated, but the turnover rate was particularly high during the Chinese New Year period. At Meteor, management estimated that every year at this time more than 20 percent of the workforce would leave for good and never come back. Thus for the producing body to be changeable, it was necessary that it be further individualized. One only took responsibility for one's own duty and only became an expert in one's own position. Everybody was useful, but not crucial; no one individual could know and affect the operation of the whole work.

Individuating the body was the principle of the economy of the production machine in order to assure the running of the whole machine, the totality. To extract labor power, and to ensure the functioning of the totality, the working body had first to be dissected and individualized, and then reconnected on the line. The dialectic of individuality and totality was controlled by the art of spacing, the art of positioning the social body in the workplace. The principle of positioning was the principle of individualized disconnecting and reconnecting, as stated by Foucault: "It was a question of distributing individuals in a space in which one might isolate them and map them; but also of articulating this distribution on a production machinery that had its own requirements. The distribution of bodies, the spatial

Table 1. Work process of functional test (III). This work position layout was posted in front of Damei, a quality controller on line A.

Model	Route-finder	Quality controller:	Work number:
Facilitators	car kit 12V, JIG short line, 2A 1.5V battery, ROM card	Speed	
Work Process	COMMS functional test		

Content:

1. Put on battery, insert COMMS card, and then switch the power on. The LCD glass panel demonstrates the following:

    > ROUTE FINDER   00:00
    > NEW JOURNEY

2. At the same time, press the " ↑ " + "T" buttons. The picture panel will be changed to:

    > TEST ROUTINE OPTIONS
    >
    > →KEYBOARD TEST
    > LCD TEST
    > ROM TEST
    > COMMS TEST
    > QUIT

    Then press the " ↓ " button, move the "→" button to the position of "COMMS TEST" and then press the " ↳ " button on the right-hand side. The picture panel will show the following:

    > COMMS ROUTINE OPTIONS
    >
    > →RUN LOOPBACK TEST
    > RUN SLBUG
    > RUN ECHO TEST
    > QUIT COMMS TEST

Table 1. Continued

3. Press " ⌞ " on the right-hand side; the plane will show: "PRESS ANY KEY TO SEND LOOPBACK Q TO QUIT," then continuously press "w" twice, LCD panel will also show the word "w."

4. At stage 3, press the "P, I, M" letter keys one by one to do the test.

5. At stage 3, press "Q" key; the panel will show back stage 2, then press "V," move "→" to the position of "QUIT COMMS TEST," and then press " ⌞ " button on the right side, the panel will resume the following picture:

    TEST ROUTINE OPTIONS

    KEYBOARD TEST
    LCD TEST
    ROM TEST
    →*COMMS TEST*
    QUIT

    Then press "V" and move "→" to the position of "QUIT." Then press " ⌞ " on the right side, and the panel will return to stage 1.

6. Switch off and then take out the ROM card and battery. Check whether there is any defect in the LCD glass.

arrangement of production machinery and the different forms of activity in the distribution of 'posts' had to be linked together" (1979, 144–45).

A Technique of Power: The Assembly Line

If we say the disciplinary spacing of the body results in the individuation and fragmention of labor power, the assembly line devised in modern industry is a technique of power reuniting individualized bodies in a concerted action.[5] All ten assembly lines at Meteor were equipped with moving conveyor belts. The moving of the belt was, simply, the movement of power. Like a chain, it coupled an individualized body with a specific position, but at the same time it linked the individuals to form a collective social body devoted to the singular aim of maximizing production.

The operation of the moving belt was not only cooperative and productive but also symbolic. The flashing light set at the head of the belt signaled and dictated the actions of each body and combined individual energies into a collective labor force, thus showing its power to control. The light acted like a conductor directing an orchestra, and each individual act formed part of a symphony. It flashed once every two to two and a half minutes, telling workers on the lines that a new set was being run. It controlled speed, time, and bodily movement. The working body was thus individualized, yet paradoxically not one of the bodies could be individualistic, idiosyncratic, or different. Ultimately it was the collective labor and cooperation of the line that mattered. It was ritual, rhythmic and totalizing; the despot of directing, the art of disciplining.

Unlike musicians in an orchestra, however, there was no need for the Chinese dagongmei to be trained for a long time before they were put on the assembly line. Taylorist methods of production were still deployed on Meteor's shop floor, so although skill was involved it was kept to a minimum. The principle of division remained the first principle determining the organization of work. Work was dissected into tasks as minute as possible, and every piece of work was precisely studied and carefully devised, as shown in table 2. For example, in the bonding work process, machine 502 was set to produce 2 lines per second, while machine 509 was set at 1.5 lines. Thus for a piece of 363 bonding lines, the required time for the first machine was 3 minutes and 5 seconds; the second would take 4 minutes and 4 seconds. Workers were under great pressure to meet the speed and timing of the work processes, and those who failed to catch up the work were thought of as lazy or incapable.

Table 2. The timing of the work process, showing division of labor.

Work process: bonding
    Model: MWD-440
    No. of bonding line per piece: 363
    502 Machine: 2 lines/sec   time/pcs: 3 min and 5 sec
    509 Machine: 1.5 lines/sec   time/pcs: 4 min and 5 sec

Work process: bonding
    Model: SA-95
    No. of bonding line per piece: 130
    502 Machine: 2 lines/sec   time/pcs: 1 min and 5 sec
    509 Machine: 1.5 lines/sec   time/pcs: 1 min and 44 sec

Work process: brushing soldering liquid
    Model: MWD-440
    Time: one minute

Quantity:	7	8	10
Sec/pcs:	8 min 57 sec	7 min 50 sec	6 min
Average sec/pcs:	8 min		

Work process: brushing soldering liquid
    Model: ROF-CPU
    Time: one minute

Quantity:	10	7	12	12
Sec/pcs:	6 min	8 min 57 sec	5 min	5 min
Average sec/pcs:	6 min 12 sec			

Work process: fixing IC die
    Model: ROF-CPU

Quantity:	2 dies			
Sec/pcs:	14 min	9 min	7 min	11 min
Average sec/pcs:	11 min			

Work process: soldering contact pin
    Model: ROF-CPU

Quantity:	6 points			
Sec/pcs:	23 min	43 min	23 min	39 min
Average sec/pcs:	32 min			

Besides the staff in the personnel section, those whom the workers disliked most in the company were the time analysts—all of whom were men. Again and again they came out from the engineering department holding a timing calculator and stood behind the backs of the women workers to measure their time. Male power and female subordination were vividly contrasted. The analysts made suggestions and sent orders, and female bodies would need to catch up to the pace again. The time analysts studied not only the amount of time the work required but also the workers' bodily actions—the gestures and the gaps between bodily movements. No time was wasted; every bodily action had to be accurate and correct. The distance between each body, the distance between the body and the conveyor belt, the height of the chair, and the table and the shelf were all carefully measured and planned. Time and space were all to be used economically; there was to be no waste of surplus bodily actions and no waste of surplus labor force. This was, at least, the dream of the production machine.

On line B, the work of assembling the ROF, the final processing product, was divided into twelve processes (see table 3). Once a new lot arrived on the line, the time analysts would again measure the work pace. The data they collected would be analyzed by computer to calculate the target for daily production, the speed of the conveyor belt, and the work pace of each individual body. Work speed was reviewed on a weekly basis, which put pressure not only on individuals but also on the line as a whole. Comparisons were made between the lines, and if the gap were too large Mr. Yeung, the chief of the timing analysts section, would personally issue a warning to the workers. The foreperson and the line leader, who were responsible for keeping the line operating, would also share the same pressure. They were assigned to train the workers, keep discipline, and arrange work positions and raw materials. But they also had to keep the line working smoothly by eliminating or controlling human factors such as slow down, sickness, temporary leave to use the washroom, and whatever unpredictable human elements might escape the dictates of the moving line (Cavendish 1982; Glucksman 1990).

We complained every day about the work speed and the unequal arrangement of jobs and time. Although every work process was "scientifically" studied and carefully measured, the simultaneous ordering of a multitude of individualized bodies was not an easy task. Despite the fact that each job was dissected minutely, it was still impossible to keep each work process within a similar amount of time. Some were forced to work faster than others, and some were required to perform more difficult work than others. However,

Table 3. Breakdown and timing of jobs on line B.

				💡 FLASHING LIGHT	
Puixi 20 pcs/min	Checking materials		Checking materials	Lingyue 20 pcs/min
Landi 35 pcs/min	Moulding rubber button		Moulding rubber button	Ganzhu 35 pcs/min
Li Ping 1 pc/min	Fixing characters, cushion, and plastic legs		Fixing characters, cushion, and plastic legs	Lu Fang 1 pc/min
Nannan 3 pcs/min	Moulding switch button		Assembling LCD with top case	Daiwu 1.5 pcs/min
Fuxing 1.5 pcs/min	Assembling LCD with top case		Assembling LCD with top case	Jiafai 1.5 pcs/min
Xiling 2 pcs/min	Screwing LCD plate		Screwing LCD plate	Baimei 2 pcs/min .
Dongjin 1 pc/sec	Checking LCD semi-product		Functional test LCD semi-product	Lanting 1.2 pcs/sec
Fuhui 0.2 pcs/sec	Assembling bottom case		Screwing ROF product	Shutong 1 pc/min
Pan Yi 1.5 pcs/min	Screwing ROF product		Screwing ROF product	Meifang 1 pc/min
Pingping 1 pc/min	Functional testing product		Functional testing product	Sinhuo 1 pc/min
Meilan 0.3 pcs/min	Repairing		Functional testing product	Yun Ling 1 pc/min

the assembly line simply sped on its way, indifferent to the nature of the work and human differences. Individual bodies were required to accommodate to the line, rather than the line to individual bodies.

Time and time again it was impossible to avoid the units piling up in front of our table. Shutong, who was nicknamed "Fatso" because of her boyish character, sat in front of Meifang and shared the same work process with us. One day she complained: "People can't work at this sort of killing speed. The line should not run so fast. You ought to know that our task requires more time. I am already killing my body." Bailan, our line leader, quickly came and hushed her. "Don't shout. The line is not under our control." This was true; the running of the line had nothing to do with the workers, not even the line leader or the foreman. As a technique of power, the assembly line was completely autocratic; the movement of the belt had a will of its own once the line was set up by the engineering department.

Maximum bodily force could be extracted if the moving machine was organized on the principle of autonomy. Work was repetitive and monotonous, and once one became accustomed to it, one's hands, eyes, and bodily forces would autonomously react to and perfectly match the rhythm of work. It seemed that the more time one devoted to the work the more free one became. No matter how many grievances the body might have, in the end the body could and did find its way out. Because the more one worked, the more efficient one became, the job would be finished and one would feel free again. Work was repeated in cyclical intervals of seconds and minutes. It ran and ran without requiring anybody's active attention. But without such attention it seemed one was free to move one's body because the mindless work process meant there was no obstacle in the mind.

The moving line was meant to produce not only an automatic body but also a free body—a body free to live up to the force. It was a paradox but a perfect one, another dialectic of discipline and freedom. The principle of the automatic body was not only the principle of the autocracy of power, but also the praxis of the freedom of the body. It was a wonderful creation of the production machine. My experience in the workplace reminded me of the Hungarian writer and dissident, Miklos Haraszti, who worked in the Red Star Tractor Factory in 1971 and from that experience wrote his famous book *A Worker in a Worker's State*. In it he states:

> In the end, the only way out [of the factory] is to become a machine myself. The best workers are very good at this. It is as if an immovable mask was glued to their faces, whatever the type of work they are doing. Their eyes

seem veiled, yet they never miss a thing. Their movements don't seem to require any effort. They follow predetermined trajectories, like inert objects under magnetic control. Throughout the whole day, they keep a fast, even pace. Just like the machines, they don't rush into things when they are feeling fresh, nor do they slow up when they're tired. They give way to "nerves" only when the proportion of "good" work to "bad" is really grim. Otherwise, their behaviour reflects reality: "good" and "bad" jobs, "paid" and "unpaid" work, run together in the course of a day. The benefits they squeeze out of them and the wages which come from them are equally indifferent to such distinctions. (1978, 54)

Speed, Control, and Defiance

Where there was power, there was room for escape, defiance, and transgression. Fatso, the boyish dagongmei, was a hothead and usually the first one to react to power. The moving line was set to homogenize the work pace, but the work itself was heterogeneous and variable. It was nearly impossible to unify the speed of each process. In relying on human elements to create the homogenization, the process was subject to uncontrollable human differences. No matter how despotic and powerful were the Taylorist methods in the workplace, the production machine was not omnipotent in controlling working bodies. Rush orders and frequent changes in production models were characteristic of Meteor because it was a subcontracting factory. So the management had to rely on workers' cooperation and their willingness not only to work overtime but also to finish the work on time. The working women thus held a certain power, albeit interstitial rather than formal, to negotiate their work situation (Knights and Wilmott 1986). This form of interstitial power often created hidden subversions and informal ties in the workplace.

Tactics of defiance often targeted work speed. The production machine tried in manifold ways to turn the human body into a working machine, and the dagongmei on the line learned very quickly that the moving line was an electric despot, binding their bodies to work as fast as possible for the least amount of money. Fu-hui, the worker stationed in front of me, talked to me one drowsy afternoon: "I dream about the line suddenly stopping for a while. I simply can't take a breath. It drags us to work faster and faster. But the more we work, the more the boss earns. They give the workers a little more, yet they make big money." Class-consciousness was articulated thus in the workplace from time to time, although typically in an individual and passing way. The pressures of the assembly line and the work tensions it produced led the women each day to confront their own exploitation in a very immediate way.

Although the work speed was predetermined, the women nevertheless could exert a certain influence on the pace at certain moments. Sometimes, especially at night, when the work speed was unbearable to overstressed bodies, or when a new speed was set for new products and the workers had not yet gotten used to it, all of the women on the line would suddenly slow down at the same time, demonstrating a silent collective resistance to the line leader and the foreman. Nobody would utter a word but simply let the jobs pile up like hills while someone else was left with empty hands. Thus they let the line alone to run itself, making it like a "paper tiger" (a powerless despot). In response the foreman would say a lot of "good words" to persuade the women to be tolerant and catch up on the work. He would say, "Girls, the more you work, the more bonus you get. So why don't you catch up?" Or, "Have some patience, you are all girls. The more you work, the more you can handle it." But if these "good words" were not heeded and the slowdown persisted, the foreman's only recourse was to report to the supervisor and have the time analysts readjust the pace.

Needless to say, the women would view these moments as victories. They knew the rush seasons were the most appropriate moments to exert their bodily power by simply letting their bodies relax and earn time to breathe. Rush periods were the times that the new pace of work and amount of the bonus were often bargained over and fought for.[6] Sometimes other working and living conditions were challenged as well. However, once the busy period was over the women's bargaining power was dramatically weakened. The workers knew too well that their bargaining power, although recurrent, was ephemeral. They had to seize the right moment or it would be gone.

Controlling pace was an effective strategy for resisting the overwhelming domination of disciplinary power in the workplace. At Meteor, nonassembly line workers, such as in the bonding room or functional testing room, had more power to "hustle and idle" the work speed according to their own interests. As Hua, foreman of the bonding room, told me one day: "If there is a moody hour, the girls will assemble the components slowly and then pass the work to the next girl slowly. They work as slowly as tortoises. If you force them to do it quicker, they can sometimes make it all wrong and you need to redo it. Or they can all pretend to be ill."

Collective illness was common if the speed were set too fast and the bonus rate was too harsh.[7] The bonus rate was an incentive mechanism that supplemented the fixed hourly rate paid to all of the shop floor workers. Every worker in the workplace knew that the bonus system was designed to induce him or her to work as fast as possible. So when the rate of pay was good, they worked faster; if not, they simply slowed down. Thus, in certain ways, the workers were able to find interstitial power to exert some control over the work pace and maximize their own interests. Hidden transgressions were everywhere, even though these transgressive acts were somehow perceived and anticipated by the management. When there was a slack season and Meteor did not have enough work, the bonus would be set lower so that the workers would automatically slow down their work pace and the factory did not need to stop production. Defiance and incorporation thus seemed to be two opposite strategies continuously enacted in the workplace in every corner and every moment.

Programming the Work Habit: The Daily Timetable

The basic technique of disciplinary power was the regulation of the body by placing it in a disciplinary space, then measuring it and analyzing it. But this technique was insufficient to produce a disciplined and yet productive body. The management of time was far more important (Thompson 1967, 56–97). An automatic body, a body machine, was not the sole aim. What global capital needed was not a Chinese docile body but a modern and efficient working body, a body of praxis. Filling this need was, however, far more complicated. Rural country girls, the disciplinary power imagined, were free to breathe the fresh air and wander in the mountainous land with nothing to do, and thus with no sense of time. They were fresh, young, and wild. How to install a program of disciplinary time into their minds, their psyches, and their unconsciousnesses in order to incorporate them into the rhythms of strict industrial life was a singularly important project for management. Thus, the timetable was used.[8] The timetable, a basic technique, was simply deployed to manage and then change everyday life practices. Programming a new factory life, building up a work habit, and self-technologizing the body, the mind, and the habitus were all the effects of practicing a timetable.

Table 4 represents a typical timetable for the dayshift workers at Meteor. The usual working day was eleven or twelve hours. If there were a rush order, however, workers were required to stay until 11:00 P.M. or 12 A.M. The nightshift workers started work at 8:00 P.M. and finished at 8:00 A.M. with one rest hour between 3:00 A.M. and 4:00 A.M. Overtime work was considered part of normal working hours, directly violating the Labor Law of 1995,

Table 4. Standard timetable for Meteor factory workers.

6:30–7:00 A.M.	Wake up
7:00–7:30	Go to the factory
7:30–7:50	Breakfast
7:50–8:00	Punch timecard
8:00 A.M.–12:00 P.M.	Work
12:00 P.M.–12:50	Lunch and rest hour
12:50–1:00	Punch timecard
1:00–5:00	Work
5:00–5:50	Dinner
5:50–6:00	Punch timecard
6:00–9:00 or 10:00 P.M.	Overtime work

and the Regulation of Labor Contract of Shenzhen Special Economic Zone (1995). These regulating documents address overtime as follows:

1. The working hours of the worker should not be over eight hours per day; the weekly average working hours should not be over forty-four hours.
2. The worker should have one rest day per week.
3. The normal overtime work should not be extended over one hour; for some special reason and with consideration of the worker health condition, the prolonging of working hours should not be over three hours each day.
4. The total overtime work per month should not be over thirty-six hours (Shenzhen Labor Bureau 1995).

No factory in Shenzhen took these regulations seriously, Meteor included. During my time there, half of every month we would be working at night for over three hours. Moreover, although it was called overtime work, the company planned it as normal production.

Daily life was rigorously regulated by the timetable and everybody struggled to live up to the strict schedule. It was particularly tough for newcomers and urban girls who might come from relatively wealthy families. Variations of adaptability to cope with the industrial rhythms were observed, and while some took a few months' time, some could only take a week's time. The section following is from my field notes—one of my many attempts to capture a day in the workplace and how the workers struggled to meet the work schedule.

The Sense of Time: 19 January 1995

It was a cold and windy winter day. The sun was still sleeping and the sky was dark, but we had to wake up. The alarms of clocks in my room sounded at 6:30 A.M., some a few seconds faster or slower. Six people, six clocks, and I was definitely sure that with only my own alarm I could never have gotten up. Yunling, Fang, Yue, Huahong, and Mei were my roommates. Yunling slept above me on the upper bunk; she was usually the last one to get up. She murmured in a sleepy voice: "Gosh! What kind of life is this! Wake up at half past six. In winter I thought I'd never experience this kind of bitterness. Only my mum in the village would do it. She's great, getting up to feed us and the pigs." We all laughed and told her it was better to act than talk.

After waking up, we rushed for the toilet, brushed our teeth, washed our faces, and changed our clothes. We had to take turns because there was only one toilet and one washroom. "Hurry up, hurry up"; there was shouting everywhere in the room, but none of the arguing that often occurred in other rooms, especially when someone lost their temper. In our room, the situation was still bearable because we had all learned to keep our patience with one another. Time was pressing and we could not afford to waste a minute, so while someone was using the toilet, others would wash themselves in the washroom, while still others would change their overalls or comb their hair on the bed. Turns were arranged silently and we lived on consent rather than written orders. To make life easier, self-disciplining was nurtured from the moment we woke up.

About 6:45 to 7:00 A.M. we began to leave the dormitory. We could reserve fifteen minutes for breakfast if we could make it to the factory in less than twenty minutes. I often walked with Yunling and Mei, two Cantonese girls from rural Guangdong. Yunling complained of the harsh life in the workplace: "At home, I got up when the sun rose and it was time to be hungry for breakfast. But here, we are all forced to wake up to the alarms." I asked her, "Don't you need to help your mum cook or feed pigs in the morning?" "Sometimes," she replied, "but I was not the one supposed to do so." Yunling had two elder sisters and one sister-in-law who helped the family do domestic chores and farm work. She was the free hand at home, which was why she was able to do factory work in Shenzhen.

Rural life rhythms were somewhat varied. Although specific times for sowing, fertilizing, and harvesting were recorded in detail in the Chinese lunar calendar, there was still no strict disciplinary machine to guide everyday life. The work time and duties of individuals varied according to family economy, sibling order, and gender. Pressures were felt, especially by the mother or eldest daughter who were required to manage the daily food for the whole family and often had to get up at a very early hour. But rarely did I hear anyone complain of not getting enough sleep in the village. In the workplace, however, the biological clock was completely socialized and reset to industrial time. Too little sleep was a serious problem; every day workers slept about six hours or less. Not enough sleep, plus a long and harsh working day, made the disciplinary time seem external and alien. The working body was dragged along to meet the timetable imposed from the outside by the despot of disciplinary time. Yunling was the one who found it most difficult to cope with the work schedule. She therefore often emphasized that she could sleep as much as she liked when she was in her home village, but there seemed no way to escape once one was subject to industrial time.

At 7:50 A.M. we had to queue up, enter the factory gate, and punch our timecards. Security guards stood at the big gate carefully checking company permits, which had to be pinned to the chest pocket of one's overalls. Those who forgot to bring the permit would not be allowed in, even if recognized as a company worker by the security guards. There was then no recourse but to go back to the dormitory and find the permit, which would make one late for work and result in a fine and condemnation: five minutes late would be counted as one hour late and wages would be deducted for two hours. The wage at Meteor was based largely on an hourly rate, around 3 renminbi per hour for production line workers. Such serious punishment reflected the saying that every minute of labor was crucial to the functioning of the entire production machine.

"Time is money" was the new disciplinary discourse prevailing in the rapidly developed industrialized areas. It was much highlighted in post-socialist China with the rapid growth of global production and the attempts to articulate a global consciousness of speed and money. Work quicker and work harder was the secret to producing wealth and the primary ideology of global capitalism. Losing time was losing one's money along with the company profit. Workers were thus self-technologized with this time/money sense that money was assigned to time and labor in their production process. It was felt not only that the disciplinary techniques would induce them to work, but more fundamentally that money and wealth inspired them to work harder and longer. Because at Meteor as well as other workplaces in Shenzhen the basic monthly wages for an eight-hour working day was as low as 300 renminbi, overtime work at night and on holidays became a self-motivation project that could result in a doubling of wages. Time therefore was to be deliberately planned and controlled, not only by the production machine but also by the producers whose prime aim was to make money by selling their laboring bodies during their transient stay in the city.

With our overalls, caps, and gloves in place and our work tools and materials prepared, the factory clock bell rang at exactly 8:00. The day would start with a ten-minute meeting reporting the output performance and commenting on each line's productivity and quality. After the workers returned to their positions, the light flashed, the line started running, and our morning work began. Music—popular Cantonese songs—was played for fifteen minutes to freshen our minds to work more efficiently. It was said that the workers could work faster in the morning with their energy refreshed by a few hours of sleep, so discipline in the morning was often strict and it was difficult to find a chance to talk or joke. There was a common understanding on the line that the higher management was in a mood to keep things straight in the morning hours. Talk and laughter caught by the foreman or supervisor often was not tolerated. Silence, fast-moving lines, and the speed of time out of control—this was the feel of morning work.

Five minutes before lunch at noon the line would stop and we started to finish up our jobs. Talk immediately mounted and all kinds of noises filled the silence. We had kept quiet for the whole morning, and it seemed that everyone had to talk at once. We were not permitted to leave the shop floor at the same time. Each line took turns to leave because there was only one staircase for all of the shop floor workers. Rushing to eat lunch in fifteen minutes, we would then come back to our seats to take a nap. All of the lights were switched off and the bright workshop turned to a dark world. Because we were exhausted every day, all of us would fall asleep. The afternoon nap is a habit in China, in both rural and urban areas. In the Mao era industrial enterprises would close at lunch and not reopen until 3:00 P.M., so that workers at least could have two hours of sleep after lunch. This habit has been altered in urban China in the past decade, however, because the mode of economic life has been dictated by private capitalist practices rather than state management. In the eyes of Meteor's management, it seems unbelievable that workers in China might have had such a leisurely life, one that Hong Kong managers could not enjoy or even dream of. Indeed, the saying that "time is money" was not a false consciousness tailored to cheat the workers. Rather, the managers themselves as the bearers of the axiom had to live up to it too.

At 12:50 P.M., the lights were turned on and we awoke to punch our time cards. At 1:00 the clock bell rang, music was turned on, and the line ran again. Work was repetitive and never-ending. The closed environment, with all of the windows sealed and covered by a plastic curtain, kept the workers from being distracted by the outside world. We could not judge the time by seeing the rising and setting of the sun, nor could we breathe natural air. The workplace air was regulated twenty-four hours a day by the central air conditioning. The temperature was kept at 68° F throughout the year, which was low enough not only to cool the electronic parts but also to wake up drowsy eyes. Talking, gossiping, joking, and secret snacks were sometimes allowed in the afternoon on the condition that they not affect the speed and running of the line. And it seemed that noise and laughter also served as an effective way to keep the workers awake.

What the girls complained about most was not the low wage or harsh workload, but lack of adequate sleep sustained over months and years. An eighteen-year-old worker, Li Peng, told me, "Everyday I can only sleep for five or six hours. It doesn't drive me mad, but makes me like a sleeping pig. Whenever there's a chance. I fall asleep. I can't help but be drowsy." What the girls could do was making an effort to cheer themselves up. Every chance to have fun and share snacks was taken, each little moment was important to keeping up spirits. Another way of killing drowsiness was to take a short break by going to the washroom. But workers could not leave their work seats unless granted an out-of-position permit by the assistant line leader, and five minutes was the maximum allowed. Workers often complained about the time limit, especially when they were menstruating. Drowsiness was the contagious virus that the disciplinary machine found most diffi-cult to deal with: work pace would slow down and the jobs piled up on the line, and some workers would slip and get hurt by the soldering gun or the molding machine. Small accidents such as hurting a finger often oc-curred in late afternoon or at night, when workers did not have enough concentration. When somebody suffered more significant bodily pain and was sent to the hospital, the others on the shop floor would suddenly wake up to their work.

By 5:00 P.M. we could all hear our stomachs rumbling and we were hungry for dinner. Work started again at 6:00 P.M. and the time card was punched again. We were then told what time we could end our work that night. If it was at 9:00 we thought we had a lucky day. Normally we stopped work at 10:00, and sometimes the shift extended to 11:00 or 12:00 for a rush production order. Night work was comparatively more relaxed, and the radio was turned on for the duration. The workers listened to the Hong Kong channels, which they found more interesting than the Shenzhen or Guangzhou channels. Chatting about popular film stars and favorite singers helped to pass time quickly; dreaming of the romance provoked by the love songs or stories from the radio helped to kill time in the extreme exhaustion and boredom of night work.

Inspections by the personnel department or higher management in the production department seldom occurred at night. As Fatso explained to me on the line, "The white-collar staff members, with their good fate, need more time to take care of their bodies; they don't have time to inspect us." At 9:00 or 10:00 we stopped for the day and dashed back to the dormitory, queuing up for hot water to bathe. After bathing, we still needed to wash our clothes, and someone with a free hand would cook some snacks because we all felt hungry after working three or four hours after dinner. Eating and talking took another hour. After midnight we all went to bed. This type of hectic day, with every minute and second fully utilized and organized, definitely differed from the rhythms of rustic life in the village. Although the six hours of sleep was inadequate, day after day we all got used to it. At the very beginning of my work in the factory I thought it would be impossible for me to stand it for more than a week. But then after one week the cycle of repetition, the constant regularity, and the well-written rhythm of life and work penetrated not only into my body but my soul and my psyche, and I found that I could cope fairly well. However, life was manageable only by a strict timetable.

At Meteor it was clear that the capitalist mode of construction of temporality overrode peasant time in regulating daily life. The relation between human life and time thus became one of aggression and conquest (Thompson 1967, 90). It became an alienating relationship in which life was forced to catch up to time as if it were an external object to conquer and possess. The timetable, with its ethos and practices, was undoubtedly the essence of the capitalist mode of temporality. It provided a new frame of timing for the individuals to program a new pattern of life, which had to take the notion of time is money into its very heart. Life itself thus became an alien flow of fragmentary time; the working day was disguised minute by minute by the renewed effort of will that the workers incessantly squeezed from themselves (Haraszti 1978, 57). But with the uncompromising, severe, and demanding nature of time, workers found it easy to notice the despotic power it imposed on their bodies, their movements, and their everyday life.

The timetable thus was a contested terrain, the acute point of labor subconsciousness before forming the work habit. The timetable was so strict, so rigorous that everybody could feel it—could know and experience it. Life was dissected into a series of timed behaviors, rigidly patterned and stored in the body and mind of each worker. It was precisely at the moment when the transaction between the disciplining power and the workers occurred that women workers, including myself, came to realize our labor value and the different lifestyles we had constructed. Accommodating, resisting, and understanding the power from the side of capital and from ourselves were all nested in the workplace. No one was a dupe.

Institutionalizing Everyday Life: The Factory Codes

If the timetable was the heart of the disciplinary power regulating factory life, then the factory regulations were the heart of the timetable. A strict timetable needed a severe prosecutor to enforce it. The modality of power itself was extremely despotic, but it was justified by the nature and massive number of the workers that had to be governed. There were over five hundred workers, and all were from diverse places of origin, spoke different dialects, and had different habits of life and codes of behavior and standards. To order these heterogeneous migrants into one standardized set of behaviors, and mold the confused mind into a well-disciplined psyche, the disciplinary machine needed ingrained techniques of power. It also needed an impartial and equitable legislator machine to set unbiased codes and state clearly how to punish and reward. This universe of punishment and reward was established in which everybody knew what to do and how to do it.

New workers were asked to read the factory regulation handbook before they could start work on the shop floor. But in our weekly precept time on Wednesday afternoon at 4:30, factory codes were frequently repeated and warnings were given from time to time.[9] On the staircase landings and in the canteen, important factory regulations were framed under glass on the wall. Six times a day, nobody could escape seeing them. Of course, one could see without looking and hear without listening, but day in and day out the regulations would simply be instilled into one's unconsciousness, no matter how much one found them disgusting or thought they had no effect on one's mind at all.

At the landing of the second-floor staircase, every day we could see the following:

PRODUCTION REGULATIONS

1. Workers should do all preparations such as wearing work cap, electronic-prevention belt, gloves, and so forth five minutes before the on-work time. To prevent any dirt on the products, no one is allowed to comb their hair or do anything that may cause dust or dirt. Each violation is fined 2 yuan.

2. All workers should obey the production arrangements of the higher authorities. If anyone has a different opinion, complete the job first before seeking out the authorities.

3. Workers are not allowed to leave work positions or change work position during work time unless approved by the supervisors. If leaving the work position for personal reasons such as going to toilet the worker must apply for a *out-of-position permit.* Each violation is fined 2 yuan.

4. No one will be allowed to leave the factory unless there is a *company exit permit* signed by the affiliated department manager and the personnel department, and examined by the security guard before leaving the factory. Leaving the factory without permission will be seriously punished and each violation is fined 50 yuan.

5. Punching a timecard for others or asking another person to punch a timecard for you is prohibited. The first time of violation will be given serious warning and fined 20 yuan; the second time will be fined 100 yuan and the worker will be dismissed at once.

6. All workers must arrive at work on time. Arriving over five minutes late will be counted as late for one hour, while wages will be deducted at two hours rate.

At the third floor and in the canteen, the following framed rules were on the wall:

DAILY BEHAVIOR REGULATIONS

1. No talking, eating, playing, chasing, or fighting is allowed on the shop floor.

2. No dumping waste and no spitting. Each violation is fined 5 yuan.

3. Receiving or making personal phone calls is not allowed. If discovered, no matter how long the call, the worker will be immediately dismissed and all wages deducted.

4. For stealing factory property the worker will be dismissed at once and fined 50 to 500 yuan. If the case is serious, the offender will be sent to the Public Security Bureau.

5. The normal period of wear for an overall is one year. If one requires a new overall, there should be a reasonable explanation; otherwise, 50 yuan will be deducted from the wage.

6. The normal period of wear for a pair of work shoes is eight months. If there is unreasonable damage, 12 yuan will be deducted from the wage.

JOB LEAVE AND RESIGNATION REGULATIONS

1. No job leave unless there is permission from the line leader, foreman, and department manager. A leave permit should be signed by all of them and then sent to the personnel department for approval. The leave permit should then be signed by the applicant to make it effective. Otherwise, all leave will be considered as absence.

2. For those who are ill or on personal leave who can not attend overtime work, prior permission should be gained and the proper procedures completed. Otherwise, all such leave will be considered as absence. Absence for one night of overtime work will be deducted half a day's wage, absence for one day will be deducted three days of wages.

3. Absence for two days will be deducted six days of wages. Continuous absence for three days will be considered as voluntary leave and all salary voluntarily given up.

4. Basic workers who intend to resign should give notice fifteen days before leaving; staff should give one month's notice. Otherwise, wages will be deducted for fifteen days.

5. For those new workers and staff who resign before completing two months of work, seven days of wages will be deducted for training costs.

These framed codes, of course, did not have a dramatic effect on factory life. We felt their existence only when we were on the verge of violating them or actually violating them. It was possible to find ways around these codes, as there is with any law. No talking, eating, or playing in the workplace was one of the primary regulations. But as I have described above, talking, eating snacks, making jokes, and teasing were all done openly in the late afternoon and on night work. Workers simply could not help but violate the regulation if they were to kill the boredom and drowsiness. Individual defiance like deliberately not performing the job, speaking loudly, making fun of others, or leaving the work seat without waiting for a permit happened from time to time as well. Passing jokes on the line, sometimes overtly, sometimes covertly, could be seen as resistance to the extreme work conditions and as a chance to refresh an empty mind. Sexual innuendoes directed at the male technicians or supervisors were the funniest type of joke on the line. Who forgot to close the zipper of his trousers, or who had a new haircut or wore new clothes were all fodder for assembling jokes. Foremen and line leaders tended to ignore such behavior because they knew that the daily operation of the line could never be guided by factory regulations that were too adamant and relentless. The willingness to give labor power and the cooperation of the workers had to be taken into consideration. As Bailan, the leader of my line, told me, "It's no use being too harsh. We need to understand the workers' situation and individual problems. I would prefer to ask the worker to leave her seat to wash her face with cold water than to see her yawning all the time. . . . Sometimes I don't prevent them from talking or daydreaming, you know, it is the only way to keep the work moving." Even to the foremen, stringent disciplinary techniques seemed despotic, external, and impractical in regulating the human world of action, agency, and limitation.

There were also other clever tactics, often invisible and unrecorded, that workers in the workplace developed to cope with the work pressure and to humanize the harsh conditions (Kondo 1990). While some preferred daydreaming, others passed around sweets and snacks, and still others listened to tapes and radio broadcasts. Some women workers also brought photos of loved ones or pictures of favorite stars and placed them on their work desks. At Meteor and elsewhere workers were interested in asking me about Hong Kong singers and film stars (Pun 2001, 103–16). Juan, the twenty-three-year-old leader of the QC line was a fan of Andy Lau; under the glass of her work desk there were over ten different pictures of him. She told me she liked him so much that she would save all of her money to buy his current album. Daydreaming of handsome and alluring idols helped to kill the boredom and fatalistic feelings of factory work. As Juan mused, "When I was a child in the village, I often dreamed of becoming a singer and having performances everywhere in the big cities. It would be so great." Both line workers and line leaders all enjoyed daydreaming in the workplace, a tactic of psychological escape to alleviate the pressure, tension, and boredom of repetitive work day after day (Pun 2001, 114).

Although there was no strict code against listening to the radio during work time, the practice was that music was played only for fifteen minutes at the start of work each morning and afternoon. For overtime work at night, the radio was often on for the whole session; but it was a common consensus and expectation rather than a rule. Indeed, the workers had to struggle to keep it as an expectation. The radio was crucial in alleviating the harshness of working life, and despite the fact that indulging in music was an individual strategy to cope with everyday work pressure and tension, any opposition to this individual act could develop into some sort of united defiance. Defiance in this vein is a good example to show that workplace transgression is not always oriented toward economic interests. It is not always about bread and dignity but pleasure and work as well.

One interesting struggle I observed at Meteor involved the radio. Because different lines were loyal to different channels, sometimes the flows of sound fought with each other because the volume of each radio was often turned to the maximum. The foremen or line leaders often needed to shout when they talked to the workers, which to some extent caused interruptions. Sometimes the volume would turned to a lower level by the line leader, but very quickly the workers would be turn it up again because of the noise from the adjacent line and the machines. The situation was noticed one night at 8:15 by Tin, the assistant manager of production department, and he suddenly ordered the line leaders to switch off all of the radios. The workplace resumed its silence, but with the queer atmosphere of silence at night. An extraordinary mood prevailed on the shop floor; grumbling and discontent were intense and widespread. Then, spontaneously, all of the workers slowed their pace at the same time. Moving lines were forced to stop and workers started chatting and laughing as they did in the leisure time. At first some new workers did not dare to stop working, but when they looked at other workers idling and chatting they felt compelled to stop. Following quietly, workers elsewhere on other lines joined in the slowdown. Foremen and line leaders knew that there would be no use in trying to persuade the workers to work.

I was shocked by the situation and excited to see how it would turn out. But nothing happened. The workers continued talking and joking, with some singing in low voices. The foremen were called in to the office of the production department to discuss with Tin how to deal with the situation. Tin was not willing to give up and allow the radio on again because it was too great a challenge to his authority and his face. But Tin could not order production to stop, because only Mr. Wu, manager of the production department, had the power to do so and he was out of the factory at the time. The impasse thus continued, and it seemed that all of the laughing and joking were mocking Tin's authority. At 9:00 P.M. we were asked to leave the workplace. On the way back to the dormitory the workers were excited, talking loudly and freely on the street. Nobody mentioned the event directly; although everyone knew it was an open confrontation with the despotic production machine. Conversations instead focused on the workers' favorite stars, and once the talk centered on their idols, they would not stop talking for another hour. The next night the radios were on and production resumed as normal.

This case illustrates that the workers would act militantly not solely for economic reasons but also for cultural activities that they saw as an important part of their daily life. Love songs and stories, full of romance and fascination, were the most fertile soil for daydreaming, alleviating work pressure, and lessening nostalgia for home. The alienation of the labor seemed lessened by popular songs and singers. The radio provided not only entertainment for enduring long working hours and harsh working conditions but also opportunities to hear about the outside world, the only way to loosen the binds of bodily imprisonment in the workplace. Although strictly regulated by factory codes, the workers nevertheless were free in their daydreams and imagination. Stopping the radio meant intervening in their private lives and thus into the rights on which they would not compromise. During the radio event, even the foremen and the line leaders were on the side of the workers. Bailan said, "The radio program provides the inspiration to stimulate the girls to work fast. I am sure that without the radio I couldn't get them to work."

The victory here was limited: factory regulations were still too detailed, too stringent, and too intrusive in the daily lives of the workers. The residence and living regulations were posted on the wall on each floor of the dormitory. Again: no spitting, no fighting, no gambling, no drinking, no faction gangs, no change of beds, no talking, laughing, or visiting after midnight, no visitors staying overnight, no use of cooker, heater, personal fan, and many other codes regulating daily behavior, with fines ranging from 5 yuan to 500. Nevertheless, there were more violations of regulations in the dormitory than in the workplace. Workers frequently changed beds to form kin and ethnic clusters because they found it easier to cope with each other. Moreover, it was impossible to stop cooking in the room because all workers were hungry at night after overtime work. Visitors from the same villages often stayed overnight until they could find jobs elsewhere. Sometimes, even, a man was found in a woman's bed; if reported, the worker would be dismissed at once. Gambling and drinking, albeit less of an issue in the women's rooms, were common in men's dorms. Daily life transgressions were innumerable and in general were tolerated if the acts did not seriously threaten the order of dormitory life.

The Electronic Eye: The Principle of Panopticism

Despite the discursive, spatial, and institutional controls on the women workers in the workplace, the production machine could not find itself secure and certain in its techniques of power. Chinese rural bodies were not easy to deal with, and a more encompassing and penetrating force was needed, one that was not a human being or even present. Such requirements could only be filled by an electronic eye. The assembly line and the timetable were the visible and conspicuous forms of power at work on the body, but there was also an invisible and untouchable part of disciplinary power. The power of the electronic eye was always obscured, hidden in the general office. The workers could not see it or touch it, but they all knew it existed, always gazing at them. It was somewhere and everywhere.

At Meteor an electronic eye was installed at the corner of the wall on each floor. But none of the workers could see it actually work and no one knew when it was on or off. Although some workers completely ignored it, others were highly sensitive to the electronic eye, worrying that their behaviors in the workplace would be recorded in detail through the camera. One day Fatso told me, thinking that I did not know of its existence, "There's an electronic eye hanging on the wall, always checking our behavior. The director doesn't need to keep a watch on the line. He just sits there but he can watch every one of us. The pictures are flowing before his eyes and he can control the computer and have the picture focused on anyone." She kept her voice as low as possible, but it seemed that the eye was gazing at her. The presence of the unpresence, the fictitious image of the panoptical eye, seemed highly effective at controlling workers' behaviors.

It was hard to know when this supreme power was articulated and re-enforced among the workers in the workplace. But once the story of the panoptical eye started, its power was penetrating, and most of the workers thought about its control every now and then. The production line workers sometimes would point to the electronic eye to remind adjacent workers if they worked too slow or sneaked away to take a rest, as if upper management was watching them. There were also rumors that once the director noticed who was talking or laughing on the shop floor, he or she would be dismissed immediately without warning. I also heard it said by some line leaders that it would be more difficult for workers to steal production materials in those workplaces where an electronic eye was installed. "It is expensive, perhaps. But it is worth it," said Bailan, the line leader. The power of the eye as the symbol of supreme power was actualized in the way that it helped to induce self-discipline and mutual control in the workplace.

With the eye poking through the wall, workers were forced to think that they were all continuously under supervision. One evening, I saw an argument in the QC room on the shop floor, where one woman worker argued with her line leader about checking a model. The woman's voice was loud enough to raise the attention of other workers, who kept murmuring about the issue. I asked one worker if they were worried about the electronic eye recording the argument and the worker's challenge to management. The worker said, "Of course, we are afraid. Who knows when the supervisor will use the record and fire us? Only those who have guts will defy. I would rather keep silent." As usual, the disciplinary power would be eased a little in the evening, but the highest authority still needed to find a chance to demonstrate its power, which was to be impersonal, invisible, untouchable, and even remote from the imaginations of the workers. It was above, it was everywhere, it was very threatening, but it did not exist until the workers told themselves that it was there. Sometimes the workers would totally forget about it, but other times they kept on telling each other that it was there. The object of the gaze was the subject of power; at the heart of the disciplinary machine it manifested the subjection of those who were perceived as objects and the objectification of those who were subjected (Foucault 1979, 1984–85).

———

This chapter articulates the microtechniques of power over the female body and the everyday defiance and transgressions against the production machine in the workplace. Homogenizing the social body involves techniques of power ranging from the sophisticated and despotic to the primitive. Initially I showed how the technique of strict spatial positioning fixed on the shop floor the nomadic bodies not trusted by management. The detailed study and analysis of the work process of each individual body, aimed at maximizing labor time, resulted in the fragmentation of labor power. Then the assembly line, with its moving and consistent exercise of power, linked a multitude of individualized bodies into one collective automatic function. The timetable and factory codes simultaneously strove to install a new program of daily factory life into workers' psyches to help them acquire a new habitus of everyday life.

The praxis of spacing and timing, the technique of dissecting individual bodies, and the power of composing collective energies thus function together to produce a new social body—dagongmei—imagineered to be under control by the electronic eye. Extracting and maximizing labor power is shown to be the sole aim and sole economy of the production disciplinary machine. These microtechniques of power speak against the findings of recent management-labor studies that argue for notions of the "new management," "new work relation," or "new workplace" in the post-Fordist era.[10] Conventional Taylorist principles, albeit twisted and warped, are still prevalent in global factories in China (Chan 2001), and we can see a high degree of hybridity when Taylorism meets the new work system and production requirements. We also see a low-trust management culture that can easily slip into what Lee Ching Kwan (1998a) calls the localistic despotism of factory regimes, or what Anita Chan (2001) describes as the authoritarianism of China's workplaces. The minimal state intervention in management-labor relations in most of the developing zones, along with the lack of independent labor forces, means that practices of excessive control, long hours, low wages, and poor living environments are often the rule in contemporary China.

4

BECOMING DAGONGMEI:

POLITICS OF IDENTITIES

AND DIFFERENCES

Dagongmei, the working daughter, is a newly embodied social identity emerging in contemporary China, produced to meet the changing socio-economic relations of the country and the needs of capital. A new identity has been crafted, accompanied by a new ethics of self, which is inscribed on young rural female bodies when they enter into a particular set of pro-duction relations, experiencing the process of proletarianization and alien-ation.[1] At first glance, this construct looks inevitably to be a disciplinary project that works with homogeneous and reactive forces to interpellate the self with a modern worker identity. With insights from Dorinne Kondo's *Crafting Selves* (1990, 16), a disciplinary project on identity, which implies unity and fusion, often goes together with a fragmentation of the self. The process of constituting an identity is imbued with a politics of difference that offers a vivid configuration of self and identity in everyday life struggles situated in particular moments and occasions. This politics of difference highlights a heterogeneous, incoherent, fluid, and conflict-laden process of identity-making on specific bodies in distinct situations.

In this chapter I describe the process as it builds a social identity; I look both from the side of power and the side of the subject, and I examine regulatory and identificatory practices inside and outside the workplace. Dagongmei is a specific ethics of self, construed at the particular moment when private and transnational capital emerged in post-Mao China. As a

condensed identity, dagongmei reveals the story of how a state socialist
system gives way to the capitalist global economy and how capitalist practices depend entirely on a complex web of regulations, and on class, rural-
urban differences, kin and ethnic networks, and sexual relations.[2] In particular, I will look at a play of difference in the process of producing the
subject dagongmei in the workplace, and how social and historical differences along the lines of social status, class, and gender differences regulate a
work hierarchy that, in turn, is reinforced by a workplace distinction system
in terms of work position, wage and bonus, accommodation, and even work
clothing. Along with the politics of difference, I also highlight a politics of
discourse in which we see how disciplinary production deploys the art of
metaphor, the power of language, and the politics of othering and differentiating in crafting a new identity, that of dagongmei. The "manufacture" of
identity involves both the politics of discourse and the politics of difference.

By writing on the politics of difference I do not intend to look at the
inherent fragmentation of the psychological self in its signification process
of becoming a subject. Rather I locate a play of difference in the process of
creating the subject dagongmei in the larger field of social and cultural
meanings embedded in a rapidly reconfiguring Chinese society. I highlight
the social and historical differences in the self-internalization of the new
identity of dagongmei as it appears in the significatory chain and strives to
emerge into the symbolic world. At the core of the regulatory and identificatory practices in urban and industrial China, there is a politics of difference
that establishes a violent hierarchy between the rural and the urban, the
northerner and the southerner, and the male and the female. In the workplace I was informed by this politics, and it let me see and experience how
regional, kin, and ethnic differences were imagineered in crafting the identity of dagongmei.

———

As a newly coined term dagongmei embraces multilayered meanings and
denotes a new kind of labor relationship fundamentally different from that
of Mao's period. *Dagong* means "working for the boss" or "selling labor,"
thereby connoting commodification and capitalist exchange of labor for
wages (Lee 1998a). It is a new concept that contrasts with the history of
Chinese socialism. Labor, especially alienated labor, supposedly emanci-
pated for more than thirty years, is again sold to capitalists, this time under
the auspices of the state machine. In contrast to the term gongren, or
worker, which carried the highest status in the socialist rhetoric of Mao's day,

the new word dagong signifies a lesser identity—that of a hired hand—in a new context shaped by the rise of market factors in labor relations and hierarchy. Mei means younger sister; it denotes not merely gender but also marital status—mei indicates single, unmarried, and younger (in contrast to *jie*, older sister), and thus mei often signifies a lower status. Dagongmei therefore implies an inferior working identity inscribed with capitalist labor relations and sexual relations.

The term dagongmei, paradoxically, did not necessarily carry a negative sense for the young rural girls themselves; rather, it provided new identities and new senses of the self to be acquired once they worked inside a global factory. Self-subjectivization was crucial to the power of capital that needed willing labor. As Foucault (1994, 81–82) has said, the project of political technology or governmentality is at the same time a project of self-subjectivization. It is fascinating to see how these two conflicting forces converge and contrast in manufacturing consent and identity in the workplace, and how these contestations can be understood within the larger dynamics of Chinese society that highlight shifting hegemony, values, and social forces in the postsocialist period.

A Fumbled Identity: My First Day on the Shop Floor

At 6:00 A.M. in late autumn 1996 I awoke while my dormitory roommates were still sleeping. I was a bit excited because after two weeks of reading company archives and other documents in the general office at the Meteor electronics factory, I was finally going out to work on the assembly line. In order to look like a factory girl, I bought T-shirts, jeans, and shoes in a local market in the Nanshan district. I also had my hair curled—at the suggestion of Tall Ling, the director's secretary. Arriving a bit early at the factory, I saw Jun from the personnel department eating breakfast at a small food shop just opposite the factory building. "You don't need to hurry," Jun said, "I know you are going to work on the shop floor today." With a smile, she added that today, in my new clothes, I looked like a factory worker. "Without your glasses, you are our double."

Jun led me to the department of general affairs where I signed some paperwork and received my factory uniform: two sets of blue overalls, a blue cap, a pair of white gloves, and a pair of slippers. Blue was the color that designated the production department. Before I went upstairs to the shop floor, I changed my clothes in the washroom. Jun was still with me and she laughed at my appearance. I somehow felt that although I was in overalls, my image was awkward and my newly assumed identity had not crystal-lized. Jun brought me to assembly line B on the fourth floor. It was about 8:00 A.M. Except for some echoes of machine sounds, silence reigned on the whole shop floor. I was shocked, not by the silence but because the moment I appeared on the shop floor everyone stared at me. With my heart throbbing, I wondered, did my appearance in my overalls look bizarre? Didn't I look like a dagongmei? Was I not expected to work on the shop floor? He-chuan, the foreman of line B, looked at me as if he were expecting me, and he was the only one to welcome me. He led me to my seat on the middle of the line, a position on the screwing station, and asked me to sit down. I did as he asked, knowing that all gazes still fell on my body—a body unfit for an identity.

My identity as an ethnographer, albeit ambiguous and unstable, was certainly too reified for me to adapt to a new identity. Time after time I wondered and asked myself: Was I anything like a factory girl? I knew all the workers could never acknowledge my appearance as a dagongmei, even if in the end they accepted me as someone who worked with them. My past identities did become diluted and ambiguous as time went on, and I found myself totally lost in the industrial world, toiling twelve hours each day without knowing what was going on in the outside "civilized" world. Yet I still dared not ask the question of whether or not I was a dagongmei. People treated me differently on the shop floor, which reminded me of my past identities. No one, not even myself, was able to inscribe on me the proper identity of dagongmei. Indeed, from the beginning the production machine had no interest in incorporating me; I was left alone.

Different Fate, Different Identity: Meifang's Coming

The fate of my coworker Meifang greatly contrasted with my fate. The production machine held a strong desire to turn Meifang into a dagongmei, a modern female worker. So did Meifang herself. None of us was born to be a worker, especially those like Meifang who were born to be "peasants." Grant-ing oneself an identity that could find no residue—no cause and effect and no justification in biological factors or any born-to-be attributes—involved particularly sophisticated techniques and strategies of power. Internaliza-tion, on the other hand, required further meandering, painful, and even perverted ways of technologizing the self.

The day that Meifang started she was brought to a seat opposite me. Un-like my training period, she was given serious warnings and strict instructions before she could start working. Bailan, our line leader, first checked her overalls, cap, and gloves, and then told her to have her hair neatly tied up and completely covered by her work cap: "Make sure not a single string of hair falls on the desk, the chair, or the floor. Short hair is easily dropped in the product and can't be easily noticed. Your fingernails should be trimmed, otherwise the gloves will tear and cause flecks on the product," Bailan said.

Then Meifang was instructed to wear a static electricity belt on her wrist to prevent her body's static from interfering with the electronic products. She was also given a metal recorder and told to tap it before she put the product onto the conveyor belt: "You should never forget to tap it. The recorder not only counts how much work you do, but also the amount that the entire line produces. All the numbers from each recorder should be the same at the end. You should not make any mistake," Bailan said, and then started to teach Meifang her assigned task.

I noticed immediately a basic difference in the way the management treated Meifang and me. He-chuan had told me to take care of my fingers and not to be hurt by the screwdriver, whereas Bailan told Meifang to take care of the driver and not let it get worn. Moreover, it took me a week to understand that Meifang was hired to supplement my work because management thought I could not keep up with the work pace and that it was likely that I would occasionally leave the line for other reasons.

Meifang was given on-the-job training for a three-month probation period before she was granted a work contract for one year, which was the practice for all newcomers. In our work process, four miniature screws and two even smaller ones were used to attach a main board to two outer cases. Picking up screws from the box and putting them in the appropriate positions required nimble fingers and a quick hand; otherwise one might pick up more than one screw at the same time because they easily stuck to the fingers, and they easily could be lost. But this was not the difficult part—the element that required the greatest skill was handling the electric screwdriver. The amount of force necessary mattered most: different sizes of screws or the same sizes in different positions involved different amounts of force. Too much force would result in small cracks in the case; too little force and the screw might tilt and require repositioning. It took me three days to become adept at the work process.

Although Meifang took nearly as long as I to learn the work process, a few days later she was able to work much faster. But she was silent all the time. Even after working for two weeks she still often just nodded and smiled at me and then went back to work. "She seems unhappy. She doesn't utter a word for a whole day. How odd!" my coworker Fatso gossiped to me at lunch one day. What kept Meifang quiet? What worried her when other workers relaxed and fell into laughter from time to time? Was a fairly fit body to do the job still not good enough for her?

Indeed, a fairly fit body was not enough because it was not complete; it was unsatisfactory to both the production machine and the workers themselves. For survival in a modern factory one needed something more, something fundamental to one's sense of self. Meifang was unhappy and I was uncomfortable. There was something we felt lacking and this lack was unarticulated. We were both capable of doing the work but we were not well equipped to be workers, dagongmei, who strived to live in a modern industrial space.

If it is correct to say, as do Gilles Deleuze and Félix Guattari (1984, 28), that the creation of lack is a function of the market economy, the art of the dominant class, and that it is deliberately created, organized, and produced in and through social production, then we need to know how this primary fear of lack in Meifang, as well as in others like her, is produced and how they are induced to live with it. Dagongmei as a cultural-symbolic artifact contains a set of reactive forces that try to homogenize human activities and senses of self that should be plural, fluid, and fragmentary. The process of homogenization is a process of exclusion and displacement, which produces anxiety, inflicts pain, and drives individuals to integrate into the collective will of the hegemonic construct.

To Be a Worker: The Politics of Rural-Urban Difference

The politics of labor identity in China is linked not only to the project of industrialization but also to a distinctive spatial rural-urban dichotomy. As I demonstrate in chapters 1 and 2, the rural space could only nurture peasants and the urban space workers. Three decades of Chinese socialist history did not imagine a modernization project but rather a curtain between rural and urban and thus between peasants and workers. Chinese socialist beings were born to have an identity not from biology but from locality, and by their locality were designated either urban or rural. Mao's industrialization required the extraction of rural resources to support the urban establishment; rigid plans for rural and urban development; and thus a strict control on individual status and identity (Solinger 1999). The art of naming and classification thus was central to Mao's politics; the hukou system of registration was one such creation. Deng's industrial development and ways of realizing the market economy, on the other hand, demanded not only raw material but also human power from the rural areas, which is why Meifang and millions of other rural women were needed as dagongmei.

Among the 550 workers in the Meteor factory in early 1996, only eleven held an urban hukou; all of the rest came from rural villages or rural towns all over the country and were listed as peasants in the official registry classification. These migrants were born in rural areas, and as such they were not workers but had already been named as peasants. Yet they were needed as laborers. This time the state socialist machine, burdened by its past history, was powerless to regear itself and it gave way to the capitalist machine. The identity of the dagongmei echoed a relationship to the urban, to capital, but not to the state. There was, and there had to be, new models of workers in the new era. The machine of capital thus felt free to reterritorialize the urban-rural boundaries and to mimic the politics of naming and exclusion.

At first newcomers like Meifang were not considered by Meteor management to be qualified workers but rather workers to be. Even after they had worked for a few months in the factory, young women were often still considered to be from the country. They were easily identifiable not because of their lack of skill or speed at work but because of their appearance and their inappropriate behavior in the industrial space. They often looked fresh and quiet, and although they wore T-shirts and jeans they did not put on face powder or lipstick and their jeans were a bit out of style. Their main pastime—knitting—further imparted a distinctly rural image. Still, not only did the production machine aim to transform them into dagongmei, modern working daughters, but the girls themselves also aimed for this goal.

I always kept my work pace as slow as possible to ensure that every piece I produced was of good quality. I was afraid that any defect for which I was responsible would cause my coworkers, especially Meifang, to be reprimanded. Still, mistakes could not be avoided. In the late afternoon of Meifang's fifth day, still within her training period, I became very drowsy and hoped that someone would start talking. Our foreman, He-chuan, holding a route-finder, suddenly showed up in front of Meifang and yelled, "What the hell are you doing? You are going to spoil this casing. Such a big scratch here (he pointed to the case of the route finder). Did you learn something by heart? You know you are not ploughing a furrow, don't you? These products are very expensive, you couldn't pay for it even if you worked in the fields for a year. *Cushou cujiao!* (Rough hands, rough feet)." Then he turned his eyes to me, and showing embarrassment, added, "These village girls are always like that, difficult to teach."

He-chuan left. I saw Meifang's face grow flushed and her eyes fill with tears. I was angry at He-chuan's sudden and irresponsible reproach: he had not tried to determine who had caused the scratch before shouting at Meifang. But then I understood that he actually could never know who was responsible. He just came to the most likely target, shouting so that all of us doing the same work process could hear and share the responsibility. In shouting to express his authority, He-chuan was in effect defeating himself, showing that he could not totally control the labor process. But his language had another function. It produced a surplus value that the disciplinary power did not expect: helping to craft the identity of dagongmei. The metaphor he used—ploughing a furrow—signified the low value placed on farm work and hence a lesser working identity. Such metaphors were invoked time and time again on the shop floor: to make a scratch on the case is like ploughing a furrow on the land, and thus one is a peasant, not a worker. But even though one is only a peasant, one should behave like a worker.

In the metaphor that He-chuan used in his reprimand, he did not mean to imply that working in the factory was like farming on the land, but he could not escape the same paradox: industrial work was not agricultural work, but in some sense it might still be like it. Otherwise how could the metaphor be effective? Invoking the metaphor did show the contradictory nature of the discourse, but it never wasted energy. By juxtaposing farming and industrial work in this way, a hierarchy of values was reinforced in which factory work occupied a higher rank. A gap was produced, a void that allowed power to produce abject subjects.

Meifang was not the only girl subject to this kind of reprimand and the power of language. Every day on the shop floor I heard discriminatory language directed toward the workers. The Cantonese term *xiangxiamei* (village girl) was often used to depreciate the status of the women from rural areas. Phrases like "xiangxiamei, you know nothing except farming," "xiangxiamei, what else can you understand? Learn the rules and behave in a civilized way," "a xiangxiamei is always like a xiangxiamei, cushou cujiao," and "xiangxiamei can never be taught! [They are] foolish and stupid" were frequently heard in the workplace, especially when a male foreman or line leader came to criticize or scold the workers. The metaphorical meanings hidden in these daily usages were the great contrasts between the body and the space: unfit xiangxiamei living incompatibly in the modern industrial world. On the one hand, were the stupid, uneducated, and uncivilized rustic women whose labor was cheap and despised. On the other hand, was the modern technology of the factory, whose products were valuable and exported internationally. Intense anxiety was aroused by such remarks, making some people feel lacking, unfit, or not properly suited to the life of the factory. Women like Meifang felt frustrated for not living up to the demands of a modern world and for not being modern themselves.

Shop floor conversations, arguments, and reprimands always served to remind Meifang and other recent hires of their past identities as peasants. "Cushou cujiao" was the physical stigma of the person as a peasant, whereas xiangxiamei was the abject identity that had to be polished and upgraded. It took me quite a long time to understand why Meifang was not happy. To avoid being discriminated against one had to try hard to change oneself. Self-technologizing, as Foucault (1988) said, is the core of power and a product of modern subjectivity. To make war with one's past identity was for the sake of establishing a new identity; to cut the umbilical cord of one's past life was to create a base for building up a new self. Industrial work was desired not only for the wages but for the new identity and the new sense of life that it created. The imagined peasantness of cushou cujiao was the constitutive outside, or the negative otherness of the new identity. Without mirroring and then negating one's past identity it was difficult to make a new life.

One chilly evening in spring 1996 I had a chance to talk to Meifang in her dormitory. At first she remained timid and kept her head low. I tried hard to start a conversation by asking general questions about where she was from, how old she was, and how many siblings she had. She told me she was from a village in the north of Hunan Province and then gave me a few details about her family situation. Then, without warning, she started crying. I was upset by seeing the tears flowing down her face.

"I really want to go back home."

"Why? You work so well in the factory."

"I don't know, I miss my home. I feel that I don't fit in the workplace."

"But why? You are not working slower than the other people."

"I don't know why. I just feel I don't fit here. I feel I'm too different from the others. Next month after I get my wage, I'll leave."

The month passed, however, and Meifang did not leave.

Later she told me, "Life is hard here, but if others can stand it, why not me?" Moreover, Meifang had started to go out with other workers on their days off, and at night she listened to Cantonese popular music with them.

She bought more current fashions and she asked me to help her buy hair shampoo, facial cleaner, and a lipstick from Hong Kong. Buying cosmetics was one of the ways I did favors for the workers, although not without a sense of guilt over introducing more commodified goods to them.

The Admonition Meeting

Our line had a fifteen-minute "admonition meeting" (*xun dao hui*) every Wednesday at 4:30 P.M. A few minutes before it started, Bailan, the line leader, would stop the line in preparation for speeches by members of the personnel and production departments. Tin, the production department assistant manager, always came. If there were serious production problems, the department manager himself, Mr. Wu, would show up. Tin was a university graduate in his early thirties and had worked at the Meteor plant for over four years. In the eyes of the line women, he was a sharp and capable figure of urban background. We also sometimes thought he was attractive, if he was in a good mood. He was urbane and educated; in a world of few men, he was often a target of fantasy.

One Wednesday Meifang and I were musing about what would happen at the afternoon admonition meeting. At 4:30 Ying, from personnel, along with Tin, He-chuan, and Bailan appeared, and all the line workers, except me, were asked to queue up in front of the line. I was told to stay in my seat. Again I felt like an outsider; time and time again I found that the production machine had no intention of disciplining me. On this day Ying wore a three-piece outfit with a skirt and looked like an urban career woman. At Meteor, she was classified as clerical staff. Her status, wage, fringe benefits, and living conditions were all different from the line workers. In a managerial tone, she stated:

> This week a worker was caught punching another worker's timecard in her absence. This is a serious violation and we reserve the right to dismiss her at once. There is no excuse for anybody to clock on for best friends or fellow villagers. The helper will be punished more seriously than the one who asked for help. In the factory one should be responsible for oneself only. If you are so used to helping each other in the village, remember that now you are in the factory. . . .
>
> The company inspected the workers' dormitory on Monday. Production tools, such as scissors and adhesive tape, were found in two workers' bunks. Although they are not expensive things, these are acts of theft. In

accordance with the factory regulations, these two workers each have been fined 50 yuan. Again, we consider these serious offenses. If they violate the rules again, these two workers will be dismissed immediately. ·

During the inspection, I found cartons that had been brought out by the workers to make benches in their rooms. I emphasize that workers are not permitted to bring any production materials outside the factory gate, even if they are waste. Waste is not your property, it belongs to the company. You have no right to use it. To put it seriously, I can treat that as stealing too. Your habit of taking waste back home should be changed. Let me repeat, you are working now in the factory; the bad habits you bring from the country should be given up. No spitting on the floor, and keep your bunk and room clean.

Ying's speech did not surprise anybody; it was the usual stuff. The workers simply stood quietly, some showing no interest in listening. Information circulated among workers through gossip and rumors, not through this kind of formal address. All the shop floor workers already knew who had been caught clocking on for another worker and who was fined for possession of company materials. The common feeling toward the workers who were caught was that they were "unlucky." Meifang kept her head low and did not look at Ying. But Ying's words had their function. Even if she could not uphold the factory regulations and impose them on the workers, she nevertheless could sometimes put into words the nature of peasantness. *Hu-xiang bangzhu*—helping each other—was perceived to be an attribute of village life that had to be given up to live in an industrial world. Workers were to be responsible for themselves alone: the production machine wanted isolated individuals only. Industrial women were to learn to compete with each other and not help each other.[3]

Stealing, too, was often taken to be a bad habit common to country people. Ying and other staff of urban origin often warned me not to leave valuable things in the dormitory. Workers were not allowed to bring bags into the workplace. All workers were inspected going in or out of the gate because each one was considered a potential thief. Bad characteristics of human nature like stealing were thought to be nurtured in rural areas. The notion of private property thus became a complicated issue for the peasant workers. They were told to give up sharing resources and were even taught to despise the practice because sharing was related to stealing, as in the repeated emphasis that factory waste products were company property that workers must not take away to reuse. The logic of capitalist practice needed to win out against any noncapitalist reasoning in order to assert its hegemony. To gain the power, to win the battle, all other lifestyles had to be destroyed.

Tin's speech focused more on the production target and work discipline on the line. He said that our line had more rejects than the other lines, which negatively affected production speed. He reminded us not to talk while working and said that everybody should be more attentive. Next Monday, Western customers from Europe were scheduled to visit the company, and he told us to behave ourselves: "Everybody should wash their overalls on the weekend. We don't want the customers to see a speck of dirt on your body or in the workplace. No one is allowed to leave his or her work seat until the end of the tour. Materials and cartons should be well allocated and labeled. Company policy is to show we have a completely modern and well-trained work force and a technologically advanced factory." Workers were asked for cooperation. It seemed that a sense of belonging to the company and a sense of self-esteem as a modern worker were to be articulated in front of the foreign customers.

At dinner the women on our line discussed the speeches. They accepted much of what Tin said, but they laughed at Ying. She had at least ten nicknames, such as "Miss Canton," "tall mei," "bossy cat," and "chicken." Posing as a "modern lady," she was less an admired figure than a target of jeers and innuendoes. She was often mocked behind her back, when tone and attitudes were mimicked and made fun of. Immediately after her sudden inspection of the shop floor, laughter would erupt and rough language would spread down the line: "The bossy cat dresses up so nice. What is she going to do tonight? Flirt with men?" or, "Miss Canton really thinks she is Miss Canton. I can't stand the way she walks." As a figure standing for modernity and urbanity, Ying was seen to be on the side of management and capital. It was a negative image, and not one the women workers wanted to imitate.

Inventing Local, Kin, and Ethnic Identity and Inequality

The politics of difference and othering in crafting subjects are further complicated by the intertwining of local, kin, and ethnic relations in the workplace. Women workers were not merely identified and classified as urban or rural people, but also more specifically by region and ethnic group (Lee 1998a). In the Meteor factory, one-third of the women were from villages or towns in Guangdong Province. These Guangdong women were linguistically and regionally divided according to whether they came from Cantonese-dialect areas, Chaozhou-dialect areas, or Hakka areas (only two of the women workers were Shenzhen locals). The remaining two-thirds of the total female labor force came from other provinces across China and were, both inside and outside the factory, referred to as *Waisheng ren* (provincial outsiders). They were commonly nicknamed by province of origin: Sichuan mei, Hunan mei, Hubei mei, or simply Bei mei (northern girls); whereas women from Guangdong Province were called Chaozhou mei, Canton mei, and Hakka mei. These were all common terms used in the workplace to identify individuals, especially in daily language when workers addressed each other.

The identification of a person according to region or ethnicity embodies a sense of spatial inequality far more subtle than the rural-urban disparity. Where one is from and one's dialect foretells one's status and wealth, and thus one's bargaining power and position in the workplace hierarchy. The rural-urban distinction, as a soil for nurturing differences, is deliberately divided into finely stratified hierarchies through its intersection with locality and with kin-ethnic identities.[4]

The most common question in the workplace, which was often used to start a conversation or make friends with strangers, was "Ni shi shenme difang ren?" (literally, "A person of what *difang* [place] are you?"). Difficult to paraphrase, it carries a much richer meaning than the English phrase "Where are you from?" *Di* means the place, the locality, while *fang* embodies a cultural meaning of *di*, connoting specific kin and ethnic relationships. Thus the question asks not only where you are from, but also what is your kin-ethnic identity and which local dialect do you use. In daily conversations workers in the Meteor plant seldom directly asked each other their names but rather asked about affiliation to local and kin-ethnic groups. With few exceptions, workers were grouped into different locality or kin-ethnic enclaves, and were enmeshed in different networks of obligation and authority in the workplace.

Regional and kin-ethnic networks were often manipulated by the production machine to create a division of labor and job hierarchies. In the Meteor factory all of the important and supervisory positions were to some extent affected by local and kin-ethnic power. A line leader was chosen not only for her work capabilities but also for her network affiliations and prestige among the workers.

Siu Wah, the line leader of line C, told me that the control of everyday operations on the shop floor was not as easy as it might appear. It involved the cooperation and consent of every worker in each seat. For a rush order, the work pace had to be increased, which required the women's cooperation. Thus, the most reliable workers were from one's own kin group and area, and the best thing to do was to enlarge one's own group. Such enlargement thus was the most important political way for dominant groups to maintain their status or for weaker groups to struggle for enhancement of their position. The weakest groups were the outsiders to the province, especially those from north China, who were often called Waisheng mei or Bei mei. They were forced to take jobs packing or soldering, the drudge work. Competition for "good jobs" was a daily occurrence on the shop floor, and workers relied on local or kin-ethnic power for these job negotiations.

The Meteor management skillfully made use of local and kin-ethnic relations to facilitate production efficiency and profit maximization, and to facilitate the control of workers. Locals and kin were considered responsible for each other's performance. In cases where unskilled new workers were hired on a relative's recommendation, the relatives often served as trainers, which saved the management time and money. Sometimes kin were made to take responsibility for those newcomers who did not conform to factory discipline or violated some of the basic rules of workers' behavior.[5] The workers were afraid that if their recommendation proved unsuitable, they would not have another chance to introduce a kin or a friend and their own reputations would be affected as well. This self-disciplining within localistic and kin-ethnic circles heightened the efficiency of labor control, and to a certain extent enforced the submissiveness of the female workers.

Regional and kin-ethnic differences among workers were further exaggerated, invented, and manipulated to divide and rank the workforce. A work hierarchy was developed along the lines of the imagined cultural traits of each individual. The director of Meteor, Mr. Zhou, said that in his ten years of work experience in Shenzhen, he had developed a particular knowledge about each kin-ethnic and locality group. He believed that different groups had different sorts of personalities and work capacities that were suitable for different kinds of jobs. His imagination, or invention, of their traits shaped the hierarchy of the labor force inside the factory. For example, he viewed the Chaozhou mei as submissive and attentive but clever, and thus suitable for accounting and personnel work. The Hakka mei were shy and reticent but industrious. They were good listeners and good followers, and so after training they were fit for midlevel management such as foremen or line leader. Zhou said the Hakka mei were often seen by other employers in Shenzhen to be inferior to the Cantonese, but he himself thought they were better because the Cantonese had more choices for upward mobility and so were not as loyal as Hakkas. At Meteor, most of the supervisor and line leader positions were filled by Hakka and Chaozhou people, while almost all of the Waisheng mei were on the production line.

The Waisheng mei, those from outside the province, were eager to show off their capabilities, Zhou said, given that the local government and local people discriminated against them in job hiring, promotion, and right of residence. Zhou thought that the Hubei mei were better than the Hunan mei because poor regions made for hard workers. Hubei mei were considered good operatives—they were dexterous and willing to work hard. Certainly it was obvious that they had less bargaining power, especially because they were only a small group in the workplace.[6]

The manipulation of kin-ethnic groups was further complicated by the production machine's use of them against each other to prevent labor resistance. Mr. Wu, the production manager, said that although local groups seemed to dominate in certain positions, he would not let them totally control any part of the work process. Locality groups placed on the same production line were easier to control and train, but he would insert an individual from another group as a counterweight. Wu said he did not trust these groups because they had many tricks and they could resist at any time by collective illness and slowdowns. In line B where I worked there were twenty-one workers, including eight from Chaozhou, five from Hakka areas, three from Sichuan, three from Hunan, and one from Guizhou. Our line leader, Bailan, was from Chaozhou. Bailan tried to keep a balance between each group and rarely showed preference for any particular group, but in times of difficulty or for rush orders she relied on her own locals, the Chaozhou mei, to help her. In daily conversations Cantonese and Mandarin were the two dialects most often used in our line as official languages, but when Bailan asked for help from her locals she would use the Chaozhou dialect. Distrust among groups was serious. Communication was not only hindered by different dialects but also by the constructed bias and discrimination from the production machine. A divided workforce was created as locality and kin-ethnic relations were mapped out and reinforced to shape a hierarchy of jobs and to facilitate labor control.

The Wage System and Differentiation

The divisions in the workforce were further enacted and codified by the wage system. Excluding the Hong Kong managers, positions such as those occupied by He-chuan, Ying, or Bailan received the highest salaries. The wage system was central to the production and reproduction of workplace life because it was the most obvious and crucial mechanism in playing out the politics of difference and differentiation. Conspicuously organized on a hierarchical basis, the wage system contributed to a kaleidoscope of power and status along lines of locality, kin-ethnicity, and gender. The wage system at Meteor was very complicated because it simultaneously deployed various payment methods, like monthly pay, daily pay, hourly pay, overtime work pay, and production bonuses. The pay one received spoke for one's status and identity and was self-explanatory, although the exact amounts were confidential.

Daily talk about wages was, however, frequent in the workplace and would mount when payday approached. Despite the policy on wage confidentiality, most of the workers actually knew each other's salary, either through their own networks or through rumor. The incomes of the five Hong Kong managers were in amounts often beyond workers' imaginations, but could be judged by the managers' daily expenditures (such as frequent eating out in the restaurant or calling taxi services) as somewhere in the range of fifteen to twenty times that of local managerial staff. Most of the mainland Chinese workers showed no interest in comparing their wages with the Hong Kong managers, because they were, in effect, from another world. All of the office and supervisory staff members above the grade of line leader were paid at a monthly rate. These urban people or college degree holders earned a monthly income in a range between 1,000 and 1,500 yuan. Envied by the majority of workers who were paid a mixture of hourly rate, overtime rate, and production bonus, these office and supervisory staff members enjoyed a privileged position with a stable income and good prospects. They were also housed in a different type of dormitory that usually was composed of units with cooking and water facilities. Of these positions the dagongmei could only dream, as they knew their rural and education background inscribed on them a different fate.

The line operators and manual workers were generally paid at an hourly rate. In 1996, normal working hours in the daytime were paid in renminbi, at a rate of RMB 2.4 per hour. Overtime work at night was paid in Hong Kong dollars at $3.6 per hour. Such wage practices induced these workers to work as long as possible at night for overtime work pay. If they did not work overtime, their wages could be as low as 300 yuan, and such amounts in Shenzhen could only support their daily basic expenditures on food, rent, and clothing. A lunchbox meal cost 2 yuan, and dinner at a food store could reach as high as 5 yuan. The price of a pair of jeans varied from RMB 20 to RMB 50 at the local market. The company charged each worker fifty yuan monthly for staying in the factory dormitory. "We all hate night work, but it is the only way to earn Hong Kong dollars and the money," the line women on the shop floor often said to me.[7] With overtime pay and the production bonus the line workers could have an average pay of around 500 to 600 yuan a month. Some workers told me that they moved to the Meteor plant because of its abundant overtime work paid in Hong Kong dollars, which accounted for up to one-third of the line workers' wages.

Besides overtime pay, the line workers received a bonus share that made up about one-fourth of their monthly wages. These bonus shares often were the most contested terrain in the payment system because they induced favoritism and clientalistic networks on the shop floor. The amount of production bonus received by each line worker was determined by his or her line leader based on an assessment of individual performance and productivity. The workers often complained to me that the assessment of the bonus was not "scientific" because it was subjective and hence it was hard to challenge the assessment scheme. The common understanding was whoever has a relative as the line leader gets a "good bonus," and such an arrangement was crucial to safeguarding one's salary. Power struggles along locality and kin-ethnicity lines were waged on these concrete monetary rewards. From the perspective of the line leaders, these production bonuses provided her or him room for manipulating line workers' consent and cooperation, especially when meeting rush orders.

The wage system for paying the line leaders was the most complicated one. It was based on neither monthly pay nor hourly rate but rather was directly linked to the line's productivity, and was composed of a mixture of a basic salary and the median income of the workers on the specific line. The basic salary of the line leaders ranged from 400 to 600 yuan, and by adding the median income of the line's workers, the leaders' wages were often double those of the workers'. A line leader at Meteor could earn as much as the supervisory staff if his or her line performed well.

This system induced line leaders to raise the productivity of their lines as high as possible. Struggles to be line leader were intense in the workplace. Capability was a necessary but not sufficient factor for promotion to line leader. Work experience and strong workers' support, usually along lines of locality and kinship, were another must. Three line leaders, from Canton, Chaozhou, and Sichuan, respectively, were friendly toward me. All of them had been working at Meteor for over three years and had been promoted to the position from line worker. Each had a "big sister" image that was supported by strong kin-ethnic networks in the workplace. One night my line leader, Bailan, invited me to her room to have soup, and I noticed that she was provided with better dormitory conditions than were the line workers. The line operators' or basic workers' room were shared by eight persons, while Bailan's room was shared only by four. All dormitory rooms had one toilet and one balcony for hanging washed clothes, but Bailan's room also had a TV set, which was collectively owned by the roommates. A higher wage, plus a better living environment, all contributed to the workplace heirarchy.

Daily Prejudice and Accommodation

In general, workers entering the factory were preinscribed with a local or ethnic identity that dictated a set of invented cultural traits and a presumed work capability. They also were judged by their dialect and accent, both within the factory premises and outside. At work, cultural traits were manipulated and mixed up with economic interests, and thus individual workers were snared into a hierarchy and then a conflict among themselves. Privileged groups such as the Cantonese and Chaozhou internalized the management's favoritism by mirroring a model image and living up to that invention. The abject groups, especially the Waisheng ren, resisted management's derogatory images of them either by working hard to show their industriousness and looking for chances to show their capabilities or, alternatively, by adopting the stereotypes imposed on them. Everyday tactics were fluid and strategic, and on different occasions individuals would react differently. The following passage is taken from my field notes, recording a complaint by a Sichuan worker:

> 10 April 1996: Li Ting's Anger
>
> At about 11 P.M. I'd finished taking a bath and looked around to join in on some women's talk before going to bed. I passed Li Ting's room, and noticed she was angry with her roommate Yue, a Cantonese woman. On fire, Li Ting shouted, "Don't think yourself extraordinary for being a Cantonese! You always bully people." Yue did not argue back but ran off to the other room. I calmed down Li Ting and asked her what happened. She said, still angry: "This woman always runs wild and does whatever she wants to do. She never considers others and she looks down on people. I

Figure 5. Migrant women workers in the Meteor plant dormitory. (photo by author)

can't stand her any longer. Because she's a Cantonese, she thinks she's big. She broke my bowl, and has no intention of buying me another. Instead she said my stuff blocked her way . . . She never cleans the room but always criticizes others for making the room dirty and always thinks that waisheng ren are much dirtier than any other people.

Different local or ethnic groups in the workplace seldom made friends across their boundaries, and the distrust was worsened by the lack of spare time to communicate with each other. Daily conflicts escalated due to the tight space and rushed time, aggravated by the mutual creation of negative images toward each other. In the eyes of Cantonese or Chaozhou groups, Waisheng mei were often portrayed as uncivilized persons and as much lazier and dirtier. Waisheng mei, who although poorer were often better educated than the Guangdong people, regarded the Cantonese as rude, proud, crafty, and never to be trusted. "These are the people who tread on my feet and remind me daily that I am a lesser human," was the common feeling of Waisheng mei toward the Cantonese. At work, Waisheng mei were allocated work at the bottom of the job hierarchy. In daily life they were excluded and bullied. Mutual exclusion based on a construct of local and ethnic elements into a "personhood" was arbitrary and violent.

Language and Identity: The Cantonization of
the Workplace

The struggle over rural, urban, regional, and ethnic identities was further exacerbated by the struggle over languages, specifically the politics of dialects in the workplace. Language is a system of differences produced and reproduced in a spider web of social differences, hierarchies, and distinctions that construe social reality.[8] The struggle over legitimate language, as Bourdieu (1991, 52–54) notes, is highly political because it encompasses a struggle over identity, status, and power. The politics of identity is enmeshed in a politics of language. It matters what dialect one speaks, and with what accent. In the factory a hierarchy of dialects was deployed in a "language war" that was linked to the struggle over work position, resources, and power.

This language war was launched in the workplace in different arenas and was aimed at different goals. First, it involved the rivalry between Mandarin and Cantonese. Mandarin is the official language in China and is politically superior, but in much of Guangdong it has lost its legitimacy. The subordination of the national official language to the local dialect is due in part to the fact that the importance of state power in regulating social life has given way to local market forces. The war between the two languages does not merely reflect the intense combat between the state and the market machines in regulating social life but also makes it and shapes it. In the workplace Mandarin is still commonly used, but it is no longer endowed with power, superiority, or a hegemonic position. Cantonese, on the other hand, as the commercial language has the upper hand in shaping the workplace hierarchy. Although the members of the factory's upper management are from Hong Kong, those in middle management are mostly Cantonese speakers from cities like Guangzhou, Zhongshan, and Shunde. The managerial language thus is Cantonese, which was normally used in managerial meetings, in passing orders from a higher level to a lower level, and in daily encounters among those in positions of management and supervision.

A command of Cantonese, then, was a must for climbing the hierarchical ladder. It improved the chance for promotion, because in Cantonese one could not only converse better with superiors but also be part of the same habitus and the same expressive style, and thus be more readily assimilated into managerial culture. Mr. Zhou and the four Hong Kong managers never uttered a word in Mandarin. Even when they knew that an individual's Cantonese was poor, they still insisted on using it. For them Cantonese was cultural capital: it was a symbol of superior status and identity that helped them to exercise their authority more effectively. This power of language was neither invisible nor silently exerted on individuals but rather was explicitly demonstrated. Subordinates who were not native speakers yet learned to speak Cantonese fluently were appreciated and had a better chance of promotion. Those who did not know Cantonese had to bear the costs in misunderstandings with superiors or others, and the anxiety that such misunderstandings created. If one did not want to remain at the bottom of the work hierarchy, one was induced to learn Cantonese, or at least to understand enough to survive in the workplace.

Although the language war had resulted in a victory for the commercial language of Cantonese, there was still defiance and transgression from time and time. Tensions were particularly acute when a Mandarin speaker in a high position in the workplace came into contact with a Cantonese speaker, notably in the case of communications between the engineering and production departments. The staff in the production department, both Cantonese speakers and non-Cantonese speakers, were totally assimilated to Cantonese. The engineers and technicians in the engineering department, however, were mainly university graduates from northern cities and exhibited a rather unyielding attitude to Cantonese. For them, accurate Mandarin, with a Beijing accent, was still an emblem of their credentials, status, and self-dignity, and these young male professionals persisted in using Mandarin even though they all could understand Cantonese. Interesting encounters were found when the engineers spoke to the staff in production department; one side spoke in Mandarin, consciously maintaining the superiority of the national language drawn from its political capital, and the other side persisted in speaking Cantonese as the official language in this workplace and the local industrial world. Needless to say, both sides understood each other well, and neither was willing to give in.

Communication on the production lines was more complicated, although the tensions were somewhat less acute. When the line leaders reported to their supervisors they usually spoke in Cantonese. But when they talked to the women on the line they preferred to use Mandarin when speaking to Waisheng workers. Most of the line leaders were not native speakers of Cantonese; some were from Chaozhou, some from Hakka. For them, both Mandarin and Cantonese were foreign languages and they used each in appropriate situations. There were exceptions, however. San, the leader of line D, was from Hunan; she had been promoted to her position after working for more than four years on the production line. She seldom spoke in Cantonese to supervisors or to other line leaders. As a tough and capable figure in the workplace, San had been promoted to the position not because she could assimilate herself to the managerial culture or because of any particular relationship with the upper management, but rather solely because of her work capability and her rigid discipline. She was one of the most disliked people in the workplace; she was never softspoken to women on the line and she often reprimanded workers loudly in Mandarin. They, in turn, often made fun of her, particularly the Cantonese-speaking workers. They mimicked her Mandarin speech and tones, drawing attention to her "unmanagerial" language to undermine her status and authority.

Intrigued by San's persistence in talking in Mandarin, one day I asked her, "San, why do you always speak in Mandarin? You know Cantonese, don't you?" She replied, "I can't help but speak Mandarin. I don't know why. I knew Cantonese after one year of working in Shenzhen. But I don't want to speak in Cantonese unless I am forced to. Probably I don't like the Cantonese. They are always too proud; they think they are rich, so everyone should use their dialect." But San was idiosyncratic; she was an exceptional case of resistance to the dominant language. The majority in the workplace were busy at, and induced into, the play of language politics.

The second dimension of the language war was the internal conflict within the Cantonese dialect. The language machine was not satisfied at creating a hierarchy based simply on the differentiation between Mandarin and Cantonese; rather a more subtle struggle was built on the internal divisions within Cantonese itself. The Cantonese spoken in the workplace was further differentiated into different styles and accents, such as Hong Kong Cantonese, Guangzhou Cantonese, Hakka Cantonese (rural Cantonese), and Guangxi Cantonese. Accents were the embodied stigma of cultural capital, inscribed with a hierarchical access not only to covert power but also to overt institutionalized power. The more one could mimic Hong Kong and Guangzhou Cantonese, the more one was granted status and authority in the workplace. Indeed, it was clearly noticeable that the higher the managerial hierarchy, the more Hong Kong or Guangzhou Cantonese was spoken. The assistant managers and the supervisors were fluent in Hong Kong Cantonese because they were often in contact with the Hong Kong managers, most of whom were native Guangzhou Cantonese. The foremen and line leaders had learned Guangzhou Cantonese because they often communicated with their Cantonese superiors. Different accents of Cantonese endowed people with different cultural capital, and thus affected their bargaining power in fighting for a higher work position and negotiating a new identity. If workers did not make an effort to change accents and instead stuck to rural Cantonese, then no matter how superior they might feel to the Mandarin or other dialect speakers, they were still at the bottom of the internal hierarchy.

Yiping, a Guangdong Hakka, was the receptionist and phone operator when I started at the Meteor factory. She was a friendly, pretty girl who had been promoted from the production line to the counter. But after her one-month probation period she was moved back to the line again. "She can never pronounce Lin and Ling accurately, nor can she hear any difference between the sounds. She always connects the phone line to the wrong person," Ling, the secretary in the general office grumbled to me. "She is a Hakka from a rural area and she can't speak Cantonese properly. What's more, she doesn't know how to handle unwelcome phone calls and people." Ling spoke proper Hong Kong Cantonese, despite the fact that she was a Chaozhou person.

One night I found Yiping in the dormitory, listening to Hong Kong Cantonese popular songs. She was still hurt by her demotion and she planned to leave for home: "I don't want to work here, they made me feel inferior. If they don't give me a chance, I will go elsewhere." But in fact, knowing that her Hakka Cantonese accent counted against her, Yiping tried hard to change herself. She took every chance to talk to me, hoping that I could inculcate in her a more urbane and highly valued Cantonese. Listening to Cantonese songs was another favorite way to learn Cantonese, and she often sang loudly.

———

On the passage to becoming dagongmei, self-technologizing was complete when one dreamed, desired, and determined to live up to the hegemonic mode of life—to acquire a modern identity and to command a superior dialect of Cantonese. To become dagongmei, one had to change not only the "bad" habitus of one's lifestyle but also one's dialect. The price of symbolic power was great, and there was no choice but to scramble for it. Language was, as Bourdieu (1991, 52) has said, a hidden political mythology prophesying, coding, and legitimating a system of social differences. The play of difference is highly political. Rural life was imagined as an alterity so that it could be undervalued. For a rural being to become an urban industrial subject, he or she had to be divided from the totality of her or his past life—habitus, disposition, accent, and identity. The rural world had to be imagined as a deficient reality that could not give birth to complete human beings or modern subjects. First, the capitalist machine invented the rural beings as incomplete, as "lacking." Then the rural beings thought and saw themselves as such. There is a process of double displacement at work here. As stated by Huck Gutman: "Deficient reality is transformed into the imaginary and the imaginary is superimposed upon the real in such fashion that the imaginary transforms, takes over, becomes, the real" (1988, 112). Thus the real is not impossible; it is simply more and more artificial (Deleuze and Guattari 1984, 34).

Dagongmei, as a new social body, thus contains multiple reactionary forces that work to produce a homogenous sense of self that is nevertheless fragmentary, fluid, and entangled. Becoming dagongmei is a dual process of displacement and replacement that produces anxiety, uncertainty, and pain for individuals in their daily struggles, and drives them toward a self-technologizing project, helping to accomplish a hegemonic construct. Selves are not inherently fragmentary but are socially negated and divided in order to give birth to a new subject. The workplace here is not merely a microcosm of the dual society at large, but part of the process of production and reproduction of an increasingly polarized society. It is through the everyday practices of such an environment that the politics of identification by which the production machine could command the microphysics of power over the self were governed. The production machine, in making use of existing social relations, simply reproduced itself as one part of the system at the same time that it built the system. The factory regime itself was not a pyramid of power hierarchies but rather a kaleidoscope of power and hierarchies created by weaving together identities of gender, kin-ethnic ties, and rural-urban disparity.

5

The second hand, minute hand, ticks and ticks in my heart
My eyes glisten and glisten with emptiness
My heart goes pit-a-pat, pit-a-pat, throbbing all the time
I ask myself how much I love you
How eager I am to live with you and fly far way
My heart's throbbing up and down, up and down all the time

Tomorrow I am going to marry you
Tomorrow I am going to marry you
If the everyday traffic doesn't disturb my dream
(If not at that night the electricity stopped, I discovered my loneliness and emptiness)
Tomorrow I am going to marry you
Tomorrow I am *finally* going to marry you

If you do not ask me
If you do not persuade me
If you don't do it at the right time, you leave my heart throbbing
(But at this particular moment, I feel frightened and afraid)

—A popular song, "Tomorrow I am going to marry you"

During my stay in the Meteor factory, I could not avoid hearing a popular song that was played every day in the workplace. Sung by a Taiwanese male singer, the song, "Tomorrow I Am Going to Marry You," expressed well the dagongmei's yearning for love and sex and their daily struggles between factory work and marriage life. I use this song to open this chapter on the gender identity of Chinese women workers from the subject's side, and the technology of sex and gender in the factory regime from the side of disciplinary power. Central to the making of a kaleidoscope of power and hierarchies in the workplace are the gendered subjects who are by no means preset or conventionally registered. Following the last two chapters, if subjects, as Foucault (1979) states, are themselves the effects of disciplinary actions—fully embedded in and produced by matrices of power and discourse—then I seek a feminist critique that questions the notions of sex and gender in postsocialist China at the conjunction of its self-incorporation into global production, and that traces and reveals the political operations that produce and conceal who qualifies as a proper Chinese dagongmei.

Constructing women as a coherent and unified identity is a project of power that aims to feminize the labor force in the service of the new international division of labor. In chapter 4 I stressed that a coherent social body like dagongmei was only a mirage, and that the differences between and within women in the workplace were obvious, especially along lines of class, locality, family, age, and stage of lifecycle. In this chapter I look at how heterogeneous social subjects were constructed as a unified social body in the workplace and how the gender identity of dagongmei/zai was construed in contrast to the Maoist term gongren, which was an asexual subject. The process of sexualization of dagongmei/zai, as a project of capital, mirrored the process of the desexualization of gongren, which was a project of the Chinese state in the socialist period.

Emerging with the reactivation of sexualization as a general process in the transnational period, I will show how the politics of gender identity was contested by workplace disciplinary power and rural family life, both of which were somewhat reactionary forces that the women workers had to live with in their daily lives. As I discuss in chapter 2, the rural patriarchal family and marriage were the primary and reactionary forces within which the lives of women workers were embedded, and the women's struggles to enact and renegotiate their new gender identity was no doubt delimited by this larger context. In negotiating their modern gendered selves, working in the factory and in the urban area was an escape from the patriarchal family life, to which, however, they returned home after experiencing the dictate of disciplinary power in the factory. The dagongmei dreamed of marriage and of returning home when they tired of wage labor and were suffering from industrial drudgery. In this chapter, I look into this paradox and examine how women workers enacted, contested, and transgressed the tropes of factory and married life.

In my work I also noted that the contestation of gender identity was further caught up with urban consumerist desires and a yearning to become a modern "cultured" self, a vital part of the passage to becoming a modern Chinese dagongmei. I explore here how the women workers struggled to be modern selves by participating in an urban consumerist life that entrapped them within, instead of allowed them to transgress, the power of capital.

The Dagongmei: Who is not One

I was often teased by women workers in the Meteor factory when my fellow worker "Fatso" held my hand as we walked together. "Like a real couple or a pair of mandarin ducks" was the common response to our intimacy. The teasing would never happen when I went out with other women workers or even went to dine with a male worker. Fatso was a nickname given to Shutong, and it was intended to highlight the male side of her appearance and her personality. With her short hair, Fatso's round face had big eyes, a straight nose, and a thick-lipped mouth. Stout, energetic, and talkative, the twenty-one-year-old Fatso was famous for her quick disposition and her courage in confronting upper management on the shop floor. In contrast to the other girls' decorations around their beds, Fatso pinned up pictures of cars and planes instead of flowers, film stars, and singers. She also preferred sportswear to more feminine clothing. I was close to Fatso because we worked on the same production line and because she was much more active than the others in making friends with me. We often walked together to the factory or back to the dormitory, and we had meals together as well. The friendly gossip about our relationship did not irritate Fatso, and sometimes she seemed to enjoy the joking that she could have me as a "girl friend."

I was somewhat educated by our relationship not only because I was Fatso's "girl friend" but because Fatso's "perverted" sexual identity disrupted, and thus opened up, my ideal construct of dagongmei, an embodied identity of both class and gender. Earlier, in chapter 1, I discussed dagongmei as a class identity, and here I will tease out the intricate processes of gendering lived bodies in the workplace. How do we understand dagongmei, a gendered subject in general, and through Fatso, an individual with conflict-ing identities, in particular? Too often in my work I was perplexed by the complexities and contradictions of gendered identities and sexualized bodies that often were unarticulated and lacking in self-reflexivity.

The identity politics of Chinese dagongmei was essentially engendered in their struggles between wage labor and married life, both of which fought to be the primary source of the women's identities. This contestation of women's lives generated the inconsistencies, contraventions, and fragmenta-tions that are inherently embedded in the gendering process, construing subjects who are always decentered, unstable, and multiple. Feminist an-thropology has helped to formulate a notion of the "dividual" self and has argued that both Western and non-Western subjects are often divided, frag-mented, fluid, and multiple (Moore 1994; Strathern 1988, 1991). The category "woman" is inherently decentering and unstable, and designates a field of differences that cannot be totalized or summarized by a descriptive identity. The very term woman, according to Judith Butler and Joan Scott (1992, 15–16), becomes a site of permanent openness and resignificability. Gender, sex, and body can be themselves fictive, articulated, and constructed as if all have their own limits and materiality in specific matrices of power and discourse.

It is this critique of gender, sex, and body—sometimes called the political anatomy—that provides the greatest insight for my own ethnography of the workplace (Foucault 1978). The biopower of the factory machine is not only interested in molding a general body but also a particular sexed body, a feminine body to fit the factory discipline.[1] In this chapter, I will try to link up the process of political anatomy in the workplace with the process of sexualizing female bodies and registering multiple feminine identities. These entangled processes, nevertheless, have to be understood against a wider history of the Chinese family and work context that provides the terrain on which biopower and identity politics were contested and negotiated, and on which the lives of women were enacted, negotiated, and transformed. Social discourse, consumerist culture, and everyday practices worked together in a rapidly changing Chinese society in which conflicting processes and per-verse workings of gendering were enacted on sexualized bodies.

Desiring Sexual Subjects

In Shenzhen, as well as in other economic development zones, stories about dagongmei in popular magazines such as *Shenzhen Ren* (Shenzhen people), *Nü Bao* (Women's magazine), *Dagongmei* (Working daughters), and *Wailai-*

gong (Migrant workers) were booming in popularity.[2] Tropes, metaphors, episodes, and story plots centered on imaginations and themes such as the struggle of life and death in the modern industrial world, changing attitudes toward sex, love, and marriage, and the desire to become a modern man or woman. These magazines helped create a variety of lively images of dagong-mei. Not without exaggeration and exception, the working daughters were portrayed as sexual subjects who were prepared to leave their villages to look not only for jobs but also for love and men. Often cast in a sad tone, predicated on the difficulties of pursuing "true" love, the stories nevertheless provided a new construction of female subjectivity—one in which dagong-mei were active and bold in seeking love, in contrast to the traditional image of submissive Chinese women. In a column in *Shenzhen Ren* (Shen, October 1994), titled "Special Economic Zone Cannot Take Care of Dagongmei's Love," several short stories appeared, as follows.

One Male Line Leader and Ten Line Girls

On her first day working on the packaging line, Ping said, "The male line leader is so handsome!" After working for two years in six factories, it was the first time she had met a handsome line leader. Ping's words threatened the other nine girls on the same line, for the line leader had become the little prince of ten hearts.

The line leader was from Guangdong. He had not completed his university studies but instead had gone off to work. At 5′ 8″ tall, he was not too fat and not too thin. He had light skin, wore glasses, and seemed mature and a little bit shy. His actions were sharp and his words generous; he played no favorites among the ten girls or said anything unnecessary to anyone. For what needed reproach, he reproached all. For what needed concern, he showed concern to all.

The ten love seeds sprouted at the same time. Those who were bold wrote love letters and sent gifts to him; those who were timid loved him secretly in their hearts. Among the line girls, a war of love was launched openly, seriously affecting production. The male line leader could not deal with the situation and was forced to leave the factory. Without a word to the line girls, he was gone.

One Foreman and Six Working Daughters

A foreman, named Lai, could not compete with the other boys in the company because he was short and quiet. From day to night he toiled hard on production. He was only age twenty-two, but the workers all called him "old boy" or "work maniac."

However, six pretty young women in the workplace all loved him. They had all written love letters to him and waited for his reply. But he never uttered a word, as if nothing had happened. Cing was the prettiest woman in the workplace. Unlike the other women, she was not disappointed by his lack of reply and never stopped writing letters to him. Every day, she was the first one on the shop floor and worked very hard to increase her output in order to attract foreman Lai's attention. Yet he still made no move.

Eventually, Cing was in despair and could not face her foreman. She quit her job and became a salesgirl in a hardware store. However, the foreman often came to the store to buy materials. She quit the job again and wrote to him: she would go somewhere he could not see her. She went to work in a big hotel as a waitress. Unfortunately, there was nowhere she could hide; every Sunday, the foreman went with the boss to have breakfast in the hotel. They met again . . .

Cing wrote another letter: "You don't love me. I can't see you again. I have to go." She left town.

One Boy Worker and a Woman Supervisor

Coming from Guangxi as a boy, it was not easy for little Tao to find a job in a craft factory. He worked as an assistant. He cleaned the shop floor and the toilets, and loaded materials and products. He received a lower wage than anyone else and often felt inferior. However, as the saying goes, a fool has more happiness. He received a love letter from Miss Chan, the famous production supervisor in the factory.

Little Tao was throbbing and could not believe it. Yet after a couple of letters from Miss Chan to "invade" him, he finally "surrendered."

They rented a flat and lived together. Miss Chan took the role of breadwinner. She paid for all little Tao spent and helped him to send money back home regularly . . .

Little Tao could never believe in the "love" he had found. Refusing to take advantages from the woman, he left quietly. His hot and sincere lover was in tears.

All of these stories are made up of desiring female subjects who are far more active than men in expressing and pursuing love. If conventional discourses continued to portray women as passive sexual objects waiting for men, popular culture favored the image of a modern, young working woman who challenges traditional sexual relations and takes an active role. Young Chinese rural women no longer stayed at home, following their parents' arrangements or waiting for a matchmaker to decide their fate. Instead, in the magazines they were encouraged to go out: to leave their villages and look for their own love and life. "Your body is your own," "Hold tight to love," and "Control your own fate"—all of these hidden messages were conveyed through popular culture and became mottos for modern female life. These liberating messages, on the surface, encouraged challenges to the traditional sense of Chinese women's lives and their defiance to the patriarchal family. However, at the same time they were manipulated by the hegemonic project of modernity and power to produce laborers for private and transnational capital.

The Proliferation of Sex and Sexualized Bodies

The feminization of labor use in the industrial export processing zones in Shenzhen, as elsewhere in China and other developing countries, was often linked to a project of renegotiating women's space and power, as well as to a politics of reimagining sex and gender in general. These larger discourses and politics could provide new elements for subverting conventional norms and values, but also simultaneously leaving women's agency submerged in the new matrix of power and subjugation. When I look at the contemporary Chinese scene with its shifting images, it is characterized by the proliferation of sex talk, sexual discourse, and consumerized female images (Evans 1997). Signs of sex are everywhere, inviting us into a Baudrillardian (1993) world where female bodies are commodified and fetishized to such an extent that only a mass grave of signs remain. Nudes, erotica, and all kinds of sexy, seduced female bodies, both Western and Chinese, are found in magazines, posters, newspapers, book covers, calendars, and even academic books and periodicals. On every street corner in Shenzhen, as in other Chinese cities, advertisements on the lampposts tell passers-by that some families have secret, local knowledge of an operation to heal sexual diseases. Stories of sex and violence, uncontrollable sex drives, and sex outside of marriage are voiced in novels, video shows, TV programs, and films. Painting, other visual arts, and avant-garde dance performances all focus on the theme of the "sexualized body." As Elisabeth Croll, after her experience in numerous field trips to China over the past decades, states:

> The Reform period is thus marked by a new interest in the image and presentation of the feminine, focusing first on physical appearance and adornment. This is not surprising given that one of the most important characteristics distinguishing reform from revolution is the new interest in consumption, in consumer goods and in their style, colour, material and brand name, all of which have generated a new phenomenon—consumer desire. . . . The new interest in commodities and lifestyles has brought about a new relation between people and things, so that persons have become classified not so much by their class background or "work" or occupation as previously, as by the possession of objects or their evaluation, so that identity has become associated with lifestyle rather than class label. (1995, 151)

The all-pervasive interest in female bodies in reform China is conjured up by all-powerful consumer desires, whose gazes are not only sexy but further sexualized. The technology of consumption power, in contrast to production power, is not interested in producing disciplined bodies but rather libidinous, lascivious, and lustful female bodies. The calling of feminist politics in Chinese society,[3] paradoxically, meets with the political maneuvers of sex and gender at the very moment when the Chinese female body is highly regulated, twisted, and subsumed by capital and power in the transnational period. The discourse of the Chinese body, presumed docile and gentle, is turned upside down, not only for the use of production power but also for consumption capital. Now the Chinese body has to be vibrant, sexualized, seductive, and liberated enough to release all forces of libido.

Shenzhen nightlife—nightclubs, karaoke, wine bars, and hair salons—has flourished since the mid-1980s and is marked by its extravagant sexual appetite, especially for female bodies. Workplaces where women were predominant—such as garment, electronics, and shoe and toy factories—were often called "peach orchards" in popular magazines and stories. The notion of peach orchards imaginatively evoked and signified female places of sex, love, and joy, in spite of the fact that it was a male-oriented if not sexist metaphor of men pursuing erotic objects. While a workplace full of young women might be an orchard of peaches for men, it was definitely not a world of joy and happiness for women, at least not for the women workers at the Meteor factory.

Here Foucault (1978, 154) is particularly correct to say the body is never preset but rather "sexed" within a discourse of sex to produce a monotonous modality of sexuality, which is itself an effect of a historically specific organization of power, discourse, and pleasure. It is not because one has a body that one has a sex but that one has a particular notion of sex so that one obtains a certain type of body. The modality of the body is of course the effect, but not the origin, of the sex, which is constructed in a specific set of social regulations and power relations.

Sex talk was also thriving in the workplace, and my coworkers always warned me not to go to hair salons or hotels, especially small ones, because they were often places for exchanging "illicit" sex. In the factory workers' eyes, *bei mei*, the girls of the north, were prostituting bodies whose world was highly differentiated from working bodies, dagongmei.[4] Young and beautiful girls from north China (the place they were from was highly emphasized and then degraded), were told to wait in hotels and search for men alone. The phone would ring late at night and ask for "lonely heart" services. In contrast to a pure and productive dagongmei working in the factories, beimei, the term denoting perverted Chinese female bodies, was invested with more abject and yet rebellious meanings. Beimei were younger, fresher, more lush and virginal, and therefore they were more sexually arousing and desirable, easily disrupting the patriarchal order of society. For my coworkers these prostituting bodies were not their "family resemblances," and even though these beimei were trapped in a situation of oppression worse than dagongmei, the unity of sisterhood was still highly segregated and exclusive.

Amidst beimei, in the process of sex trading regional disparity between the north and the south was again produced and reproduced. Sex was not only inscribed with inequalities between male and female but also marked with economic discrimination between north and south. Prostitutes were themselves hierarchically differentiated: those who came from richer areas were worth much more than those from poorer areas. These differences between and within women again spoke of a self-defeating project in arguing for a universal category of women. The politics of identity is always the politics of difference. These subjects should be seen as the effects of power and as discursive constructs with their own possibilities, through a process of signification, differentiation, and exclusion (Butler 1990).

The "sexy" scenes in open-door China make me wonder if global capital particularly needs sexualized subjects. It seems clear that where private and transnational capital goes there is a proliferation of sex trade and sex discourses in towns and cities. Time after time since the early 1990s the central Chinese government has launched antiporn movements in the cities. The official discourse continues to promote a regulatory mode of sexuality, and according to Harriet Evans (1997, 156), state discourses on sexual issues are largely a response to changing popular beliefs and practices. Although no longer effective, never has the state lost its interest in regulating individual sexual conduct and marital behavior. With deflated and worn-out ideological apparatus, the failure of the central state to safeguard the "virginity" of Chinese society is all too plain to see. The local state, however, was far more tolerant, because they saw the sex industry closely linked to local economic development. As one local cadre in a southern Chinese town openly told me: "No sex, no video shows, no clubs, no hair salons, no restaurants, no hotels, no money!" Sex linked up the entire chain of economic activities, just as corruption facilitated political life in China. No sex, no money. In contemporary China, discourses on sex—official and civil, and at odds with each another—fight hard to grasp and produce the reality in which the real, although impossible, again becomes more artificial.

Invoking Sexual Subjects

It seems that for private and global capital, "sexualizing the subject" is crucial to the creation of the modernity project. The political technology of capital involves a series of maneuvers of hierarchization and division of society, of which sexual difference was one of the major regulatory targets. As noted above, dagongmei stands in contrast to gongren, the nonsexualized subject in Mao's era, and entails a process of sexualization within laboring bodies. Mei explicitly means a young woman and a sister. The feminization of labor has proceeded rapidly in Shenzhen and in other economic development zones, clearly illustrating that basic industrial laborers, especially cheap and unskilled workers, are mostly female. Male workers, dagongzai, are not excluded, but once they are needed they are given different positions in the sexual division of labor in the workplace, as we will see later. Labor is thus no longer taken as an unsexed body but as a gendered subject exhibiting itself more as a "sexual being" than as a "class being" in postsocialist China.

Sexualizing laboring bodies in this manner is a project of capital rather than the state. This can be seen if we compare the two social subjects: the gongren of Mao's period and the dagongmei/zai of today. With gongren, sexual difference was submerged and made redundant in socialist labor relations. Women were introduced into the "world of men," be it in light, heavy, or military industries. The official rhetoric proclaimed that women could hold up half the sky in socialist China; that they could do whatever men could do. In official regulatory practices sexual difference was diluted

and made meaningless through propaganda and institutionalized arrangements. With the dissolution of socialist practices in general and the bank-
ruptcy of state and collective enterprises in particular, the gongren subject
was disappearing and the term became an outdated mode of everyday discourse, especially in south China. The disembodied world of industrial labor
was to be sexualized; its sex was not to be veiled but had to be reinvented and
regulated.

In the Meteor workplace it was not difficult to find that the regulation of a
sexed body was fundamental to the control of labor. Given that the workplace was a world of young women who occupied almost all of the seats of the
assembly operation, it was always a headache for the upper management, the
foremen, and the line leaders, often male, to manage the workers. None of
the foremen or line leaders, male or female, assumed that dagongmei were
submissive females waiting to be regulated at their will. Complaints about
the discipline of dagongmei were frequent when I talked to any supervisor.
Indeed, submissiveness, often with an imaginary feminine identity pinned
on the workers, needed to be articulated and rearticulated in the everyday
language of management to facilitate labor control. Here are a few vignettes
used to invoke sexualized bodies that I recorded from management:

> Shun (foreman of line c): Mei, you're a girl, how can you speak to me like
> this? Didn't your parents teach you how to be a woman? Do you speak to
> your father like this?
>
> Hong (assistant manager): Rough voice, rough *qi* [energy], don't you want
> to marry yourself out? Behave yourself, since you're still a young girl.
>
> Li (foreman of line a): Girl, do you have ears? You never follow exactly
> what I tell you to do. Where is your heart? Gone with your lover?
>
> He-chuan (foreman of line b): Mei, don't you know you're a girl? You
> should treat the work more tenderly. How many times do I have to remind
> you?
>
> He-chuan (foreman of line b): Look at yourself, like a *nanren po* [butch
> woman]. Can't you learn to be like a woman?

Such remarks were often heard in the Meteor workplace, particularly
when workers' discipline had to be tightened. What is especially interesting
was that in the eyes of management their identity as laborer was less important than their identity as female. The regulation of gender was invoked
when labor control was at stake. The workers were often reminded of their

femaleness: "You are a girl." As a girl in the process of becoming a woman, one should behave as the culture required: submissive, obedient, industrious, tender, and so on. The underlying implications were: "You are a girl, you should be obedient enough to do what the management tells you to do. You are a girl, you should not be defiant to your superior by speaking in a loud voice. You are a girl, you are going to marry someone, serve someone, so you had better train yourself to behave properly. You should take care of the job you do as you one day will take care of your family. As a girl you are going to be a woman, a wife and a mother of men."

The ascription of these feminine attributes to a woman and the regulation of a woman's behavior did not, of course, concern her future life in general. Rather, her future life as a wife and as a mother was deployed for the present technologizing of bodies as docile labor. As Judith Butler (1993, 1) puts it, "sex/gender" not only functions as a norm but is part of a regulatory practice that produces the bodies it governs, that is, whose regulatory force is made clear as a kind of productive power, the power to produce the bodies it controls.

Also of note is that maleness was posited as a degraded opposite in warnings to the workers: "You should not act like a boy, a boy is lazy and troublesome, careless and rough. Otherwise, you can't marry yourself out." Maleness was thus articulated as an oppositional and inferior sexual attribute that a woman should not have if she wanted to become a good female and thus a good worker. The subject, in Butler's words, is "constituted through the force of exclusion and abjection, one which produces a constitutive outside to the subject, an abject outside, which is, after all, 'inside' the subject as its own founding repudiation" (1993, 3).

Despite the implication that maleness was supposedly contradictory to dagongmei self-esteem and self-identity, it always seemed that those who possessed the power to speak were free of gender constraints. When Hechuan, our foreman, condemned workers for manly behavior, he seemed to forget that he himself was a man. It was so naturally practiced that nobody could cast any doubt on the legitimate correspondence between being a female and a good worker. Discursive power was not only pervasive, but also elusive. Further, those who held regulatory power tried hard to create anxieties among the targets of their condemnation—they would be shamed if they, as girls, behaved like boys. "Dividuals," as Marilyn Strathern (1988, 19) states, were often taken as individual wholes, and one could only choose or be forced to choose, either as a female or as a male.

No internal ambivalence inside the individual is allowed; femaleness and maleness were created as a fundamental binary opposition in human beings. The women workers, however, cared less about being unable to get married than about not living up to the imaginary feminine. They could seldom fight back if their foremen or line leaders attacked their sexuality as being too male. They were induced to fear any evidence of their own gender ambiguity or perversity. Gender thus became a means of discipline and self-discipline, invoked so that they would learn to police themselves. The feminine was not only imagined and inscribed but also self-desired, and its mirroring other was the opposite sex—male (Irigaray 1977, 25). In this way, dagongmei was never only a subject of power, but an object of one's own desire.

Sexual Division of Labor

Femininity was always imagined and linked to performance as a good worker. But women workers in the Meteor plant knew quite well that in the pyramidal hierarchy inside the workplace, the female, not the male, was the inferior sex. While they might not fully understand how their femininity was articulated, imagined, and engineered time and again in everyday disciplinary practices, they knew well that the division of labor was rigidly segregated by sex. Out of more than five hundred workers in the workplace, about 75 percent were female. They were predominant on the assembly lines, and were placed in all kinds of work processes: assembling components, screwing, air seasoning, soldering, molding, function testing, quality control, and packaging. Above them were men as their foreman, their managers, and their director. Meteor was a world of women, but not for women. No matter how often they were reminded not to be mannish—"don't behave like a boy"—it was the male who had the power and status, with a higher wage and more benefits. Women workers in the workplace had to live up to the ambivalent realities construed by disciplinary discourses, daily language, and institutionalized power, which often were inherently split and self-contradictory.

The worlds of management and assembly workers were strongly stratified along sexual lines. The management strata were not entirely men but were males and masculinized females. In the eyes of the line women the top level of management was a world of masculinity—cool, deep, and untouchable. Although two managers and three supervisors were female, they were all taken as men or as being "as capable as men." The director, Mr. Zhou, and

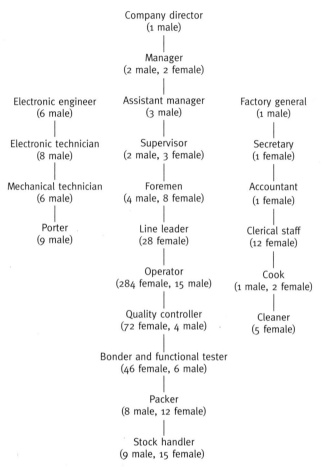

Figure 6. Gender division of labor in Meteor Electronics Company (from data collected by author in 1996).

the four managers—Mr. Li of the engineering department, Mr. Wu of the production department, Miss Tang of the quality control department, and Miss Ren of the material stock department—were all from Hong Kong. As in all of the large foreign-owned corporations in China, the most important posts were not given to the mainland Chinese. Mr. Zhou, the founder of Meteor, had a firm and disciplined paternalistic image. He was an untouchable authoritarian figure in the workplace, especially for the women workers on the production lines. He seldom appeared on the shop floor except when accompanied by representatives of Western businesses touring the company. If he did show up on his own, it meant a serious problem had occurred.

Mr. Li, who was over fifty years old, was a Hong Kong–born professional; he could not speak Mandarin well. In charge of the engineering department, which was full of male university graduates, he was seen in the eyes of the women workers as a somewhat respectable person of expertise and knowledge. Mr. Wu, in his early forties, had immigrated to Hong Kong in 1987. He was one of the first generation of university graduates when China resumed university education after the Cultural Revolution. He was hired for the important position of production department manager because of his particular background. According to Mr. Wu, the production department was the largest section of the company and thus its heart. It had more than 350 workers, and managing it well required someone who was not a mainland Chinese but knew how to manage mainland Chinese workers. "The bosses thought I was an expert in Chinese economics and knew how to control the mainland workers' psychology," Mr. Wu said to me one day. After graduating from the Economics Department at Nanjing University, he first worked as an accountant in a state-owned enterprise in Nanjing. In 1985 he was promoted to secretary, the highest position in the enterprise. However, he chose to leave China because status and power could no longer satisfy him, and he was looking for a higher living standard in Hong Kong.

Miss Tang was employed as the quality control manager, probably because she looked like a man and was sufficiently strong and authoritarian. There was a widespread rumor that she was a lesbian, and nobody could control the gossip about her throughout the workplace. People called her "Mr. Tang" to her face and *nanren tou* (man head) behind her back. The manager of material stock, Miss Ren, was a stout mother type who had left her husband and son in Hong Kong to work in Shenzhen. As with other Hong Kong staff members, she had to stay in Shenzhen during the week and could only go home on Saturday afternoon, whereupon she had to return to Shenzhen very early on Monday morning. Mr. Zhou told me he preferred to find men from Hong Kong to take up managerial posts in Shenzhen, because men carried less of the family burden. Women, even when they were strong like Miss Ren, still considered their families as their first concern.

For production line women in their everyday sexual fantasies, the engineering department was the place that conjured up dreams and desires. In the department, all positions—engineers, technicians, work analysts, and machinists—were occupied by men. These men appeared young, handsome, urbane, and professional, and most important of all they often had urban hukou and hence higher social status. As such, they filled the women's dreams of escaping rural poverty and moving up the social ladder. Rumors would enthusiastically spread throughout the workplace if an engineer dined with a production line woman, or if they went out together to see a film. But these sexual fantasies were full of ambivalent feelings in the everyday struggles when the women had to confront these men as the ones in power and in charge of their daily production. The electronic engineers were the people who designed the operation of the assembly lines and decided how each work process on the line should run. The work analysts studied and determined the time, speed, and pay rate of the line. The technicians and machinists would maintain and repair the conveyor belts and all of the machines and tools. Orders and production designs were then sent to the production department, which undertook the actual daily operation of production.

Under Mr. Wu, Tin and Shen were the assistant managers in charge of the production lines and the bonding department, respectively. These two men were also university graduates from big cities, with qualifications that the women dared not envy. On the shop floor it was actually Tin and Shen who held direct control of production and thus the highest authority over the female line operators. It was thus clear that the entire production process was under the control of men, who gave orders and decided the work speed and wages for the women. No one complained about male authority in the workplace because gender issues were subsumed by rural-urban differences and educational level. In the eyes of line women, Tin and Shen were not only male but urban born and highly educated, and as such it seemed difficult to organize any fundamental challenge to male power in the workplace, in spite of the fact that spontaneous and momentary resistances to male authority were frequent in the women's daily lives.

The assembly operators, although predominantly female, were not a homogeneous group. They were categorized into three grades: the basic operators concentrated on the job; the second-grade operators were competent in at least three jobs; and the first-grade operators knew almost all the jobs and could be moved up and down the line as required. Some of the first-grade operators were called "flyers" because they were trained for all of the work processes and could be called up for any position in the event of absence. Most of the time assistant line leaders were chosen from among the ranks of these "flyers," who were considered capable and experienced and who dared to speak out. "It is difficult to find the right people for leaders among the line girls. Girls are so talkative when they crowd together. But at work, they are so timid and afraid to criticize the others," Tin tried to explain when I asked why management was dominated by males.

Men were not totally excluded from the assembly lines, but over 90 percent of the positions were occupied by women. As usual, assembling tiny electronic components was often considered women's work because it required patience, care, sharp eyes, and nimble fingers. At Meteor the management emphasized that the reality was that they did not have a totally submissive workforce under control. While upper management would typically imagine women to be more submissive, attentive, dexterous, and thus more reliable than men, the middle-level management, nearer to the actual shop floor, often held different views.

Due to the sexual segregation of jobs, the wage system, organized on a hierarchical basis, was also favorable to male workers. Male staff had a more stable form of wage, and the average wage of male workers at Meteor was about 30 percent higher than that of female workers. Furthermore, the uniforms and overalls worn at the factory helped to symbolize and draw the laboring bodies into the world of sexual hierarchies. Men and women, in different work positions, were put in different types and colors of uniforms and overalls. Management by color, understood as a new workplace management practice, signified position, status, and power. Except for the director, everybody—managers, office staff, shop floor staff, and workers—were asked to be properly uniformed.

But there were great differences between those who wore uniforms and those who wore overalls. The male engineers and technicians had to wear white shirts, whereas the male supervisors had blue shirts and the female supervisors blue dress sets. Shirts and dress sets were formally recognized as uniforms, clearly articulating the symbols and representations of power that belonged to the management strata. Despite the fact that the foremen and line leaders might sometimes be considered representatives of management, they nevertheless were dressed in overalls rather than uniforms, although in a different color, yellow, from that of the operators, who were dressed in white and blue. Operators on the quality control lines wore white overalls, symbolizing a slightly higher status than the production line operators in blue. Uniforms and overalls thus marked the line differentiating between managerial staff and basic workers, male and female, and controller and controlled, and the gender hierarchies were covertly revealed and reproduced in uniforms and overalls. Women, either consciously or unconsciously, came to a realization of themselves as an inferior sex with a degraded body when they put on a pair of blue overalls and worked on the shop floor.

Perverted Bodies

Dagongmei as an obedient and submissive social body was, in spite of everything, merely a hegemonic imaginary: although powerful enough, it was often contradicted in real-life struggles. The technology of power over female bodies was often self-defeating or sometimes even impotent. This impotence of the all-powerful matrix of power and language was, for example, acutely revealed when the factory disciplinary machine repeatedly failed to co-opt Fatso's sexual identity. Fatso was always a headache for management. She refused to feminize herself, and she openly acted butch. She was quick to air grievances and express her opinions when she saw unreasonable arrangements or unfairness. But she was loved as well as loathed by our line leader and foreman. She often worked faster than anyone else on the line and thus was able to help the others when their work was piling up. She rarely asked for sick leave; rather, she often helped to take women suffering from menstrual pain or other bodily discomfort to the restroom or the hospital. It was considered inappropriate for male supervisors to touch the female body, especially when the woman was menstruating. Everybody knew Fatso's important role on our line, and thus the regulation of sex did not work on her. This is not to say that the disciplinary machine completely failed to regulate her behavior, but to do so it needed to resort to other strategies.

Although she had to face much gossip and innuendo, Fatso insisted on having her own way: "I don't mind that people say that I'm mannish. I don't like girls to be timid, screaming, and fussing all the time." Fatso liked to make friends with the men rather than the women in the factory, and she often went out with male workers to see films or videos with violent and heroic plots. Women's talk at night, the most common entertainment after working, did not particularly attract her because she often thought that women gossiped and murmured too much. Young women in the workplace, on the other hand, accepted her as butch and treated her as a boy. They came to her when they needed help. In this case body, sex, and identity, had no one-to-one correspondence; for Fatso, neither body nor sex could provide legitimacy for sexual identity. Her sexual identity was not yet split, but ambivalent and somewhat different.[5]

A Fight

The ideal construct of dagongmei as a docile feminized body was further disrupted and shattered in my mind when one day I witnessed a terrible scene. It was a winter night, windy and cold. At 10:00, after overtime, I went with Fatso back to the dormitory, dragging my exhausted body. Fatso told me she would queue up for hot water for me to bathe, and she told me to have a few minutes of rest in bed. Every night we would struggle over whether or not to bathe, especially on cold nights. If we decided in favor of the bath, we needed to queue up for hot water, sometimes for more than half an hour. At the end of our dorm rooms was a room with a big stove that heated water between ten and twelve at night. Because hot water was provided within limited hours, women frequently helped relatives, fellow villagers, and good friends to wait for hot water. Sometimes one person would bring four or five buckets from the long queue. Needless to say, queue jumping happened from time to time and squabbles and arguments followed. It was a site of contestation.

When we entered the dormitory gate, approaching the stove room, I heard loud noises and surmised it was an argument. Fatso screamed: "They are fighting, they are fighting with each other!" We ran to the spot, where two groups of women were wrestling. In a rage, one woman hit the other woman's face with great strength; the other woman fought back by pulling her opponent's hair. As Fatso tried to stop the fighting, she was forcefully pushed away by a thin young woman. I stood still, terribly frightened by the violence.

I couldn't sleep that night, haunted by how it was that these women could engage in such violence. Violence is often believed to be a male attribute; that is, that it belongs only to men and does not happen except among men. But this fierce women's fight disrupted my thoughts. It seemed silly to ask why these young women could act as brutal and aggressive as boys. It was also senseless to think about "human nature" as such. Forced to live in a harsh and inhuman environment, these women did not know how long they could tolerate such a life. Suspicion, quarreling, and even fighting were ways to release grievances, especially those suppressed for a long time. It was the outside environment that acted on the subject. What was the point if I retreated back to the "inside" of the subject, the "nature" of a human

Figure 7. Women workers
in the Meteor plant
dormitory queued up for
hot water for bathing.
(photo by author)

being, male or female? Violence is a performance of social relationship, embedded in specific historical and social contexts and often gendered in nature. Yet, it is never sexually prescribed.

The fighting women were all dismissed by the factory the next morning, without any investigation of who might be right or wrong. These workers all knew factory discipline and they all knew this fact: they did not behave like girls but rather like unruly boys or animals. Defiant bodies were punished and, again, they were disciplined through the discourse of sex and gender.

Women's Talk

For a few nights in the dormitory, talk centered on the women's fight. After bathing, at about 10:30 P.M., was often a time when women talked. Talking was an important fact of life after the workday because of the ban on speaking while working. Women congregated together based on ethnic-kin lines and, when the time came, chatting everywhere would start. I often heard men complain that when several women came together, you could never stop them talking. "Qi zui ba she" (seven mouths and eight tongues), was a Chinese saying about talkative women who were eager to speak out. "Qi zui ba she" was, of course, a term of denigration; its meaning showed overtly the desire and power of men to silence women because women's talk had long been seen as a threat to both the patriarchal order and the managerial order.[6]

At night the women gossiped about management; exchanged information on personnel policies; and discussed who was punished by confronting the factory rules, who succeeded in finding a boyfriend, and who was so disgusting and always flirting with women. They chatted about sex, childbirth, family, and sometimes complained about food. Because I could speak Chaozhou dialect, sometimes I joined in the talk among the Chaozhou women. One time, two Chaozhou women, both over forty, who worked as cooks, were talking with several other women. Lan, a young girl from Chaoyang asked, "Aunt, do you think the food in our canteen is too poor?"

The younger cook instantly replied, "Daughters, I never want you to eat poor rice. But what can I do? I did my best to serve you."

"But aunt, the food is really rotten, not even my family's pigs would eat it." Another woman, named Jin, interrupted.

"Oh girls, don't say something bad that will spoil your fortune. You are all young, you all have never swallowed bitterness and gone through hard times. At the time of the famine in the 1960s we all ate wild vegetables and tree leaves." The older maid spoke in a rather sentimental way, recalling her memories of hard times so as to convince the young women.

"Wow, aunt, you are talking about something terrible. But times have changed," said Tongtong, interrupting the cook.

"You are too lucky, and too happy in this generation. You've got no sense of women's bitterness in the past. You now have pretty clothes, earn your own money, and go where you want to go. Who could be like you when we were young? We never dreamed of leaving the family and the village. Women, always kept at home, did all the cooking and chores, waiting to get married and give birth to sons," the cook continued. All the women chuckled, but the cook felt a bit more at ease and continued to talk about "women's bitter story."

"You don't understand women's lives, do you? You won't know what bitterness is before you taste it. Mei, there is still a long road ahead of you. In the future, when you think you can marry a husband and enjoy happiness, you will find yourself alone in a man's family that is not your own, never. Your mother-in-law will keep a strict eye on you, and even your husband can't help you. And within two years, if you still can't lay eggs (give birth to sons), then you will know what kind of life will follow you. All the gossips in the village will target you . . . Then comes the big stomach, the ten months pain and the extraordinary pain at the moment of delivery. You are all young, you can't even imagine the pain. It kills you, it kills you, but every woman will go through it. It is women's destiny, you never know."

"Oh, oh, aunts, your time is past. Nowadays, we can run away from our families and find a job in the factory." Tongtong showed her optimism. Escaping to the workplace was often seen as an alternative to a coercive married life for the young women. But for the older women, escaping to work in the city was temporary and their gendered role as wife remained unchanged.

"You are telling children's tales. How about when you get older and older? Will the factory still want you? Women's place is in the family. You don't believe me, do you?" the older cook said.

One of the main plots of the women's talk in the workplace was the articulation of a subaltern "herstory" of women's lives—albeit often imagined, exaggerated, and victimized—that was narrated to the younger generation through the spoken word (Anagnost 1997). Often excluded by the formal and official written records, women's experiences of their own lives were marginalized, trivialized, or simply seen as nonexistent in history. But stripping away women's right to write or to be written could not silence them. It was not true that the subaltern could not speak and that women trapped in a patriarchal order could never express themselves, or, in the words of Shirley Ardner, could only have "a problem without a name" (1975, 10). The issue at stake here is who can hear? Who is willing to listen carefully at the fissures of dominance and power where voices of subalternality can be heard? Female histories in China constitute a long oral tradition that is memorized, imagined, and passed on from generation to generation (Croll 1995, 11–12). It was these kinds of women's stories that helped to construe the worlds of women's lives and helped women make sense of their own experiences. This women's talk, a rich cultural capital, provided not only stories, examples, and models but also a lively genealogy, from which women could learn about and negotiate themselves as female subjects.

Gossip and Romance

One night I was invited to eat soup with a Cantonese group. The women were all from Qingyuan, the poorest rural area in Guangdong Province, and they all worked in the quality control department. During our meal gossip and rumor flowed naturally and wildly and, as on many occasions, came to focus on Miss Tang, the manager of quality control, who was from Hong Kong.

Qing started gossiping about Miss Tang: "I saw her eating with her girl-friend in the McDonald's."

"When? Did you see her girlfriend? Is she pretty?" all the other women asked.

"Last Sunday. I could only see the side of her face, you know, I dared not enter. I looked from the glass wall. I guess she doesn't look bad. Very well dressed and thick make-up. Dong told me that one day she saw them walk-ing in the street. Her girlfriend was taller than her," Qing answered.

"But Tang looks quite handsome, doesn't she?" Bin said.

"Wow, somebody is secretly in love with our Tang!" Qing teased, and all the women laughed.

Bin responded instantly, "What rubbish are you talking? Will I love a person who is so harsh to us? I think because she treats people so hard and so emotionlessly, that's why she became abnormal. Can I love a pseudo man, who is in fact a woman? Can I?"

We continued to laugh despite Bin's explanation. A woman named Hua cackled "Why not? She is rich, powerful, and handsome. I bet if she chooses you, we can all get promoted. Please do sacrifice yourself!"

"But how can a woman love a woman? I am asking seriously. How can two women have sex? Can they give birth to a baby?" Bin turned her head to me, expecting an answer and trying to divert attention from herself. Unwill-ing to intervene in their talk, I simply said, "They can have sex, but they can't have a baby that way."

Qing added, "I saw a magazine one day. It said that in Western countries they have a lot of gays and lesbians who don't care about social and family pressure and insist on getting married to each other."

"How strange! They can marry. But it's good for them, isn't it?" another woman named San said.

"But it's still a pity they can't give birth to a baby. I think a woman's life can't be complete without going through marriage and the delivery of babies," Bin muttered.

"Oh, Bin, your thoughts are a little bit outdated. Today, who will care about the stuff of delivering sons? Happiness is more important!" Qing responded.

"Yet finding a good man is still important, isn't it?" Hua asked.

"Oh, Hua, you are dating somebody, aren't you? When are you going to marry him?" Bin asked back. All of us chuckled again and Hua blushed.

"I still have no idea. I don't want to go back home too early. But last New Year when I was back home, the man's family had already asked my father. Last month, my boyfriend came to visit me. He tried to convince me to come back home too." Hua spoke in an embarrassed tone.

"What a lucky woman! You must have done a lot of good things in your previous life. By the way, will you have sex before your married life?" Qing teased again, and we all fell into chuckles.

Hua instantly flushed and shouted, "I won't, I won't!"

"My father would beat me to death if he knew I had that relation with a man in the city," the quiet San murmured.

"Oh, I don't think it is wrong. If I really love a man, I don't mind," Qing raised her tone, a naughty expression on her face.

"Ah, what a liberated woman!" All the girls turned to laugh at Qing and the joking continued.

Gossip, jokes, and laughter centered on the topics of sex and love helped us to cope with the difficult and tedious factory life. Gossip and laughter demonstrated the power of the female workers, however minimal, to tease the patriarchal and capitalist orders. As Paul Willis (1981, 29) puts it, "having a laff" is a way to defeat boredom and fear, to ease the hardship and brutality of life, and thus is a way out of almost anything. "Having a laff" was clearly a weapon of the weak in fighting against the alienation of work and the subsumption of labor to capital. The factory daughters learned that sexuality was political and something they could decide to manipulate or not. Becoming sexually involved with someone in management, if one were willing, was a possible way to get promotion and gain advantages. Like labor, sexuality was something that belonged to the workers but could be manipulated and subsumed into the logic of capital. Sexual relationships between male supervisors and female line workers were not absent in the Meteor workplace, although they were frowned on heavily by all those not involved. Dating and sexual relations were often seen as advantageous and functional, but in the end futile, if not evil.

Another focus for gossip was the love affair between Gen, one of the supervisors in the production department, and Jing, now the secretary of the department. People kept telling me that Jing was only a line worker before she knew Gen, and that she was a nice, humble person before. But now she was completely proud and seldom talked even to her ethnic-kin group. At one point, a worker remarked to me: "You see the thick make-up, nobody is stronger than her. I am sure I won't want to learn from her, selling sex in exchange for a higher position."

Despite some bias, there were genuine social and cultural reasons for the workers to worry about any love and sexual relations they might have. First, if the man were an urban citizen, his family probably would not accept a woman of rural origin. Second, if both sides came from different provinces, the woman's family might not approve of the affair either. No family wanted their daughter to marry far away, unless they were really poor. Third, there were many rumors in the workplace that once a woman got pregnant, the man would run away and there would be no hope of finding him. It was an anonymous industrial world, not a communal village where everybody knew each other. Tragedy came once the man ran away and the woman's pregnancy was noticed by her company. Losing a job and not daring to go back home, the woman would be left alone to face her misfortune. Most women thought that it was not worth exchanging sex for short-term interest because in the end it could ruin one's whole life.

Gossip and laughter nevertheless were more than a weapon that was deployed to poke fun at the management. Jokes, laughter, and rumors were exactly where the women workers played out their gender subjectivities. Having a laugh was about having their views and ideas on sex, love, and marriage exchanged and voiced, and therefore helped to suture their female identities. During joking and laughing, women were more capable of articulating their feelings and emotions, albeit conflicting and ambivalent, such as love and hatred, desire and fear, dream and anxiety. For example, there was Bin who thought a woman could not be complete without getting married and giving birth to babies. There was Hua who took marriage as an important life path for women. But there was also Qing who said sex for happiness should be acceptable. Feelings and emotions expressed in the talking and joking were all part of a process of sexualization (Hearn and Parkin 1987). They were how women colluded in playing themselves out as sexualized subjects.

Consumerist Desire and the Modern Self

If "having a laff" in the workplace was one form of recreation, getting out of the factory premises to have fun was another alternative when time was available. Each month in the Meteor workplace we had a rest day on the Sunday following payday, and going shopping downtown in Shenzhen was one of the workers' favorite pastimes on that day. Quite often I would go with the women workers to Dong Fang Market, where a wide array of clothing, handbags, accessories, and beauty products were available. Dong Fang Market was a shopping paradise for them, a place where they could look for suitable, alluring, and inexpensive products. Fashion shops, department stores, supermarkets, fast-food stores, and cafés, all owned by local people, were clustered on both sides of the street. These shops exemplified the "vogue from the west" (*Xi feng*), offering the dagongmei a "taste" of a cosmopolitan lifestyle and, more important, their self-affirmation as modern gendered subjects (Yan 1997). In their search for "modernity" and in their hopes of improving their lives, the women workers possessed a great consuming passion. Their desire to consume was driven by their urgent desire to reduce the disparity between themselves and the city dwellers, as well as to live up to the calling of the modern model of female beauty that was increasingly imagined and imaged by the mass media and popular magazines.

The transition to being a modern lady, even if only as a matter of appearance, conjured up the dreams and desires of dagongmei as they strived to transform themselves. Deploying a touch of fashion to highlight their appearance was the most common strategy for the women as consuming subjects. In the urban industrial world the lure of consumption produced irresistible consuming desires, even for those who could not afford them. Their not being able to consume was not a problem; what was important was the power of the desiring machine to incite them to dream and to produce promises and further desires. What this promise meant to the young workers became clear to me when I jotted down this note for my field research: "28 March 1996, evening. We still have to work at night. The radio is on. There is no mood for work, we wait and dream. Tomorrow is payday. The girls on our line are talking about where to go and what to buy. While Fatso suggests buying new jeans, Fuhui, a girl sitting in front of me, thinks of buying lipstick. She asks me to suggest some brand names of high quality and reasonable price. I am at sea and wondering."

In the workplace the women workers dreamed of consumption even as they labored, as if the dreaming spurred them on despite their mood. Dagongmei consuming practices contested the assumption that consumption was an "individualizing project" invested in, by, and for capital. In the workplace, the women shared with equal enthusiasm the satisfaction and frustration of shopping as well as work. Instead of keeping them separated, consumption bound them into a collectivity through their shared dreams and desires to become a new kind of gendered subject. "Dressing up" is perhaps the most common of these practices. Returning to their workplaces after a day of shopping, they could not wait to display their transformed selves wearing newly purchased T-shirts and jeans. For those who had worked in the city for a year or two, the urban environment with its many shops was attractive. In the evenings, they returned to their dormitories where they talked excitedly about fashion and make-up and where they could find the best buys. The desire to transform themselves and have a new look was what drew them together.

Their change in appearance was pivotal to them in the workplace. As mentioned earlier, the managerial class mocked the dagongmei's "coarse hands and feet," an abject subject bearing the stigma of rural backwardness. One could not help but notice how much time they spent on their fingernails, painting them with shiny colors to make them look more glamorous. Another obsession was with products that promised to whiten their skin, darkened from long exposure to the sun while laboring in the fields back home. One had to be light skinned to be a city dweller, and thus whitening lotions and creams were among their favorite purchases. A new look and a fresh identity were not only desired but could be realized by actively working on their appearance. A rebirth could be achieved through a consumption practice that functioned as a technology of the self. Through this means, they could realize for themselves "a great leap forward" out of rurality.

Going Out Shopping

One Sunday five Sichuan women, Yue, Ling, Hong, Qin, and Ping, invited me to go out with them. As usual, we went to Dong Fang Market, and I suggested that I treat them in a café there. From the time we boarded the minibus, and in every fashion shop we went into, I could feel a sense of discrimination against my coworkers. Because they were speaking Mandarin and had strong village accents, they were told in a very impolite way to hurry up into the bus. Because they were not dressed in modern urban styles, saleswomen in the boutiques showed indifference to my coworkers' interest in their fashions. The saleswomen did not bother with them even when they asked about prices: their attitudes seemed to say that the dagongmei were too poor to buy their stock. Ping asked me to speak to the saleswomen in Cantonese when we headed for the next shop. I told her, "If you want to buy something, then I'll help you ask them in Cantonese. If not, I don't want to speak to them. We should despise them far more than they despise us." All of the women laughed; it seemed I was more annoyed than they were. Ping comforted me, saying, "You don't need to be too serious. We are getting used to the local people's attitude. They think they are richer, don't they?"[7]

We shopped in the open market and then went into a supermarket.

Supermarkets have become popular in China in recent years. To show its difference from the local family-owned grocery shops, this supermarket provided a variety of foreign goods and stressed its concern for high-quality foods. It puzzled me that security in the store was as strict as at the factory premises. Four or more security guards stood in front of a gate leading into the store, and we had to leave our handbags at the counter before we walked through the gate. And because we looked like poor rural women, a security guard followed us everywhere we went. But there was a "real" reason to take us as potential thieves; the prices in the supermarket were unreasonably high. One cup of Japanese instant noodles cost 11 yuan, the workers' salary for one day. We discussed, muttered, and chuckled, but we never bought anything. Ping asked me how much the local people earned that they could afford to buy such expensive stuff. Seeing that the workers felt awkward and out of place in this supermarket with its prohibitively expensive foreign commodities and security guards, I suggested that we go on to the café.

Surprisingly, this was the first time the Sichuan workers had gone to a café. No one had any idea what to order and the prices of the drinks were unacceptable to them, so they tried to persuade me to leave. But it was too late. A waitress was already standing at our table, looking at us with a strange smile.

Yue said, "A coke for 8 yuan!"

Hong echoed, "A tea for 10 yuan! For 10 yuan I can make one hundred cups."

Ping whispered, "What is a drink for? Just water. It doesn't fill your stomach. Should we go?"

Feeling embarrassed, I tried to calm them down and then ordered drinks for them. Two coffees, two lemon teas, and two soft drinks. As the waitress left our table I noticed that the people at the other tables all looked at us. I felt I had been unforgivably foolish to put the workers in such an awkward situation. A few minutes later, a waiter brought us one drink. It didn't look like anything we had ordered. I called back the waiter and he took it to the table in front of us. The man sitting there said loudly in Cantonese, "Their hands have touched the drink. Bring me another one. You don't know how dirty their hands are, those waisheng mei!" Waisheng mei was an abject term for girls from foreign provinces, that is, outside Guangdong Province. I was angry at his words, and burst out in Cantonese: "What's wrong with wai-sheng mei. A dog's eyes always despise a human being!" He didn't expect my sudden outburst, and so stood up and left the café, still wearing a disdaining look. Perhaps he was thinking of the Chinese proverbs, where a "good" man

Figure 8. A woman worker in the Meteor plant dormitory writing a letter to her boyfriend. (photo by author)

never fights with a woman. We all laughed, and, while drinking, we continued to make jokes about this particular local man.

Back at the dormitory, I was not able to fall asleep that night because the disgusting man's image was haunting my mind. I knew too well that the term waisheng mei carried the double negative of gender and rural-urban difference. But probably my discomfort was in part due to the fact that this was the first time I had shared the same discrimination with my coworkers. Although we enjoyed a victory at that moment, the man's silence might hide another layer of discrimination toward female subjects. Women were not worth arguing with; that was what the Chinese proverb meant. I headed over to Yue's bunk and found that she was still awake, writing a letter to her boyfriend, a recruit in the army in Beijing. In her letter she wrote: "It was exciting today. We went out to Dong Fang Market and had a drink in a modern and expensive café. An ugly local guy bullied us but we fought back. . . . Shen, why are we so poor? Why do the local people never treat us as human beings? Now that I'm out in the world, I find myself one hundred times more worthless than in the village. How do people treat you in Beijing? It's our country's capital. People there must be nicer. . . ."

In their letters to relatives, the women workers were able to state their position clearly: Shenzhen was a spectacular city, full of high-rise buildings, theme parks, expensive brand-name boutiques, luxurious hotels, and coffee shops, but it was not a place for them. And no matter how many years they spent there, in the drudgery of labor they would always be recognized as outsiders. The dream of consumerist gratification, of transforming themselves into modern selves, and their pursuit of modish feminized beauty to disguise their rural identity could only result in reinforcing their class and gender differences. When the subject of production strived to reemerge in the chain of the symbolic world, it was a process of negative hallucination, the "I" of production had to enter a process of identification or subjectification with the "other" of consumption. However, when the women workers decked themselves out to go shopping, they discovered that they failed to be recognized as the ideal consumers.

———————

In this rapidly transforming period old cultural practices; new urban cosmopolitan models, pressures, and norms from the rural society; and desires and pursuits in a modern yet anonymous industrial world are all mixed up yet work together to invoke new female subjects and sexual bodies. There are no fixed boundaries and stable reference frames, no harbors in which new subjects can take refuge. We can say that Maoist China aimed only at producing an asexual subject—*tongzhi*; a unified subject embodied with the same will as the state socialist production. No class, no gender. Reform China, however, within a global project of capital, shows interest in resexualizing the subject, most notably a new dagong subject tailored to meet the new international division of labor. In the workplace, while the homogeneous construct of sexuality seemed the dominant mode, alternative models like Miss Tang, new ideas from Hong Kong, Taiwan, Japan, and the West, new experiences of urban life, and all kinds of contradictory ideas and behaviors, are nurtured and contribute to constituting fluid, shifting, and decentered female subjects. While some of the women escaped from their rural families to work in the global factory, thus hoping to elevate themselves to being modern subjects by staying in the city, many of them would soon realize that the toil of factory work was only an alienation from which there was no rescue; some of them even dreamed of marrying out and hoped to return home as an escape from factory work. Women workers in contemporary China are induced to live with conflicting feelings, emotions, and subjectivities, far from their own making.

These Chinese dagongmei, however, were manipulated by capital not only to be turned into efficient industrial producers, but they themselves desired to become fetish subjects as elements of the project of subject and of power. As Marx (1954) has said, the production process is an alienating process, in which women and men turn themselves into objects and confront themselves as something hostile and alien. In the process of consumption, then, women and men strive to redeem their alienation and achieve a sense of satisfaction through consumption. The harder they work, the more they want to spend. The more they desire to spend, the harder they need to work—thereby mirroring the dyadic relationship between production and consumption. The desire to be rid of poverty and to become modern gendered subjects is articulated together with the desire to consume commodities. Young female workers in the factory shared the same passion for purchasing lipsticks, whitening creams, trendy watches, jeans, and T-shirts, just to name a few items. These objects conjured up new desiring subjects who only were to discover themselves still trapped in a politics of identity and difference.

In the next chapter I go on to explore, inbetween fissures of domination and resistance, dream and desire, and hope and anxiety, the journey of transgression for dagongmei in a rapidly changing China.

6

SCREAM, DREAM,

AND TRANSGRESSION

IN THE WORKPLACE

At the final stage of my fieldwork, I unexpectedly encountered the dream-induced scream of a woman worker. The scream pitched itself through the darkness of the last hours of night, at about four. I was awakened by the ghostlike voice to find it passing away, and the deep silence of the night reigned once again. The scream had come from Yan, who earlier had experienced the same dream. Because there had been complaints of her scream every night, I decided to move to her room, which she shared with seven others. Relations among the women in the room were tense, not only from the lack of space and privacy but also because of Yan's screams, which frightened her roommates and disturbed their sleep. I suffered, too, not so much from having my sleep disturbed but from my difficulty in understanding and then speaking about Yan's scream. Yan herself seemed to suffer the least; she woke up at a particular moment amid her screams, and then fell asleep again immediately. I was perplexed by the scream and anxious to understand it. Can the subalterns speak? Or do they have to scream?

The postscream silence of the night did not bring me to a standstill; rather at that moment it opened up the possibilities of new experiences of human suffering and transgression. I was thus inspired to conceive a minor genre of resistance, unconsciously at first but increasingly driven by a desire to produce a new genre of writing and be part of the current of resistance politics. What is a minor genre, or in Deleuze and Guattari's (1984) term, a minor literature? First, as they define it, the language of minor literature is affected by "a high coefficient of deterritorialization" (16). A minor literature does not come from a minor language; it is constructed by a minority within a major language. Second, everything in the minor literature is political. In a major literature, when the individual concern joins with other individual concerns, the social milieu serves as a background. Minor literature, however, is completely different in the way that "its cramped space forces each individual intrigue to connect immediately to politics, to the social it formed" (17). Finally, everything in minor literature takes on a collective value. There are "no possibilities for an individuated enunciation that would belong to this or that 'master' and that could be separated from a collective enunciation" (17). After all, minor literature, in Deleuze and Guattari's words, is the literature of people's concern: "There is never an individuated subject; there are only collective assemblages of enunciation, and minor literature expresses these acts insofar as they are not imposed from without and insofar as they exist only as diabolical powers to come or evolutionary forces to be constructed" (18).

I was fascinated by the thought of the birth of a minor genre, one capable of articulating a personal itinerary into a historical narrative and analysis. While some of the events I observed cannot be communicated, and while some are universal human experiences, the incidents I encountered in the Chinese workplace nonetheless remain rooted in a local place, shaped by a specific historical epoch and its sociocultural transformation, at the same time that they are linked to global forces. The questions I would like to pose for such a new genre include: Can there be an alternative genre of resistance—in other words, a yearning for new possibilities of resistance that might be approached through such experiences? Can dream, scream, and bodily pain, those experiences at the edge (often either ignored or trivialized in a master discourse of resistance, whether collective or individual), be taken as acts of transgression? Can I argue that in the borderland of consciousness and unconsciousness lies the very possibility of resistance?

The Scream That Broke Out

Yan's midnight screams had been going on for a month. She said she did not know why she cried out. Nor could she control it:

> I feel depressed when I hear people gossiping about my screaming. I have
> no idea what it is. When I am awake, it disappears and I sleep again. But I

have a dream that is the same every night: I dream I am going toward a pier, and that I am about to take a boat across a river. The river separates two villages, and the boat is the only way to get to the other village . . . I see that the boat is leaving and I hurry. But then I find my body can't move, it's too painful, too tired to move. I'm terribly scared because the boat is leaving. I'll be left behind and the sky is turning dark. It's the evening. I have no way to go.

Yan was too terrified in her dreams to control herself, to keep from screaming, yet at the moment she screamed, she woke up and fell asleep again. While Yan and the other women were so tired that they soon slept again, I lay awake for a while. I heard the silence, then a deep sigh from another woman, Ping, who slept in the upper deck, and the noise of grinding teeth from Bin, who was lying across from me. I found myself in a growing state of anxiety and agony because I had no idea how to apprehend the situation. I was lost in the field. I was lost precisely at the particular moment that I woke up to hear the scream.

World, self, and voice are all lost, or nearly lost, as Elaine Scarry (1985) writes, when the body experiences intense pain. In such close proximity to this pain, I found myself, a novice ethnographer, forced on a journey of novelty and otherness. It was not solely a result of being in a foreign culture, an alien place, that I had this complete sense of otherness in the field. It was the scream, the voice resistant to language, without its significance or referentiality—this scream that could neither be seen nor touched that had no "reality" when it manifested itself in the air. If, as Michel de Certeau (1984, xxi) has said, our own era is a sort of epic of the eyes, then what can an academic do with something invisible, as well as nonlinguistic? But for me there was no choice. The scream was too powerful, and with its boundless referential power it shrieked into the symbolic world and nullified any of the claims of that world. It came, furthermore, directly from the body of a subaltern; from a person who was often excluded in and from the written; from a specific human being struggling to live out her life; from a dagong-mei, a displaced yet resistant subject living in postsocialist China.

It was in the encounter of the scream and the attempt to understand, read, and codify the possible meanings of its impossibility that I was forced to realize the practices of knowing. Yan's screams tempted me to enter a foreign, risky terrain—somewhere between sound and word, between language and nonlanguage, between consciousness and unconsciousness—where I had never been before. I learned that pain and the impossibility of experience gave rise to the yearning for producing a genre of resistance. The intrusion into the gap, the fissure between the presence and unpresence, between the symbolic and unsymbolic, was the possibility of producing meanings and transgressions. The gap, the borderland, after all, was a source, a fountainhead, of desires of and for resistance, providing new experiences that awaited my exploration.

The Personal Trauma

Yan's screams and dreams in some ways appear to be the result of traumatic neurosis:

> I don't know why I have that dream, and everyday it is the same. The pier, the river is so familiar to me. It seems that I have been there before. . . . Oh, when did I start having this dream? A month ago, we were kept to do overtime work until 11:30 P.M. for three consecutive days. And we needed to move to a new dormitory on Sunday morning. I felt so tired that every part of my body ached, almost as if it was not my own body. I could not control it and stop the pain. When all my roommates went shopping and the room was empty, I urged myself to cry out, so loudly that I myself couldn't believe it. I was shocked by the sound, and ever since then I have had that dream and scream at night. It repeats and repeats.

Cathy Caruth has provided the most general summary of a trauma as "the response to an unexpected or overwhelming violent event or events that are not fully grasped as they occur, but return later in repeated flashbacks, nightmares, and other repetitive phenomena" (1996, 91). The persistent repetitiveness of Yan's screams seemed to indicate a traumatic experience. But other than her extraordinary bodily pain and fatigue, no particular unexpected or sudden event in her life could be singled out as the personal trauma suggested by psychoanalytic theory. On the surface and in her daily life, she was as ordinary as other factory workers—although each, of course, had her own personal story.

When I met Yan she had worked at the Meteor factory for more than thirteen months. During that time she had not met with any industrial accidents, nor had there been any great change in her family except the death of her grandmother during the Chinese New Year of 1996. She went home to her village in Hunan when she got the news that her grandmother was seriously ill, and she returned to the factory the day after her grandmother died, without attending the burial ceremony. Yet Yan took her grandmother's death at the age of eighty-three as natural. The death caused her pain, but it was not an unexpected shock in Yan's life. Thus, instead of looking for sudden events, I have tried to make sense of Yan's dreams and screams as situated in the present of her experiences in social life.

Although there had been no single, shocking event in Yan's life, assuredly the bodily pain she suffered from overtime work in the factory was at first experienced in the realm of consciousness. She shrieked in the afternoon when nobody was in the dormitory. Then a displacement had occurred: the experience went to her unconscious, manifesting in dreams, and was unwillingly, repetitively reenacted there. The screaming that followed broke out somewhere between consciousness and unconsciousness as she woke and then fell asleep again. The detour from the realm of consciousness to unconsciousness and back to consciousness entails a double telling of the story, which I will explore below within the larger workplace context.

Chronic Pain: Body and Work Process

Yan worked as a clerk in the production department. This was, in fact, her second job after she graduated from secondary school in her hometown and spent a year studying accounting in Guangzhou. Yan's understanding of her pain was ambivalent: "I get a nagging pain in my back. It often hurts me. After I had worked here for several months, I started to have the pain. You know, I have it better here than the assembly girls, who sit all day and night on the line. I'm just doing typing, recording, and bookkeeping in the production department. Sometimes I get the chance to walk around and take a break, drink some water. But I still suffer from the pain, I don't know why. Sometimes it runs to the back, sometimes the neck." Sometimes she thought the pain was obviously due to the stress of the heavy workload, but at other times she murmured that, at the age of twenty-four, she was too old to work in the factory. She no longer had the energy to toil for twelve hours each day. Old age in this context meant a body too weakened to endure industrial work. Most of the dagongmei, as stated earlier, with an average age of twenty, expected their health to deteriorate after working for more than three years in the factory.

The electronics industry is particularly notorious for using toxic chemicals that damage the health of its workers.[1] Based on the daily experiences I shared with my coworkers, my focus here is on the chronic complaints that were common at the Meteor workplace: headache, sore throat, flu and coughs, stomach problems, backache, nausea, eye strain, dizziness and weakness, and aggravated menstrual pain. Nearly every operation and thus every job along the electronics production line involved a complex series of chemical processes. Cleaning, the first job of semiconductor assembly, uses the majority of the chemical agents, such as solvents, acids, or alkalis for degreasing, rinsing, etching, oxidizing, and buffing the electronic chips. These solvents can be highly toxic and are known to have long-term effects on human health (Gassart 1985).

Workers on the shop floor, especially those involved in the assembly of printed circuit boards and semiconductors were routinely exposed to these toxic cleaning agents. Organic solvents such as alcohol and the aliphatic, aromatic, or chlorinated hydrocarbons were the most common (and probably the most poisonous) chemicals used in the workplace. While some were in pure solution, others were mixed with or used to dilute other substances such as inks, paints, plastics, and glues. Various forms of cleaning took place in nearly every major work process. "Dip cleaning" was the method favored at Meteor: electronics chips and printed circuit boards were cleaned in a large bath of heated solution before assembly. Because of the pervasiveness of these chemicals, the cleaning room was considered the most foul place in the factory, and workers went there only unwillingly. The chemical fumes and smells were nauseating and often caused effects that were almost narcotic, such as drowsiness, dizziness, feelings of drunkenness, and headache.

One day, after three months of working, I noticed that Hui-ping, a twenty-year-old worker at Meteor, had a terribly pale face. She had worked in the cleaning room for nearly a year, and she had serious headaches and felt dizzy all of the time. Her experience was in many respects typical: "You know, none of the workers is willing to work in the cleaning room. So they bully the new hire. When I came to work here, they placed me in the room and never let me move out. The room is stuffy, and the smells are worse than the smells in the hospital. Those acids make me feel dizzy all the time and I can't make my mind concentrate. Recently I find that my head is too painful to describe. I am thinking of going back home if my headache doesn't improve."

Bonding was another essential work process that caused chronic pains. At the heart of semiconductor assembly in electronics production, bonding connects the electronic die to the integrated circuit microchip on a frame, so as to create an electrical circuit. Performed by a machine with a computer monitor and microscope, it was a semiautomatic job (the machine required a bonding worker for its operation and maintenance). There were two types of bonding in the workplace: die bonding and wire bonding.

Die bonding was done by hand; the minuscule semiconductor dies were mounted on the frame with a transistor, diode, or integrated circuit. Die bonding involved the application of epoxy resin in the frames along with a curing agent, so that the dies could be fixed on the frames. Workers used a pair of tweezers to separate the dies, and then placed them on the frames with extreme care, lest the tiny dies should fall. These dies were the most expensive electronic component in the entire production process; workers were often reminded of this and were put under extra pressure to work with meticulous care.

Wire bonding, the next step after die attachment, used aluminum wires to connect each chip to electrical terminals on the frame, thus creating an electric circuit. Ultrasound waves were applied in this process; the sound wave caused the molecules in the wire and the contact points to vibrate and shake together, forming bonds. Because both the die and the wire were extremely tiny and thin, the workers could only perform the job by using a microscope and a computer monitor to fix the wire and the contact points. Later, drops of black epoxy glue were used to coat the bonded die in order to protect it from damage. For this process, workers held a glue gun, shooting drops of epoxy onto the frames before putting them into an oven to be baked to fully cure the epoxy. Epoxy resin has long been known to be poisonous and hazardous to workers' health—it is linked in particular to skin and lung illnesses (Gassart 1985, 122–23).

As mentioned above, bonding was a work process notable for the extreme smallness of the objects involved. Long-term use of the microscope and the intensive concentration on detail caused eyestrain, dizziness, headaches, and stress. Permanent eyesight damage would result if the worker used the microscope continuously for more than two years. Yet the bonding machines in the Meteor plant operated twenty-four hours a day: with such a large investment in its machinery the company could not afford to stop production. Accordingly, workers were arranged in double shifts. Because of my own job on the assembly line I could not observe production in the daytime, so I learned the work process at night. There were a total of forty-six workers in the bonding department, including technicians, foremen, and line leaders. Most of these workers were female and were said to be experienced workers who had spent more than two years in the factory before being moved to the bonding room. Sharp eyes, thin fingers, and good work attitudes were particularly important in these jobs, as Lun, the foreman, explained: "Damaged chips are not repairable, so we have high pressure to do everything in the right way. . . . In the night hours, workers usually don't have enough spirit to concentrate on work, so that the work pace is slower and there is more breakage . . . The wage and bonuses here are a little bit higher than for the workers in other assembly lines, because the bonding job is harder and takes more energy."

Surrounded by the rhythmic sound of the bonding machines, Lun needed to raise his voice when he spoke to me. The temperature in the room was much lower than in other rooms and lines on the main shop floor because the maintenance of chips and machinery required cool conditions. The contrast between the cool temperature in the room and the hot temperature outside, especially in the summertime, often caused workers to get flu, colds, and coughs as they went in and out for lunch and dinner. Workers' fainting spells most often occurred in the bonding room, especially during the time of women's menstrual pain.

Siumei, a veteran of the bonding room, told me one night: "We are often told that we are at the heart of production and the most important workers in the company. But what do we get? Fifty yuan more than other workers in the workplace. Yet we all know that our eyesight is becoming weaker and weaker. Sometimes when I leave the factory, I do not dare to glance at the sunlight. I find my vision blurred, and I can't walk a straight line." Hon-ling, a young woman sitting beside Siumei, jumped into our conversation: "I worry about my eyestrain; I've got headache and stomachache [menstrual pain], too. It's too stressful to work here. Night and day are turned upside down. I have demanded to move out, but there is still no answer. You know, I don't want to faint myself one day."

The belief was common in the bonding room that once the women developed eyestrain, headache, and abnormal menstrual pain, they could never be cured. Both Western medicines and Chinese herbal medicines were tried in an effort to alleviate the problems, but such treatments were said to be useless against these chronic complaints. Hon-ling said she first had the headache after working for six months in the bonding room; she had tried several measures to heal herself but nothing had helped. "Sometimes it seems that the pain is incurable," she said. "Even when I go back home, it follows me." Poor sleep in the daytime and a stressful nighttime working situation all contributed to the general weakness of workers' health and the specific illnesses of each worker. Sometimes just by looking, one could tell a fresh from an old worker. A rosy face, the insignia of a young village girl, faded after just a year or two in the factory.

The intensity of bodily pain varied among workers. There was no mechanism that could measure the pain, and the experience of pain was inseparable from personal perception and social influence (Kleinman 1992, 6). Yet the pain of one worker could easily affect other workers, especially those in the same line or room. Although headache, backache, and menstrual pain were pervasive in the workplace, these problems were also largely invisible; most women kept them private. Yet once the problems were evoked, nearly every worker could tell her own story of a similar pain or illness. The chronic pain, because of its persistence and incurability, provided an index of social alienation and domination in the workplace.

From another perspective, Arthur Kleinman (1992, 174) argues that chronic pain, as the embodiment of human suffering, can also be viewed as embodied resistance to the lived flow of one's daily experience. Chronic pain is thus a source of power; with its uncompromising refusal to be cured it can pose a powerful challenge to the micropolitics of social relations (187). Such pain, for instance, would not only lower the work pace but sometimes would cause a direct interruption or complete stoppage of production—for example, in the case of fainting spells. Less obviously, dizziness and eyestrain might affect the accuracy and efficiency of the bonding workers in managing their machines. Thus a body in pain is not simply a defeated body; rather, it might constitute a resistant shield against the micropower directly afflicting the self. The collective manipulation of chronic pain in the workplace therefore can be seen as fundamental, bodily resistance to the alienating and punishing industrial labor performed by the women in the workplace.

Menstrual Politics: Women's Time versus Industrial Time

Women's fainting spells occurred time and again in the workplace. On one hot May afternoon, a woman called Lan, on line A, fainted. Her face turned pale, her lips became bloodless, and her body was as cold as ice and trembling. No one could stop the cold and the pain. Production was interrupted. "It's the woman's issue, woman's period and woman's fate." Women on the line all knew what happened, and every time they sighed with worry that the suffering would come to them sooner or later. Every month there would be one or two women sent to the clinic room suffering from dysmenorrhea. It was a threat, a pain, an inescapable issue shared by all women in the workplace, irrespective of age (those between menarche and menopause), locality, and ethnicity. This common experience of women inevitably exposed the conflict between the uncompromising nature of industrial time and a woman's life.

The woman's period, argued Penelope Shuttle and Peter Redgrove, is "the moment of truth that will not sustain lies" (1978, 5). The truth I want to articulate here in the particular context of a Chinese workplace is the alienation—the arbitrariness of disciplinary time that intruded, dissected, and reorganized women's lives. That time was inherently contradictory to their sense of time, which was closer to their common bodily experiences. With insights from Julia Kristeva (1986), we know that women's time is particular; it can never be fully incorporated into social time because it is organized by a periodical or cyclical sense of time, as women repetitively live out changes in their bodies in everyday practices.

Kristeva argues that a feminine mode of time is inherently contradictory to historical and social time: "Female subjectivity would seem to be linked both to *cyclical* time (repetition) and to *monumental* time (eternity), at least in so far as both are ways of conceptualizing time from the perspective of motherhood and reproduction. The time of history, however, can be characterized as *linear* time: time as project, teleology, departure, progression and arrival" (1986, 187). Women's time is maternal time. The menstrual cycle, the cycle of marriage and procreation, the cycle of puberty and motherhood, are all crucial bodily experiences in making up a woman's life. This cyclical sense of time conflicts inevitably with the linear, progressive, and aggressive male industrial time. Emily Martin makes this point very succinctly when she states: "Women, grounded whether they like it or not in cyclical bodily experiences, live both the time of industrial society and another kind of time that is often incompatible with the first" (1987, 21).

At night, after overtime work, I went to visit Lan. She lay on her bed, still looking pale and weak. She was nineteen years old and often suffered from menstrual pain. "I don't know why, it's so painful that I can't control it. Inside my body, something has turned upside down. And the blood, the blood never seemed to stop flowing," Lan told me.

"What did the nurse do to you?" I asked.

"The nurse gave me an injection, and after a few hours the pain was gone; but I was too weak and dizzy so I fell asleep again. When I woke up, it was already evening and the nurse asked me to leave. . . . But I was so afraid, I could feel the blood was still flowing. It was very embarrassing that my pants were getting stained and red," Lan told me in a low tone.

"Did you have the pain when you were in your hometown?" Lan came from a village in Jiangxi. Before she moved out to work in the factory, she helped her family by doing farm work at home.

"No, I didn't feel any discomfort when it came. I didn't even know it would cause pain. Sometimes my mother asked me not to go to the rice field when the period came. She said a menstrual body was a weak body and one shouldn't let it soak in the water of the field. That would make me have pain, but I didn't feel the hurt," Lan said.

Many women in the workplace were subjected to dysmenorrhea, although the degree of pain varied from one individual to another. Menstrual pains, it was said, occurred less often when the women were in the village. Most of the women started to have the pain after working one or two years in the factory. But some told me that once they had moved out of their villages they suffered immediately from the pain. The common rhythm of suffering, while it caused pain to the women, could not help but at the same time cause trouble for the production machine. The disciplinary time was scientifically studied and deliberately organized, but the women's bodies had their own clocks and could never be totally regulated and subsumed into the rhythm of industrial production (Martin 1987). A woman's fainting often stopped the assembly line until her position was filled by somebody else. The loss of production was expected but it could strike at any time. Especially at the time of a rush order, women fainting was often taken as a bad omen foretelling the possibility that the order date would not be met. A sudden change of environment, long working hours, and extreme pressure all contributed to disturbing the women's menstrual cycles. Some women's peirods would be prolonged from five days to seven, some had periods lasting over a month, and some simply would stop having periods altogether. Menstrual disorder disturbed the women's time and yet simultaneously made it harder for the disciplinary machine to control women's lives.

As a consequence of the inner splitting and splintering originating in their bodily experiences, women came to know bodily pain other than from external social violence. Emily Martin succinctly points out that, much more acutely than men, women suffer from alienation with respect to part of the self: "For one thing, becoming sexually female entails inner fragmentation of the self. A woman must become only a physical body in order to be sexual" (1987, 21). The splitting of the self from the body, and treating the body as an object for the self, was the women's common experience, particularly when they went through menstrual pain: "It was out of my control . . . I hated it so much," "It cut my body into pieces." Thus, the body was not only taken as an object, but sometimes as an opponent to the self. In facing agony, women sometimes split their minds and bodies. If the women wanted to retain the "will to power" over their lives and bodies, dividing the self was one of the ways to resist extreme bodily pain and to prevent total self-collapse. Otherwise, the intense, extreme bodily pain would destroy the integrity of the self and result in some sort of schizophrenic experience (Laing 1967, 1969).

Because it was often out of control, the sufferers would try to exteriorize the pain as something that was opposite to their bodies, and their bodies opposite to their selves. The pain attacked the body; the body, failing to sustain the pain, in return took revenge on the self. It was the pain that caused the splitting of the body and the self. Or, it could be said that the splitting of the self from the body was a tactic for confronting unbearable pain. Such externalization formed a buffer that could prevent the complete disintegration of the body/self complex.

Inner fragmentation thus was the common experience of women in protecting themselves against the loss of self as a consequence of bodily pain. What I would like to elucidate here is how this inner fragmentation of women's bodies is related to social violence and alienation. R. D. Laing once wrote: "Torn, body, mind and spirit, by inner contradictions, pulled in different directions, Man cut off from his own mind, cut off equally from his own body—a half crazed creature in a mad world" (1967, 46–47). Besides Laing, Deleuze and Guattari (1984) also believed that schizophrenia—the splitting of the self—is not a syndrome only of a limited few. Rather it is a common phenomenon, an everyday life tactic of survival for normal people living in modern capitalist societies. To survive in a mad industrial world and in response to social alienation, human beings tear themselves apart, both mind and body. The destruction of the social, in Laing's (1969) eyes, comes through the destruction of the self. The divided self, estranged from oneself and society, he argues, cannot experience either oneself or others as "real" or "whole." The self thus invents a false self, and with it confronts both the outside world and its own despair. The disintegration of the real self keeps pace with the growing unreality of the false self until, in the extremes of schizophrenic breakdown, the whole self disintegrates.

The Ruse of Capital over Bodily Pain

Disciplinary power nevertheless had its own ruse to contain the bodily resistance of the women workers. On the shop floor, line leaders kept at hand several types of unknown pills to provide to the workers when they claimed menstrual discomfort. Nobody could ask for sick leave because of menstrual pain. As Bailan, the line leader, told me: "Too many women have this kind of problem. If we allowed one to take a rest, then all the others would ask for it as well. What can we do? Production cannot be stopped. We give the pills to the girls to stop the pain. Or, if they faint, we send them to the hospital." These unknown pills, which I guessed were painkillers and contraceptive pills, were distributed by the personnel department to the line workers. "So we keep them. Whenever the girls suffer from the pain, we give them water and the pills. Sometimes these pills really work—they can stop the pain within a short time," Bailan explained to me.

Women on the line had no choice but to depend on these pills. Some thought they were panaceas, and could not live without them: "I don't know what the pills are, but every time when I feel pain, I eat them and I feel released. . . . Sometimes I am afraid that the line leader will refuse to give them to me, so I keep some of the pills myself," said Fuxing, a woman on line B. While the company encouraged the women to take these pills when they suffered from menstrual pains, there were also worries that the contraceptive pills would be misused and sexual encounters encouraged. So they warned the women that these pills could not be used except for menstrual disorders. The line leader often reminded the workers: "These pills are not for fun. If you use them wrongly, you'll make a big mistake."

The lack of an explicit explanation for these pills stimulated the myths and rumors that obviously formed part of the strategy of the production machine for exercising control over the female body and sexual behavior. Providing the unknown pills thus was an attempt to regulate the female body, to rechannel women's time into the mainstream of disciplinary time. Marx's labor, as we understand it, is an asexual labor, and the alienation he indicated is a general experience for both male and female workers. Here, however, I would like to highlight how the alienation of male and female workers was sexually different and gendered in nature. Female workers, I argue, can be subject to more acute and deeper alienating forces than can male workers, because a woman's physiology, body, and sense of time are fundamentally contradictory to the capitalist mode of production and the industrialized mode of time. Women's time is less able to be surrendered, and women's bodies are more difficult to regulate. Premenstrual syndrome, menstrual pain, and maternity leave and sickness are all women's issues that are beyond the control of the capitalist machine. Women's labor is devalued and discriminated against precisely because of the difficulty the machine has in instituting and rechanneling women's time into industrial time. In the world dominated by the capitalist mode of production, women are second class—not only as sexual subjects, but also as laborers. Socialist feminism is right to say that women are oppressed by double alienation, as women and as workers. What we need to further pinpoint is how this double alienation is closely interconnected and mutually reinforcing (Bartky 1990). The workers as women are deeply alienated in material production, as industrial time is highly contradictory to women's time. On the other hand, the women as workers toiling in the factory are estranged from their biocultural production in their family.

But where was repression and where were the fissures of transgression? The menstrual body itself could be the body of resistance, and the failure of the disciplinary machine to control it was plain to see. No matter how deliberately bodily actions were measured, and no matter how scientifically the pace of work was calculated in minutes and seconds, the female body had its own rhythms of time and suffering. A woman is not a robot: her body is a body of flesh and blood that can be regulated but never changed and totally subsumed by the disciplinary machine. While most of the women's time was successfully rechanneled, the exact moment of a woman's menstrual period, and the outrageous pain, depression, and anger, could not be precisely anticipated. Fainting, the extreme experience of bodily pain, could be seen as a fundamental challenge to the disciplinary machine. Fainting was not only an illness but also a dysfunction of the female body that could live in its own rhythm. This obviously exposed both the violence of industrial time and its failure to turn the female body into a working robot.

Yan's Pain: Between the Body and the Social

Here I return to Yan's story of pain. We already know that working in the Meteor factory caused her bodily pain, but this pain again must be seen as embedded in a wider social and cultural context. Yan's comment that at twenty-four she was too old to work in the factory designated not only her physical state but also signified the more subtle cultural pressures in her life. In Chinese rural culture, the issue of age is laden with gendered significance. Yan was brought up in a town in western Hunan, the province where Mao Zedong was born. Although Yan's was one of the poorest towns, her own family was not impoverished because both of her parents were official cadres and worked in the township government. After secondary schooling, she tried her best to get into the university but twice failed the entrance examinations. When she was nineteen, her parents sent her to a one-year course in accounting in Guangzhou. After the course, she returned home to take an accounting job in the forestry department of the local township government.

But she was dissatisfied both with the job and the life in a small, poor town. After a year in Guangzhou, she was aware of the great disparity between urban and rural China. "I was a cadre in my hometown, but my wage was just 200 yuan. An ordinary worker in Guangzhou earned more than me," she recounted. Besides the wage disparity, there was also too great a gap in material lifestyles. None of the young people were willing to stay in the town: "Educated or not, they all went to Guangdong looking for opportunities." This was even true for Yan, who convinced me that she was not particularly ambitious. She had accompanied her elder sister to work in Dongguan, another economic development zone in Guangdong. When her elder sister married a local citizen there, their hukou were transferred from their hometown to Dongguan, at a price of RMB 5,000 for each person paid to the local government.

As I discussed in chapters 1 and 2, in Mao's China the hukou system proved to be one of the most effective mechanisms for population control and distribution during the process of constructing the socialist state. One's fate was tied to the area of one's birth. In the village, an individual's entire life would be spent as a peasant; to have the good fortune to be born in the city meant that one would be a worker, part of a privileged class that enjoyed all the produce of the peasants. In contrast however, peasants had little or no access to goods produced in urban factories. Population mobility was not permitted unless it was part of the state plan. With the open-door policy and economic reform, however, the controls on population mobility were eased, and the labor surplus from the rural areas was drawn to the cities to meet the needs of private and global capital. After being bound to the land for three decades, it was the first time that the whole of the Chinese peasantry gained the freedom to move, and thus the freedom to experience the inequality between the urban and the rural. This constitutes the "social revolution" from below.

Yan spent more than two years in Dongguan, working as a secretary in an electronics company where she earned 600 yuan each month. She felt happy in the first year because she was supported by her sister's family; she ate and slept at their home, enjoying the sort of family life that was beyond the dreams of the typical dagongmei working far from her hometown. As a secretary, reporting directly to the general manager of the company, she held a high-status job. She could learn a lot, especially about how to deal with complicated personnel matters, and in this job she matured.

But then came her affair with her boss, the general manager, a Hong Kong man in his mid-forties. Ultimately the affair forced her to leave the company and even Dongguan. Yan told me the story one night when we had gone to a bookshop:

> He treated me so nicely, like an uncle, teaching me a lot of things. I didn't hate him, frankly. We worked as a pair of good partners, and he never scolded or criticized me. . . . But he had a family—a wife, sons, and daughters in Hong Kong. Sometimes they came to visit him and had a good time. . . . He wanted to take me as a lover and promised to get me an apartment and take care of me if I was willing to stay with him. You know, a lot of girls these days are looking for this kind of relationship, waiting for a man to feed them. They don't mind the low status. But I was so hesitant, very fearful that something out of my control would happen. It might affect my whole life.

Yan refused the relationship and left the company. Asked if she regretted it, she responded with a smile and said, "Sometimes I do miss him." It seemed clear that they were sexually attracted to each other, and that the reason for her refusal involved more than an ethical issue. She was ambivalent enough that even she herself could not quite tell what she felt.

Within Shenzhen there are certain residential areas—called *er-nai cun*, concubine villages or second-wife villages—where women live who are supported by Hong Kong businessmen. To be an *er-nai* was to be an illegal wife, a woman whose immorality lay in her reluctance to work for herself and her greed in enjoying what was perceived as a luxurious life at the expense of another woman's family. When I visited these areas accompanied by other women workers from Meteor, they often made fun of the women they saw, singling out their make-up and the way they dressed. "*Bu yao mian zi*" (shameless) or "*mai shen*" (selling one's body) were common phrases used to make fun of these women. *Mian zi* indicated not only one's dignity but also one's relationship with others, especially one's family and the community. Thus *bu yao mian zi* not only insulted its target but also involved a wider network of filial and communal relations. Mai shen was a kind of exchange of one's body for a better life, also with overtones of material pursuit.

Yan often kept silent when other women gossiped about the women they saw in the street. Sometimes she would comment, "It's their business, don't stick your nose in it." In her case, it had not been money that had attracted her to the man. But her decision to leave him was not without consideration of mian zi. The presence of her elder sister, the fact that her parents were government cadres, and her relatively high educational background all contributed to her anxiety and thus the repression of her desires. "I am poor, but I am not greedy": Yan never forgot to convey this message to me. While relative poverty had led her to leave her hometown and look for a better life elsewhere, it did not impel her to love a Hong Kong man as her superior. She did not consider her love illegal or immoral, but both mian zi and the uncertainty of a future with a married man caused her to give up the relationship. In other words, the repression of Yan's sexual desire was both personal and cultural. The cultural value placed on monogamy, particularly for women, was reinforced by discrimination against the mostly poor women who entered such arrangements. This discrimination was particularly severe when the men were from the upper classes, and there was thus a huge gap between the two parties.

In leaving Dongguan, however, Yan was caught in an impasse: "I was wondering whether to go home or find a job somewhere else. I really had no idea at the beginning. I missed my hometown so much and definitely wanted to return. But I found I had no choice. My hukou had been moved out (of the village) and I no longer could find a job in my hometown government. I found myself with nowhere to settle. I could not return to my hometown in this position." At that particular moment Yan realized that once her life was put in transition, she could never go back. Her life was out of her control forever. She often told me she was just floating here and there. The paradox was that although she had suppressed her desire to love a man precisely in order to prevent the loss of control over her future, she now found her life in this state. This sudden, surprising realization, I believed, was the probable cause of her trauma. Yan realized something that she could not accept, and the process of realization involved both pain and refusal.

Yan herself saw the dream and scream as an uncontrollable evil force that was born from within her body. It had nothing to do, however, with such spirits or ghosts as are often said to haunt women workers in Southeast Asian countries (Ong 1987). Yan herself thought that she suffered from *xinbing*, the illness of the heart. Although she always emphasized that she could not understand the reason for this, she often said: "There must be something wrong inside myself. . . . I am sick, you know, that is why I have the dream and scream." For her the dream and scream was a sign of her sickness. Thus, although inner and psychological, her "heartsickness" took a form that was not separable from either the body or the social. Dream and scream was an index of bodily imbalance and cosmic disorder. The evil, as she understood it, was an external force that came to dominate her, but it had grown from her own body and mind.

In Yan's story there is a dynamic relationship between the individual and the social. The social might be "out there" but it cannot affect an individual's life unless the individual turned it inside out. The rapid social changes affecting her might be beyond Yan's control, yet such dislocations could only destroy her sense of self at the particular moment she realized and simultaneously refused this fact. But there was never truly a dichotomy between the individual and the social; the individual was always in the process, to a varying extent, of realizing the social. In this sense, we can understand that the individual is impersonal. But what is more important is to decode the process of impersonalization and to show that the social never ceases to impose its violence on the self—and the self, with its existence as being in the world, could not but realize the social existence that is not real.

Yan's Displaced Self

After she left Dongguan, Yan was helped by a relative and found the job in Shenzhen at the Meteor plant where we met and worked together. Yet Yan was far from happy with the job. As an ordinary clerk in one of the departments in the company, she enjoyed none of the status or the privileges she had had in Dongguan. Above her was a huge hierarchy. She knew she had little chance of promotion without particular guanxi—nepotistic relationships or kin in the upper echelons. Like all the other workers at Meteor, she put in twelve hours a day plus overtime. In Dongguan, she had usually worked ten hours and had some leisure time of her own at night. In Shenzhen, too, without the support from her sister's family, she had to eat in the factory and sleep in the dormitory; she had to depend on herself.

One day, when several workers were complaining about wages, Yan told me: "Previously I didn't think factory life was so exploitative. I knew the bosses always made a lot of money and the workers wages were meager. In the company in Dongguan, I knew almost everyone's wage. . . . Well, the workers earn very little, and I know that a meal the general manager eats in the restaurant costs more than a worker's monthly salary. There are also inequalities among the workers. Some earn double or triple what the others do. But at that time, I didn't question anything. I accepted it—it's a person's fate." At Meteor Yan only earned 550 yuan per month, 50 less than she had been paid in Dongguan. She believed she was worth more, because what she did for the company went beyond clerical duties. As a computer typist who knew advanced programs, along with her experience taking meeting minutes, she actually did most of the department's office work.

The sense of oneself as a commodity was quite strong among the workers at Meteor in general, and it was particularly acute for Yan. The sudden transformations of the reform era contributed to a sense of alienation as market forces replaced state command and control in regulating social life. In leaving the land and going to the industrial cities, workers experienced another life in which their labor can only be sold for cash. Significantly, mai shen, the term for women selling their bodies to men, was also used to signify the sale of workers' bodies to capitalists. Having nothing but their bodies when they left the land and the villages, these workers were forced to see themselves as part of the proletariat.

The realization of class-consciousness, nevertheless, was varied and always fluid. In Dongguan, Yan had been more willing to cope with the industrial life and felt satisfied in "selling her body" to the company she worked for. Only in Shenzhen did she grow more aware of inequality and exploitation and begin to complain about her wages. Her view of the boss she worked for changed with the situation. Now she put herself in a completely oppositional class position. Compared to her ambiguous status in Dongguan, Yan now saw her situation starkly: "Before I controlled people, now I am controlled. . . . In the eyes of the managers, workers are merely stuff that can be thrown away at will."

Given the long hours and harsh working conditions, the common feeling in the workplace was that the employees "worked like dogs." Jokes circulated to this effect: "Is your only regret that you weren't born a foreign dog?" or "Next incarnation, remember to be born elsewhere (than China), even as a dog." Some workers consoled themselves with the thought that "fate takes turns, so fate will turn one day." But while some might dream of someday becoming petty capitalists, others were more realistic; they knew that after several years of toiling in the factory they had to go back to the villages of their household registry. For the women this meant that they were going to be married before they became too old. Few of them could hope to stay in the city, unless they could find local husbands or some other way to transfer their hukou. As discussed earlier, there was still little chance for the relocated peasantry to form a real proletariat in the industrial towns and cities. Not only the hukou system but also the huge gap between rural and urban living standards presented barriers to migrant workers staying in the city.

With regard to marriage, Yan was again caught in the middle. At the age of twenty-four, she was forced to think of her marriage prospects. Especially in rural China, twenty-four was near the limit for a woman to enjoy the freedom of a single life. Celibacy was not an accepted norm of village life, where marriage was still "the big event of the entire life" for a woman and essential for settling one's future life with the family of her husband. Young women of Yan's age often returned home, whether on their own or at their parents' request. Resistance to marriage was not impossible, but it meant that a woman would have to depend completely on herself, given the families' objections and their sense of insult. Women workers were always torn: between family expectations and industrial demands, between marriage pressures and the temptations of city life.

Quite clearly, the capitalist machine manipulated these individual conflicts and cultural expectations. It was standard practice for most women to leave the factory automatically at age twenty-three or twenty-four. They had already contributed their labor at perhaps the most energetic period of their lives, from as early as the age of sixteen. The factory had by then extracted the maximum of their youthful labor capacity. Furthermore, after working as many as eight years for twelve hours a day in the factory, these women were physically worn out. It was then high time for them to get married and continue their labor by giving birth to sons and serving the patriarchal machine. The socialist machine had not smashed the patriarchal machine in the Maoist period, nor did the capitalist machine do so in contemporary China; in fact, these systems worked happily with each other, hand in hand, gear meshing with gear.

Yan had no idea about her future married life because her original hukou had been cancelled, and the last thing she wanted was to look for a husband in her rural hometown. She was lost whenever she thought of her future married life. "Why not find a man in Dongguan or Shenzhen?" I asked her one day. "It's not as easy as one thinks," Yan answered. "The men with local hukou in Shenzhen will not look for women of rural origin. There are plenty of pretty urban girls from the north, from big cities, for them to choose from. . . . In Dongguan, my sister introduced me to (prospective) partners, but sometimes I didn't like them, sometimes they didn't like me. It's not easy."

Yan said she sometimes considered not marrying, but she was also reluctant to let the time pass. "What can I do? Yet the problem is that I need to find a job to survive. I really don't know how many years I can keep working with a worn-out body. Even if my health could support it, I don't think the company wants an old woman." Yan remained silent afterward. Her anxiety about her life was not difficult to understand. The wear and tear of her life, as I have argued above, was both psychosomatic and biocultural. And if the socialist apparatus and its hukou system bounded her mobility, the capitalist machine sapped her youth and energy while the patriarchal culture helped bring her to this impasse. With these triple oppressions, we come nearer to knowing Yan's dream and scream.

Dream, Scream, and Resistance

Domination foretells resistance. Here we return to the trajectory of Yan's dream and scream. If the narrative of Yan's personal story discloses the social and cultural violence on the individual, then the final question we must ask is how the individual reacts to and resists that violent reality. Were Yan's dreams and screams acts of transgression or flows of resistant desire? If we wish to argue that Yan's trauma was more than an inner and personal crisis of the psyche, then her story must be situated in a larger social and cultural context, yet without subjecting it to a cultural determinism. And what, finally, can we learn from Yan's story? Does her dream and scream help to open new experiences of resistance, new terrains of transgression that we have not dreamed of before?

The journey of Yan's story finally leads us to Foucault's reading of dreams. The dream, Foucault believed, was not a fulfillment of a repressed desire, or "a rhapsody of images" that helped dreamers to escape reality. Rather, dreaming was a specific form of human experience, entailing the very possibility of the theory of existence. As he states: "But a dream is without doubt quite other than a rhapsody of images, for the simple reason that what a dream is is an imaginary experience; and if it cannot be exhausted—as we saw earlier—by a psychological analysis, this is because it relates also to a theory of knowledge" (1985, 43).

The dream as the imaginary experience is understood as the practice of human existence and the very possibility of transcendence. Acknowledging the dream as a sign of imaginary experience, a possible experience that might break through and transcend the dichotomy between objectivity and subjectivity (between the conscious mind and the unconscious), grants beings the experience of freeing themselves and making themselves in the world: "The dream: like every imaginary experience, is an anthropological index of transcendence; and in this transcendence it announces the world into man by making itself into a world, and by giving itself the species of light, fire, water and darkness. In its anthropological significance, the history of the dream teaches us that it both reveals the world in its transcendence and modulates the world in its substance, playing on its material character" (49). Rather than taking the dream experience as either a displacement or a wishful fulfillment of the repressed desire, corresponding to a lack in waking reality, Foucault wished to restore the very possibility of human imaginary experience, which entailed a journey of radical freedom into the world with its transcendence. As he writes, in dreams humankind "encounters what he is and what he will be, what he has done and what he is going to do, discovering there the knot that ties his freedom to the necessity of the world" (47).

Yan's dream can be read as the trajectory of realization of her being in the world and the very possibility of freedom and resistance. Caught in the triple oppressions of the machines of state socialism, global capitalism, and patriarchy, her pursuit of an industrial living rewarded her only with a torn body. Sexual desire and moral pressure alike stressed her. The cultural demand for marriage and the state control of her mobility snared her in the in-between, leaving no possibility for progress or retreat. Her individual, bodily pain, inscribed with a social and cultural trauma, was reenacted repeatedly through her individual life. Yan's dream was specific, but its specificity entailed the universal, all-too-common struggle of a female worker at the crossroads of a Chinese society transforming itself on the model of industrial capitalism.

Yan resumed the unity of body and self by driving the struggle, along with the pain, into the dream. There, rather than giving up, she continued her hopeless struggle: Yan was running across the river, trying to reach a foreign land. "Sometimes I find the scene in the dream is very familiar to me, I must have been there before. It's like a call to go back home. I am running and running." The dream, for her, was like the space of home; it was the dwelling of "Existenz," in Martin Heidegger's (1988) sense—the hope, the very possibility of the actualization of being in the world. The dream itself constituted a home for Yan, at once very familiar, intimate, and authentic, while in it she was always running toward someplace strange and foreign. "I don't know why I am so desperate to cross the river. I simply make up my mind to so do, to chase the boat. I am so determined. Seeing the boat leaving, I find myself full of extraordinary strength . . . It seems like I am going to break through something that blocks my way."

In the classical Chinese village scene, a river is the division between one's own land and that of the other. A woman crossing the river is one who is leaving her hometown and moving to an alien land; most often, it is a "crossing over" into married life. Traditionally, on getting married, a woman had to leave her own village in order to start a new life in her husband's family in a strange community. In the contemporary Chinese context, a woman crossing the river and leaving her own land might be leaving home and village to look for a job in the city. Economic reform and the infusion of global capital into Chinese society opened new possibilities and created novel desires and hopes for village girls to pursue a new life path. Put in a transcendental sense, crossing the river might mean the break between the old and the new way of life: Yan's determination was to break with her present life, with all of the pains and unbearable beingness of existence. Deciding to cross the river was to expect a future life in a new, foreign land that might open up brilliant new possibilities and opportunities for being. Twenty-four years is too young for Yan's life to be in ruins. It was her experience of being alien, of nomadism, and her call was the strong desire to look for something new, even though she was caught in the middle and torn by a painful body.

In spite of the gap between the realms of consciousness and unconsciousness, by going through the unconscious Yan saved a lost self. Her failure in her dream reproduced her predicament: she had no way forward or backward. Yet she continued her struggle to realize a worn-out body that could not move. When the projection of the future was again blocked, she broke out in a scream, that most authentic resistance, and woke herself up at the dream's end. In between the conscious and unconscious, the scream declared the very existence of her struggle. Crossing the realms between language and nonlanguage, between the imaginary and the real, between the self and the world, the scream was a final means of self-extension, beyond the boundaries of any personal and cultural limits, to occupy a deterritorialized space much larger than the world of Yan's life.

Yan was on an odyssey of human freedom and praxis, opening up a minor genre of resistance.

7

APPROACHING A MINOR

GENRE OF RESISTANCE

On a burning-hot day in mid-July 2001, in a mountainous village in Mei-
zhou, a relatively poor region in north Guangdong, I did not expect to meet
a family of five migrants from Sichuan. They had been settled in the village
for eight years, renting a room from local villagers. There they had given
birth to their youngest daughter and sent their children to the local school.
"Ha, ha, you are surprised? We Sichuan people are already everywhere, in
every corner of the whole country. We work in a brick-making plant. Look,
the compound is just over the river—you can still see the smoke coming out
from the duct. It's arduous and dirty work; the locals are not willing to do it,"
said the father, a man in his mid-thirties, who was feeding his child. The
mother was busy preparing a meal. She helped "meet both ends of the
month" by tilling farming land rented from a local household, whose own
members had gone dagong in a coastal city. A young man, the youngest
brother to the father, had just returned on his bicycle from the brick-making
plant, and he joined our conversation: "I have no skill. I couldn't find a job
in the city. Those foreign-invested companies want girls only. You can hardly
see girls in this village. They've all gone."

When I met this Sichuan migrant family in Guangdong, more than five
years had passed since my fieldwork in the Meteor plant in Shenzhen. The
Chinese rural migrants were not only everywhere becoming "floating populations" but had also settled in places far from their native villages, to which

their status, identity, rights, and means of survival were ascribed. The migration flows or mingong (peasant-worker) tides in China reached their peak in the mid-1990s and have ebbed since then, evolving into a more multicolored pattern, a vivid metaphor for Chinese society at large on the move. A part of this is a silent yet inexorable "social revolution," which foretells a great desire, the desire that gratifies, yearns, urges, and finally releases the energy of social transformation, working against the repressive socialist force in its quest for modernity. A new age of Chinese society has come. It has no choice but to disrupt, if not pervert, existing social relations, creating new modalities of political engineering and social resistance between state and society.

In using the term social revolution I mean a sort of social force springing up from the very bottom of society—the Chinese peasantry, who constituted the subaltern of Chinese socialist history and who strove for rapid social change. In contrast to the Communist revolution, or the economic reforms that followed it that were launched from above, the explosive social force of this silent revolution came from below, spearheaded by a Chinese rural population that had been tied to agriculture for over three decades. Guangdong villages were becoming increasingly empty at the end of the century, leaving aging people and children in the villages and the agricultural work in the hands of Sichuan peasants who had left their own land, searching for survival or dreaming of getting rich, either in the coastal industrial cities or in remote villages in Guangdong. New and more complex patterns within the "floating population" in the late 1990s heralded a deeper reconfiguration of social relations and social class, the nature of which still has not been adequately studied. If we say it was the socialist party-state acting as a "visible hand" to pin down the Chinese peasantry ever since the 1950s, then it was the failure of the visible hand that set the peasantry on the move in the 1990s.

Far from resulting in the demise of the state, the party-state has become increasingly stronger since incorporating a market discourse to legitimize its political power, change its political technologies, and enlarge its bureaucracy. The market, nevertheless, was a new actor on the stage, occupying a hegemonic role in constructing new imaginaries, new identities, and new desires for the new age. The silent social revolution, if we agree that it exists, has a tougher war to fight. Its enemy is not yet clear.

In this book I strive, first of all, to make sense of this silent social revolution as it emerged at the end of the 1990s, and to identify its enemy (the matrix of power and discourse), which continues to reconfigure itself as I write. I understand this social revolution as a countermovement against two reactionary forces: the changing modes of political regulation over society, and the increasing marketization of socialist society, embroidered with a hegemonic eulogy: "the quest for globality." Although I retain the word revolution, I do not do so with the intent to romanticize this new social force or to indicate that any mature social agenda against state and capital has been formed. Instead, I understand this great social force, at the very core of its ambiguities and (im)possibilities, not only as a fundamental challenge to existing social relations—the dual structure of urban and rural society and increasing social inequality (Study Group 2000)—but also as a great generator of new subjects, new dreams, and new desires that conjure up the very possibility of social transformation.

In the postsocialist period, both the dominated and the dominating forces are rapidly making and remaking themselves, searching for their own cultural identity, social status, market position, and even political legitimacy. The project of theorizing these complex processes is beyond the scope of this book; however, here I limit my attempt to understand the social revolution—its agents and actions, its subjectivities and transgressions—to the ethnography of female migrant factory workers, the making of the new worker-subject, and the dreams and desires of peasant bodies becoming "modern workers." It is the making of this worker-subject as an unfinished project that launches a journey of exploration into Chinese society.

A Minor Genre of Resistance

I started my long journey to search for a Chinese worker-subject within the trajectory of China's state socialist system's incorporation into global capitalism. I ended up with the seemingly inevitable social violence inflicted on the individual lives of dagongmei, migrant working daughters. I am aware that this journey may lead to the enclosure, if not foreclosure, of agency, subjectivity, and social change. But only by meeting that danger can it properly open up the possibilities of a minor genre of resistance in contemporary China. In fact, these incidents of social violence like Yan's dream and scream are glaring examples of an epochal trauma, and thus the social resistance that enmeshes the lives of dagongmei in this time of rapidly changing Chinese society. Reform-era China is envisioned through a lens focused squarely on the global market, a lens that not only occludes new forms of class and gender inequality—and thus legitimizes them as necessary evils—but also leaves the voices of individual transgression subsumed within the collective project. Who cares? A giant China is coming and a few million sacrifices mean little. After all, it was the West that was the first to dream of and promise the coming of a giant China in the twenty-first century. This vision then triggered a mighty desiring machine in mainland China, its effects felt especially among the middle-class elite and those newly transformed capitalists who are misplaced in a system without the proper name of capitalism: "capitalists without capitalism."[1]

The fire in the foreign-invested toy plant, the story of which opens this book, occurred two years before I started my ethnographic study in the Meteor workplace. The blaze took the lives of over eighty workers and caused the collapse of the factory building, and yet it never destroyed the dreams and hopes of thousands and thousands of dagongmei who continued to flood into the economic development zones. I feel particularly at a loss at this moment, as I arrive near the end of this project. Those of whom I write and am concerned about probably will never have the time or the opportunity to read what I write, especially in this form and style of writing. So why keep on with it? Again, perhaps it is the urge, the pain, the impossibility of not writing that drives me to the stories.[2] But most likely it will take another journey to unravel the violence of the writing, the specific power matrix in which meaning, language, academic institution, and self-colonization all contribute to this connivance—the violence of transliteration of the life of Chinese dagongmei.

In the final phase of my fieldwork at the Meteor plant I met Yan, the migrant working daughter who struggled through the journey of dreams and screams, disrupting if not threatening the disciplinary order in the workplace. As a disclosure of social violence, I dream of a politics of writing that could work to turn the pain inside out and go deeper into the technology of power that held these individual workers' lives; and if the worker-subject is the subject of human praxis, I dream of a poetics of writing that might help articulate an odyssey of social transgression and human freedom.

I also never expected to meet Xiaoming, the fire survivor I described at the beginning of this book, and Yan, whose story is narrated toward the end. Fire, pain, dream, and scream tied three lives together—bound us with a mutual imperative to find a way out. My sensitivity, if any, to the changes in Chinese society was first of all brought out by meeting Xiaoming in 1993 and the pain that maintained a ghostly hold on me. It was through Xiaoming's trauma, and then Yan's screams, that I finally realized that there was no individual story that was not political and social. It was in the encounter of the traumas in the field and the attempt to understand and narrate the lives and struggles of Chinese dagongmei that I was driven to anchor the practice of a minor genre of resistance.

By bringing the insights of a minor genre of resistance into the scene of contemporary China, we can see that Yan's scream and Xiaoming's pain, experiences of not only minority but subalternity and collectivity, are not merely oppositional to a master language but are further resistant to all language itself. Their screams and pains are fundamentally political, the subversive power of which is derived from its persistent refusal to be channeled into the signifying chain. It shrieked, destroying the symbolic order of this alienated and increasingly polarized world. A minor genre of resistance focuses on personal accounts, and its magical power lies not in generalizing individual narratives into a collective enunciation but rather in directly displaying that there is no individual story that is not also a historical narrative. Yan's scream is a cry against an epoch in which all of the Chinese working daughters are forced to live out their common existence.

Multisited Resistance

The opening of China to global capital and the introduction of market mechanisms undoubtedly inflicted more serious wounds on Chinese society and individuals than we can imagine. Notwithstanding a specific process of proletarianization in China, the persistent influx of peasant migrants into the urban areas did not give birth to a new Chinese working class in the past two decades. The making of the class force is, after all, retarded, shattered, and destroyed not only by the market apparatus but by the state machine. Dagongmei, as half peasants and half proletariat, are the displaced subjects produced by the hybrid conjugation of state and market machines.

Xiaoming's escape from the gates of hell drove the pain of writing and my urge to disclose these double wounds. Later in my fieldwork I was confronted with the delicate microphysics of power in the workplace. The production machine, plugged into the state and market machines, is the immediate means for manufacturing massive numbers of displaced selves. The human body, the producing body, is the interface or the threshold where violent forces, whether political or economic, complicit or conflicting, do their work.

But the state and market are not the only springs of power: local cultural practice—in China the patriarchal culture, although changing and reconfiguring—comes onto the scene as well. The process of gendering, the regulation of sex and sexuality, and the dominance of marriage and family life showed the great strength of power in sexualizing the dagong subjects. The rural family still provided the primary support and sources of identity to the migrant women workers who, otherwise, would be left alone to face the imperatives of capital. Where the tragedy lies is that in the passage to being modern dagongmei, the women workers would soon discover that factory work was no panacea to their displaced lives. Industrial labor was, rather, a new alienation to the married life that was still a common practice of Chinese rural women; some of the single women even dreamed of getting married as a way to escape from factory work, continuing to serve the Chinese patriarchal family on their return from the urban factory. Triple oppressions are my exegesis of the fate of Chinese dagongmei, despite the risk of overgeneralization and simplification. Yet, in the face of the inescapable oppressions, a new Chinese worker-subject is struggling to emerge despite all its very (im)possibilities: Yan's scream was the scream of our epoch, decrying the violence and absurdity of the triple oppressions.

The body in pain is bereft of sources of speech, unfolding the nature of subalternality to its very extremeness. While Xiaoming spoke out through the process of othering in a calm and emotionless voice, Yan screamed out into nothingness, attempting to ease the pain and to reunite the split body and self. Both struggle to resist a possible disintegration of the self; they uphold the worker-subject of freedom, freedom of projecting themselves in the world with human dignity, and freedom to act against the social violence inflicted on them. As Alain Touraine succinctly states, the subject is "a call to transform the Self into an actor" (1985, 260). The painful selves are never the defeated bodies, but the transgressive subjects. The displaced subjects like Yan and Xiaoming turn out to be actors of praxis.

New theorizing on resistance, not simply of the worker-subject, is urgently required, and it should go beyond conventional dichotomies of individual and collective actions, personal and social resistance, and nonpolitical and political confronting behavior. A multisited resistance is perhaps possible. The coincidental encounters with Xiaoming and Yan brought me to a concern for the social, or more specifically, to the intriguing relationships between social violence and individual lives. The trauma opened me up and I realized the rapid changes in Chinese society, the reactionary force of market and state on individuals, and the multiple arenas of reactions and transgressions of the subject that criss-cross and surpass the boundaries of conventional understandings of resistance. A complex interdependence of domination and resistance has been constituted, and as Jean Comaroff argues, "this system was a hierarchical, coordinated cluster of relations, in which the exercise of centralized power . . . impose their domination on the more diffuse domains of production, exchange, sexuality, and nurture" (1985, 260). This diffuse microphysics of power, in return, engenders a realpolitik of resistance rooted in everyday practice in all layers and, as subtle and various as it is, denies simple dichotomization in terms of resistance and compliance (261–62). A disjuncture of resistance patterns occurs, breaking through the traditional binary opposition of individual actions (which have often been trivialized and taken not as a force of resistance to social change) and collective actions (which were often highly romanticized as the only true force to challenge the established order) (Scott 1990). Dream, scream, fainting, menstrual pain, inner splitting of self, workplace defiance, slowdowns, fighting, running away, and even petition and strike are all points and lines of resistant behaviors, forming a cartography of resistance that will inevitably direct a challenge to power and control.

A minor and multisited journey of resistance aims at deterritorializing the reified spaces of control and resistance and opening up a multiple front of resistances, a new poetics of transgression, that always advances into a different war of positions. It will call up a multicellular site of social actions, a motley collection of transgressed events that eventually substantiate whole tactics of resistance countering against the whole technology of power. It is, in James Scott's (1990, 4–5) term, the valorization of "hidden transcripts" or "infrapolitics" that every subordinate group can create, not only to act behind the backs of the dominant but also to openly confront and disrupt their power. As Scott succinctly puts it: "An individual who is affronted may develop a personal fantasy of revenge and confrontation, but when the insult is but a variant of affronts suffered systematically by a whole race, class, or strata, then the fantasy can become a collective cultural product. Whatever form it assumes—offstage parody, dreams of violent revenge, millennial versions of a world turned upside down—this collective hidden transcript is essential to any dynamic view of power relations" (28). The formation of the Chinese dagongmei/zai, as half peasant and half worker, does not reproduce the structures and relations of the working class in its traditional sense. Instead, this new worker-subject invites a poetics of transgression that should be more creative, multifronted, and penetrable to the power matrix of capital, state, and the effects of sociocultural discourses in this increasingly globalized world. This new politics of transgression, of course, can never be simplified into individual or collective actions, non-political or political engagements, local or global struggles, and the like.

Throughout this book I see my factory coworkers, friends, and the people I met as pioneers who teased out the tensions in all the structural and historical forces they faced. I also struggle to see them as human subjects, as practical agents who consciously and/or unconsciously live out their body politics and negotiate with and confront those tensions and forces. For the Chinese dagongmei, caught in the impasse of triple oppressions, they did live out the class experience and interpellete their class position as part of their life struggles. Yet class differences are not the only conflict in their working lives, in part because of the hallucinating effects of the hegemonic power but, more important, because of their own subjective experiences living within a microphysics of domination and power far more complicated than class relations can contain. Rural-urban disparity, policing of the state, gender difference, family and kinship, and production relations as well as consumerism all contribute to a matrix of domination relations that could hardly be reduced to a single dominant oppositional logic. The acute terrain of contestation was the concomitant as well conflictual relations between the patriarchal family and the global production machine in creating ambivalent experiences for the women workers.

If we see that individualism is the evil product of Western neoliberal capitalism, and collectivism is the peril of Chinese socialism, then we have no choice but to look for a resistance agenda that can transgress and re-articulate both individuality and communality without privileging the former, which serves the logic of capital, and the latter, which would easily fall prey to a political strategy put forward in its name. A worker-subject seeks a space in its own right, surpassing any ideologized resistance projects that often lead to the subsumption of workers' subjectivity within the movement. A worker-subject project should therefore open up a new cartography of transgressions, taking a multiple front, criss-crossing individual and collective levels, and negotiating not only with economic and political factors but also cultural and psychic experiences.

Introduction

1   The first factory fire to occur in a foreign-invested industrial area of China was in May 1990 in Dongguan, a highly industrialized zone of the Pearl River Delta. This fire caused the death of over eighty workers in a Hong Kong capital-owned factory, which produced raincoats for export to Western markets. My first encounter with Chinese migrant workers was due to this blaze when I paid a visit to the injured workers in a hospital in Guangzhou. Later I made another visit to the hospital with my good friend Chan Yu, with whom I conducted a joint field study in four villages in Hubei in July 1990 to trace and record the home villages of the injured workers of the factory.

2   Note that pseudonyms have been used for the names of all factory personnel throughout this volume.

The quote from Xiaoming here, as well as all other quotes from factory workers and management staff members, were taken from the notes I compiled during my fieldwork in China in 1990, 1993, and 1995–1996. All translations in the text are mine unless otherwise indicated.

3   For a vivid description and analysis of the hukou system in constraining the different life chances and rights of the Chinese urban and rural populations, see Solinger 1999.

4   For a discussion of the changing forms of family in post-Mao China, see Davis and Harrell 1993.

5   Many married women in the rural areas did struggle with going out as dagongmei

in the urban industrial zones. An increasing trend, since the late 1990s, of married women working in the foreign-invested factories has been noted, but systematic research on this area is still lacking.

6   Emily Honig (1986), Gail Hershatter (1986), and Elizabeth Perry (1993) have all made excellent contributions by arguing that the tongxiang relationship was central to the making of the politics of Chinese labor in the early twentieth century.

7   See also the reporting by Hung Xiangfa (1994) in her "Taohun de dagongmei" (The working girl who escaped marriage).

8   As Elizabeth Perry rightly puts it: "Labor politics begins with the laborers themselves: their geographical origins, gender, popular culture, education attainments, work experiences, and the like" (1993, 4–5).

9   By articulating the concept of "social actor," Alain Touraine tries to decentralize the idea of a class subject that might too easily be incorporated into a state or totalitarian project. A social actor, he argues, is not someone whose action is structurally determined by the economic position he (or she) occupies, but "someone who modifies the material and, above all, social environment in which he finds himself by transforming the division of labour, modes of decision-making, relations of domination or cultural orientations" (1995, 207). A social actor is a subject struggling to be free from individualism and collectivism and ready to take action for the sake of social transformation in open-ended forms of social resistance.

1. State Meets Capital: The Making and Unmaking of a New Chinese Working Class

1   Although I do not intend here to neglect the complexities and variations of the new working classes emergent in different regions of China, migrant workers throughout the nation nevertheless share many of the same characteristics not only in terms of "mode of production" but also "mode of life." This ethnographic study, which is focused on migrant workers in south China, can only shed light on one particular form of working class emerging in the changing society of Shenzhen. However, this form of working class is becoming increasingly important in contemporary (and future) China as a whole.

2   See a critical review on the problematic of class analysis in Kalb 1997.

3   See Walder (1984), "The Remaking of the Chinese Working Class, 1949–1981," for the argument of the (un)making of the Chinese working class in socialist China.

4   On the controversy between the role of the peasantry and the working class as the leadership of revolution, see Schram 1969.

5   In the 1990s Shenzhen rearranged itself into four administrative zones; the new one was named Yantian.

6   In 1990 the total number of workers and staff was over 550,000, of whom over 290,000 were temporary workers. At the end of 1995 the number of temporary workers was over 200 percent of the regular workers and five times that of the contract workers (*Shenzhen Statistical Yearbook* 1996).

7   For discussion of the use of temporary labor in the Maoist period, see Walder 1986 (48–54).

8   However, a careful reading of the statistics can provide some clues. According to the *Shenzhen Statistical Yearbook* for 1992 and 1996, female labor, not exclusively temporary labor, in the light industry sectors made up 62.8 percent of the total workforce in 1991, while in 1994 female labor in the manufacturing sector as a whole accounted for 60.2 percent. In 1995 total female labor already amounted to 417,123 in Shenzhen. Because the statistics mix regular, contract, and temporary labor we cannot know the exact percentage of temporary female laborers working in the manufacturing sectors.

9   An analysis of the state in China should take care to avoid overgeneralization. For example, the term "the Chinese state" can mean the central government, provincial government, and local governments. The interests of each, however, are diverse and often in conflict. Moreover, the relation becomes tense when the central state tries to limit the pace of economic development to control financial disorder.

10   However, some enterprises in Shenzhen, especially small and local-capital-owned enterprises, simply neglect the labor control measures. Few send the handbooks back to the Labor Bureau. Indeed, I found a lot of original copies at the Meteor plant even though the workers had already left the factory.

11   No one can change his or her identity except under state planning. In some cases university graduates were allowed to change their hukou to work in big cities because they were considered professionals.

12   This information was provided to me at the workplace by Shenzhen Public Security Bureau, in documentation compiled by the hukou management division in 1990.

2. Marching from the Village: Women's Struggles between Work and Family

1   The imperative of the factory regime to discipline female bodies was witnessed at the first moment that the migrant workers entered the factory gate. I discuss this issue in detail in chapter 3.

2   Accurate data on rural-urban migration flows and the number of migrant workers nationwide are difficult to obtain because of the complexity of the issue in terms of the definition, nature, and composition of the labor flows.

3   As described by Elisabeth Croll and Huang Ping (1997), in 1994 the United Nations Food and Agricultural Organization commissioned a number of studies of

rural migration in China. Three macrostudies were conducted by the Research Team on Rural Population Mobility of the China Population Information and Research Centre and Chen Jiyuan, Hu Biliang, and Yu Dechange of the Rural Development Institute of the Chinese Academy of Social Sciences. These studies were mainly concerned with the policy and implication of labor mobility for social development and social order.

4   The exception is Li Zhang's (2001a; 2001b) studies on the migrant workers' community in Beijing. Zhang provides a good discussion on the issue of the spatiality, power, and agency of the migrant community.

5   This impression is echoed by Chinese sociologist Sun Liping, who points out that there is no concrete relationship between land and labor power in the minds of migrant workers. Young migrant workers knew little about the amount of agricultural land possessed by their families. As Sun states: "A few acres of farming land more or less makes no difference. Anyhow, farming can't make money" (2001, 2).

6   Rural migrants in the city are often blamed for having no planned route or destination. Thus they are referred to as being "blind" in their migration flows.

7   Regarding this view of identity, see also Honig 1986.

8   Margery Wolf's pioneering work in the early 1970s is one excellent attempt to provide insight into how Chinese women's status and power were negotiated in different life phases. The concept of "uterine family" vividly illustrates how women at their third stage of life as mothers develop informal channels to secure their position and build up female authority centered on mother-son relationships. Wolf argues that, as an outsider in her husband's family, the main strategy for a woman in struggling for some security in her day-to-day existence was to build up her uterine family deliberately through nurturing mother-son relationships, which were permanent, affective, and authoritarian. Wolf states: "Once she had established her uterine family, a woman was well on her way to subverting the men's family. In future discussions of family strategy, she might speak up for the interests of her sons if her husband would not speak for her, and as soon as her sons were able, she could speak through them. If she did her job well, by the time she was a grandmother the men's family—that bastion of male power in rural China—might in fact be dominated by her wishes, though expressed by her adult sons" (1972, 9).

9   The World Bank (1992, 57–58) also provided the following reasons for the stagnation and poverty after the mid-1980s in the rural areas: first, sharply increased prices for grain and other subsistence goods adversely affected the real incomes of the majority of the rural poor; second, the rapid growth of the working-age population, which exceeded the expansion of employment opportunities, contributed to a worsening of rural underemployment; and third, economic growth was greater in higher-income coastal provinces than in the lower-income inland

northwestern and southwestern provinces. Fiscal decentralization passed an increased share of the costs of rural social and relief services to the local governments, which were unable to support either adequate social services or economic growth.

10 The central government changed the unified procurement system in 1985, which means that the state stopped purchasing grain from the farmers at a preset price that was relatively higher and more stable than the market price.

3. The Social Body, the Art of Discipline, and Resistance

1 Previous studies have contributed to showing that women do not passively accept their working situations but rather are active agents in manipulating their work to safeguard their own rights. See Honig 1986; Lamphere 1987; Pollert 1981; Rosen 1987; and Westwood 1984. In past decades a new interpretation of women's struggle in the workplace has slowly been developed, one that tries to theorize the possibility of a multifaceted, energetic, and fluid work culture. This culture is a creative one where women try to develop everyday life tactics to assert informal controls over the work process. See Kondo 1990; Ong 1987; and Rofel 1999.

2 See Lee 1998a, 1998b, for a vivid picture of how factory regimes in South China and Hong Kong have been regulated differently. Lee categorizes the factory regime in South China as localistic despotism and that of Hong Kong as familial hegemonism.

3 Lisa Rofel succinctly states: "Factory spatial relations are not just the setting for disciplinary actions, but are themselves part of the same mode of power and authority" (1992, 103).

4 Regarding the body in the production process, see Foucault 1979, 149.

5 See the relevant studies on women and work in other societies in Cavendish 1982; Glucksmann 1990; and Knights and Wilmott 1986.

6 On rush work and bargaining, see Westwood 1984; and Rosen 1987.

7 See chapter 7 for further discussion of pain and illness in the female body.

8 Foucault (1979, 149) states that the timetable as a strict model was inherited from the old practices of the monastry in the Middle Ages.

9 Chapter 4 contains further discussion of precept time.

10 For further discussion on change and continuity in Fordist production, see Delbridge 1998, 2. Delbridge is particularly correct in saying that the new work systems, such as the just-in-time production, are designed to reduce the amount of stock, labor, and time (and hence cost) in the system. This in turn reduces the amount of buffering between processes, and hence production quality must be assured. The reduction in buffers thus places further stress on labor and suppliers to provide what is required in a timely fashion and at acceptable quality levels (4).

4. Becoming Dagongmei: Politics of Identities and Differences

1 For a comparable situation, see Kondo 1990.

2 For historical studies on Chinese workers that highlight the importance of locality, kin-ethnic ties, and gender in the process of making the Chinese working class in the early twentieth century, see Honig 1968; Hershatter 1986; and Perry 1993.

3 Helping others to clock in was a regular practice in the Meteor workplace. Sometimes workers needed extra time for activities such as sending money back home. The post office was only open during the day and most of the workers had to sacrifice their lunch time to go there. Moreover, long queues were expected at lunch time, so they got back to the factory late. Thus other workers would step in if they saw their kin or fellow villagers were not back in time.

4 For more on these hierarchies, see Honig 1986; Hershatter 1986; and Perry 1993.

5 On the disciplinary and regulatory role of kin, see Hareven 1982.

6 No doubt there were heterogeneous views among different employers in Shenzhen toward local and kin-ethnic peculiarities, and it is always dangerous to draw any generalizations. But my study of the Meteor plant relates a valuable story about how the regional and kin-ethnic cultural traits were imagined, articulated, and then lived out in a specific workplace and how they had a great impact on the job positions and mobility of workers.

7 I was the only one in the workplace who did not get paid. I refused to receive a wage from the company, but traded it in return for some rest on Sundays.

8 I do not hold the Saussurian perspective in which language is viewed as an internal linguistic structure based on a system of difference. Rather I follow Bourdieu's (1991) line that the difference is social.

5. Imagining Sex and Gender in the Workplace

1 While Foucault dealt with the body and sexuality, he has been criticized for not paying adequate attention to the gendered nature of disciplinary techniques on the body, or to a sexually differentiated body that is necessary for certain types of mechanisms or apparatuses (see McNay 1992).

2 See also the stories by An Zi (1993) in the volume *Qingchun xuyu: Dagongzai dagongmei Qingjian* (The dialogue of youth: Love letters of working sons and working daughters).

3 See Li Xiaojiang's two representative books on feminist politics in China: *Xiawa de tansuo* (Eve's search) (1988) and *Xing gou* (Gender gap) (1989).

4 Research on women and work shows that the advent of multinational capital and the industrialization of developing countries leads to the disintegration of tradi-

tional morality and the growth of a pornography culture. See also Ong 1987; and Truong 1990.

5 For more on ambivalence in sexuality, see Moore 1994.

6 For a discussion on women's talk as perceived by men, see Spencer 1980.

7 Lee Ching Kwan (1998a), as described in her ethnography of a Shenzhen workplace, had similar experiences.

6. Scream, Dream, and Transgression in the Workplace

1 With neither medical training nor firsthand knowledge of chemical health hazards, I do not explore at length here those hazards believed to cause damage or conditions such as infertility and even cancers.

7. Approaching a Minor Genre of Resistance

1 This insight is derived from Eyal, Szelennyi, and Townsley 1998.

2 On the issue of not writing, see Fanon 1952.

REFERENCES

Althusser, Louis. 1990. *For Marx*, trans. Ben Brewster. London: Verso.

An, Zi. 1993. *Qingchun xuyu: Dagongzai dagongmei qingjian* [The dialogue of the youth: Love letters of the working boys and working girls]. Shenzhen: Haitian Chubanshe.

Anagnost, Ann. 1994. "The Politicized Body." In *Body, Subject, and Power in China*, ed. Angela Zito and Tani E. Barlow. Chicago: University of Chicago Press.

———. 1997. *National Past-Times: Narrative, Representation, and Power in Modern China.* Durham: Duke University Press.

Andors, Phyllis. 1983. *The Unfinished Liberation of Chinese Women, 1949–1980.* Bloomington: Indiana University Press.

———. 1988. "Women and Work in Shenzhen." *Bulletin of Concerned Asian Scholars* 20.3: 22–41.

Appadurai, Arjun. 1996. *Modernity at Large.* Minneapolis: University of Minnesota Press.

Ardner, Shirley. 1975. *Perceiving Women.* New York: Wiley.

Barlow, Tani E., ed. 1993. *Gender Politics in Modern China: Writing and Feminism.* Durham: Duke University Press.

———. 1994. "Politics and the Protocols of Funü: (Un)making National Woman." In *Engendering China: Women, Culture, and the State*, ed. Christina K. Gilmartin et al. Cambridge: Harvard University Press.

Bartky, Sandra Lee. 1990. *Femininity and Domination.* New York: Routledge.

Bataille, Georges. 1985. *Visions of Excess: Selected Writings, 1927–1939.* Minneapolis: University of Minnesota Press.

Baudrillard, Jean. 1993. *Symbolic Exchange and Death.* London: Sage.

Bettelheim, Bruno. 1960. *The Informed Heart.* London: Penguin.

Bian, Yanjie. 1994. *Work and Inequality in Urban China.* Albany: State University of New York Press.

Blecher, Marc. 2002. "Hegemony and Workers' Politics in China." *China Quarterly* 170 (June): 283–303.

Bordo, Susan. 1995. *Unbearable Weight: Feminism, Western Culture, and the Body.* Berkeley: University of California Press.

Bourdieu, Pierre. 1984. *Distinction: A Social Critique of the Judgment of Taste.* Cambridge: Harvard University Press.

———. 1991. *Language and Symbolic Power.* London: Polity.

Bradley, Harriet. 1986. "Technological Change, Management Strategies, and the Development of Gender-Based Job Segregation in the Labour Process." In *Gender and the Labour Process*, ed. David Knights and Hugh Willmott. London: Gower.

Braidotti, Rosi. 1994. *Nomadic Subjects: Embodiment and Sexual Difference in Contemporary Feminist Theory.* New York: Columbia University Press.

Braverman, Harry. 1974. *Labour and Monopoly Capital.* New York: Monthly Review Press.

Brownell, Susan. 1995. *Training the Body for China: Sports in the Moral Order of the People's Republic.* Chicago: University of Chicago Press.

Buck, John L. 1937. *Land Utilization in China: Statistics.* Chicago: The University of Chicago Press.

Burawoy, Michael. 1985. *The Politics of Production.* London: Verso.

Butler, Judith. 1990. *Gender Trouble: Feminism and the Subversion of Identity.* London: Routledge.

———. 1993. *Bodies That Matter: on the Discursive Limits of "Sex."* London: Routledge.

Butler, Judith, and Joan W. Scott, eds. 1992. *Feminists Theorize the Political.* London: Routledge.

Cai, Fang, Guo Hanying, and Gao Jialin, eds. 2001. *Zhongguo renkou liudong fangshi yu tujing* [The mechanism and way of Chinese population migration]. Beijing: Shehui kexue wenxian chubanshe.

Cao, Min. 1995. "Shenzhen dagongmei, nimen huode zenmoyang?" [The working girls in Shenzhen, how are you getting on?] *Shenzhenren* 18 (February): 20–22.

Caruth, Cathy. 1996. *Unclaimed Experience: Trauma, Narrative, and History.* Baltimore: Johns Hopkins University Press.

Cavendish, Rosemary. 1982. *Women on the Line.* London: Routledge and Kegan Paul.

Certeau, Michel de. 1984. *The Practice of Everyday Life.* Berkeley: University of California Press.

Chan, Anita. 1998. "Labour Relations in Foreign-Funded Ventures, Chinese Trade

Unions, and the Prospects for Collective Bargaining." In *Adjusting to Capitalism: Chinese Workers and the State*, ed. G. O'Leary. Armonk, N.Y.: M. E. Sharpe.

———. 2001. *China's Workers under Assault: The Exploitation of Labor in a Globalizing Economy*. Armonk, N.Y.: M. E. Sharpe.

Chen, Nancy N., Constance D. Clark, Suzanne Z. Gottschange, and Lyn Jeffery, eds. 2001. *China Urban*. Durham: Duke University Press.

Cheng, Lucie, and Edna Bonacich. 1984. *Labor Immigration under Capitalism*. Berkeley: University of California Press.

Cheng, Tiejun, and Mark Selden. 1994. "The Origins and Social Consequences of China's *Hukou* System." *China Quarterly* 139 (September): 644–68.

Chiu, Fred. 2003. *Colours of Money/Shades of Pride: Historicities and Moral Politics in Industrial Conflicts in Hong Kong*. London: Routledge.

Christiansen, Flemming, and Zhang Junzuo. 1998. *Village Inc.: Chinese Rural Society in the 1990s*. Honolulu: University of Hawaii Press.

Clark, Jon, and Marco Diani, eds. 1996. *Alain Touraine*. London: Falmer Press.

Clifford, James, and George E. Macus, eds. 1986. *Writing Culture: The Poetics and Politics of Ethnography*. Berkeley: University of California Press.

Cohen, Paul. 1978. "Ethnicity: Problem and Focus in Anthropology." *Annual Review of Anthropology* 7: 379–403.

Comaroff, Jean. 1985. *Body of Power, Spirit of Resistance: The Culture and History of a South African People*. Chicago: University of Chicago Press.

Cook, Sarah. 1999. "Surplus Labour and Productivity in Chinese Agriculture: Evidence from Household Survey Data." *Journal of Development Studies* 35.3 (February): 16–44.

Cook, Sarah, and Margaret Maurer-Fazio, eds. 1999. *The Workers' State Meets the Market: Labour in China's Transition*. London: Frank Cass.

Cornwell, Andrea, and Nancy Lindisfarne-Tapper, eds. 1994. *Dislocating Masculinity: Comparative Ethnographies*. London: Routledge.

Croll, Elisabeth. 1985. *Women and Development in China: Production and Reproduction*. Geneva: International Labour Office.

———. 1994. *From Heaven to Earth: Images and Experiences of Development in China*. London: Routledge.

———. 1995. *Changing Identities of Chinese Women*. London: Zed; Hong Kong: Hong Kong University Press.

Croll, Elisabeth, and Huang Ping. 1997. "Migration for and against agriculture in Eight Chinese Villages." *China Quarterly* 149: 128–46.

Dai, Wei. 1991. *Zhongguo hunyin xing'ai shigao* [History of marriage and sexual love in China]. Beijing: Dongfang chubanshe.

Davis, Deborah, ed. 2000. *The Consumer Revolution in Urban China*. Berkeley: University of California Press.

Davis, Deborah, and Stevan Harrell, eds. 1993. *Chinese Families in the Post-Mao Era*. Berkeley: University of California Press.

Davis, Deborah, et al., eds. 1995. *Urban Spaces in Contemporary China.* Cambridge: Cambridge University Press; Washington, D.C.: Woodrow Wilson Center Press.

Delbridge, Rick. 1998. *Life on the Line in Contemporary Manufactory.* Oxford: Oxford University Press.

Deleuze, Gilles, and Félix Guattari. 1984. *Anti-Oedipus: Capitalism and Schizophrenia.* London: Athlone.

———. 1986. *Kafka: Toward a Minor Literature.* Minneapolis: University of Minnesota Press.

Derrida, Jacques. 1994. *Specters of Marx.* New York: Routledge.

Dirlik, Arif, and Maurice Meisner, eds. 1989. *Marxism and the Chinese Experience.* Armonk, N.Y.: M. E. Sharpe.

Dirlik, Arif, and Xudong Zhang, eds. 2000. *Postmodernism and China.* Durham: Duke University Press.

Douglas, Mary. 1966. *Purity and Danger: An Analysis of the Concepts of Pollution and Taboo.* London: Routledge.

Evans, Harriet. 1997. *Women and Sexuality in China.* London: Polity.

Eyal, Gil, Ivan Szelennyi, and Eleanor Townsley. 1998. *Making Capitalism without Capitalists: The New Ruling Elites in Eastern Europe.* London: Verso.

Fanon, Frantz. 1952. *Black Skin, White Masks.* London: Pluto.

Fardon, Richard. 1987. " 'African Ethnogenesis': Limits to the Comparability of Ethnic Phenomena." In *Comparative Anthropology,* ed. L. Holy. London: Basil Blackwell.

Fei, Hsiao-tung, and Chih-I Chang. 1945. *Earthbound China: A Study of Rural Economy in Yunnan.* Chicago: University of Chicago Press.

Fernandez-Kelly, Maria Patricia. 1983. *For We Are Sold, I and My People: Women and Industry in Mexico's Frontier.* Albany: State University of New York Press.

Foucault, Michel. 1978. *The History of Sexuality; Volume 1: An Introduction.* New York: Vintage.

———. 1979. *Discipline and Punish: The Birth of the Prison.* New York: Vintage.

———. 1980. *Power/Knowledge: Selected Interviews and Other Interviews.* New York: Pantheon.

———. 1985. "Dream, Imagination, and Existence." In *Dream and Existence,* ed. Michel Foucault and Ludwig Binswanger. Atlantic Highlands, NJ: Humanities Press.

———. 1986. "Of Other Spaces." *Diacritics* 16: 22–27.

———. 1988. "Technologies of the Self." In *Technologies of the Self,* ed. Luther H. Martin, Huck Gutman, and Patrick H. Hutton. London: Tavistock.

———. 1994. *Ethics: Subjectivity and Truth,* ed. Paul Rabinow. London: Penguin.

———. 1997. *The Essential Works of Michel Foucault, 1854–1984.* Vol. 1, ed. Paul Rabinow. London: Penguin.

Freud, Sigmund. 1976. *The Interpretation of Dreams.* London: Pelican.

Frydman, Roman, Kenneth Murphy, and Andrzej Rapaczynski. 1998. *Capitalism with a Comrade's Face: Studies in the Postcommunist Transition.* Budapest: Central European University Press.

Gan, Wujin. 1995. "Liulang de rizi" [The days of wandering] *Wailaigong* 29 (October): 9.

Gassart, Thomas. 1985. *Health Hazards in Electronics: A Handbook.* Hong Kong: Asia Monitor Resource Center.

Gilmartin, Christina K., et al., eds. 1994. *Engendering China: Women, Culture, and the State.* Cambridge: Harvard University Press.

Glucksmann, Miriam. 1990. *Women Assemble.* London: Routledge.

Griffin, Susan. 1978. *Woman and Nature: The Roaring inside Her.* New York: Harper and Row.

Guha, Ranajit, and Gayatri Chakravorty Spivak, eds. 1988. *Selected Subaltern Studies.* New York: Oxford University Press.

Guo, Haihong. 1994. "Tequ,wuxia guji dagongzhe de aiqing" [Special economic zone, no time to care for the romance of the working people]. *Shenzhenren* 15: 26–27.

Gutman, Huck. 1988. "Rousseau's Confessions: A Technology of the Self." In *Technologies of the Self*, ed. Luther H. Martin, Huck Gutman, and Patrick H. Hutton. London: Tavistock.

Hall, Stuart, and Paul du Gay, eds. 1996. *Questions of Cultural Identity.* London: Sage.

Haraszti, Miklos. 1978. *A Worker in a Worker's State.* Trans. Michael Wright. New York: University Books.

Harding, Harry. 1994. "The Contemporary Study of Chinese Politics: An Introduction." *China Quarterly*, 139 (September): 699–703.

Hare, Denise, and Zhao Shukai. 2000. "Labor Migration as a Rural Development Strategy: A View from the Migration Origin." In *Rural Labor Flows in China*, ed. Loraine A. West and Zhao Yaohui. Berkeley: Institute of East Asian Studies, University of California.

Hareven, Tamara K. 1982. *Family Time and Industrial Time: The Relationship between the Family and Work in a New England Industrial Community.* Cambridge: Cambridge University Press.

Hearn, Jeff, and Wendy Parkin. 1987. *"Sex" at "Work": The Power and Paradox of Organization Sexuality.* London: Wheatsheaf Books.

Heidegger, Martin. 1988. *Existence and Being.* Washington, D.C.: Regnery Gateway.

Hershatter, Gail. 1986. *The Workers of Tianjin, 1900–1949.* Stanford: Stanford University Press.

———. 1993. "The Subaltern Talks Back: Reflections on Subaltern Theory and Chinese History." *positions* 1 (spring): 103–30.

Honig, Emily. 1986. *Sisters and Strangers: Women in the Shanghai Cotton Mills, 1919–1949.* Stanford: Stanford University Press.

Hsiung, Ping-chun. 1996. *Living Rooms as Factories: Class, Gender, and the Satellite Factory System in Taiwan.* Philadelphia: Temple University Press.

Huang, Ping. 1997. *Zhunqiu shenchun* [In search of survival: A sociological study of rural-urban migration]. Yunnan: Yunnan renmin chubanshe.

Hung, Xiangfa. 1994. *"Taohun de dagongmei"* [The working girl who escaped marriage], *Shenzhenren* 12:26.

Irigaray, Luce. 1977. *This Sex Which Is Not One.* Ithaca: Cornell University Press.

Jacka, Tamara. 1998. "Working Sisters Answer Back: The Presentation and Self-Presentation of Women in China's Floating Population." *China Information* 18.1: 43–75.

Johnson, Elisabeth. 1975. "Women and Childbearing in Kwan Mun Hau Village: A Study of Social Change." In *Women in Chinese Society*, ed. Margery Wolf and Roxane Witke. Stanford: Stanford University Press.

Johnson, Kay Ann. 1983. *Women, the Family, and Peasant Revolution in China.* Chicago: University of Chicago Press.

Judd, Ellen R. 1994. *Gender and Power in Rural North China.* Stanford: Stanford University Press.

Kalb, Don. 1997. *Expanding Class: Power and Everyday Politics in Industrial Communities, The Netherlands, 1850–1950.* Durham: Duke University Press.

Kam, Wing Chan and Li Zhang. 1999. "The *Hukou* System and Rural-Urban Migration in China: Processes and Changes." *China Quarterly* 160 (December): 819–55.

Kelliher, Daniel. 1992. *Peasant Power in China: The Era of Rural Reform, 1979–1989.* New Haven: Yale University Press.

Kleinman, Arthur. 1992. "Pain and Resistance: The Delegitimation and Relegitimation of Local Worlds." In *Pain as Human Experience: An Anthropological Perspective*, ed. Mary-Jo DelVecchio Good et al. Berkeley: University of California Press.

——. 1995. *Writing at the Margin: Discourse between Anthropology and Medicine.* Berkeley: University of California Press.

Knights, David, and Hugh Willmott, eds. 1986. *Gender and the Labour Process.* London: Gower.

——. 1990. *Labour Process Theory*, London: Macmillan.

Kondo, Dorinne K. 1990. *Crafting Selves: Power, Gender, and Discourse of Identity in a Japanese Workplace.* Chicago: University of Chicago Press.

Kristeva, Julia. 1986. "Women's Time." In *The Kristeva Reader*, ed. Toril Moi. London: Blackwell.

Kung, James Kai-sing. 2002. "Off-Farm Labour Markets and the Emergence of Land Rental Markets in Rural China." *Journal of Economic Literature*, 1–38.

Kung, Lydia. 1983. *Factory Women in Taiwan.* Ann Arbor: University of Michigan Press.

Laclau, Ernesto. 1990. *New Reflections on the Revolution of Our Time.* London: Verso.

Laing, Ronald David. 1967. *The Politics of Experience and the Bird of Paradise.* London: Penguin.

——. 1969. *The Divided Self.* London: Penguin.

Lamphere, Louise. 1987. *From Working Daughters to Working Mothers.* Ithaca: Cornell University Press.

Lau, Raymond W. K. 2001. "Socio-Political Control in Urban China: Changes and Crisis." *British Journal of Sociology* 52.4: 605–20.

Leacock, Eleanor, Helen I. Safa eds. 1986. *Women's work: development and the division of labor by gender.* South Hadley, MA: Bergin and Garvey.

Lee, Ching Kwan. 1995. "Engendering the Worlds of Labor: Women Workers, Labor Markets, and Production Politics in the South China Economic Miracle." *American Sociological Review* 60: 378–97.

——. 1998a. *Gender and the South China Miracle: Two Worlds of Factory Women.* Berkeley: University of California Press.

——. 1998b. "The Labour Politics of Market Socialism: Collective Inaction and Class Experiences among State Workers in Guangzhou." *Modern China* 24.1: 3–33.

Leung, Wing-yue. 1988. *Smashing the Iron Rice Pot: Workers and Unions in China's Market Socialism.* Hong Kong: Asia Monitor Resource Center.

Li Peilin. 1996. "Liudong mingong de shehui wangluo he shehui diwei" [Social network and social status of migrant peasant workers]. *Shehuixue yanjiu* 4: 42–52.

Li Qiang. 2000. "Zhongguo waichu nongmingong jiqi huikuan zhi yanjiu" [The study of Chinese migrant workers and their remittances]. *Shehuixue yanjiu* 4: 64–76.

Li, Si-ming. 1989. "Labour Mobility, Migration and Urbanization in the Pearl River Delta Area." *Asian Geographer* 8: 35–60.

Li, Xiaojiang. 1988. *Xiawa de tansuo* [Eve's search]. Henan: Henan remin chubanshe.

——. 1989. *Xing gou* [Gender gap]. Beijing: Sanlian Shudian.

Lin, Nan. 1995. "Local Market Socialism: Local Corporatism in Action in Rural China." *Theory and Society* 24.3: 301–54.

Liu, Alan. 1996. *Mass Politics in the People's Republic.* Boulder: Westview.

Liu, Yingjie. 2000. *Zhongguo chengxiang guanxi yu zhongguo nongmin gongren* [China's rural-urban relation and migrant peasant workers]. Beijing: Zhongguo shehui-kexue chubanshe.

Lyon, Thomas, and Victor Nee, ed. 1994. *The Economic Transformation of South China: Reform and Development in the Post-Mao Era.* Ithaca, N.Y.: East Asia Program, Cornell University.

Mallee, Hein. 1996a. "In Defence of Migration: Recent Chinese Studies of Rural Population Mobility." *China Information* 10.3–4: 108–40.

——. 1996b. "Reform of the *Hukou* System: Introduction." *Chinese Sociology and Anthropology* 29.1: 3–26.

——. 2000. "Agricultural Labor and Rural Population Mobility: Some Observations." In *Rural Labour Flows in China*, ed. Loraine A. West and Yaohui Zhao. Berkeley: Institute of East Asian Studies, University of California.

Mao Zedong. 1965. *Selected Works of Mao Tse-Tung*, Vol. 1. Peking: Foreign Language Press.

Marcus, George E. 1998. *Ethnography through Thick and Thin.* Princeton: Princeton University Press.

Martin, Emily. 1987. *The Woman in the Body: A Cultural Analysis of Reproduction.* Milton Keynes: Open University Press.

Marx, Karl. 1954 [1865]. *Capital.* Vol. 1. Moscow: Progress Publishers.

——. 1964 [1844]. *Economic and Philosophic Manuscripts of 1844*. New York: International Publishers.

——. 1968. *Selected Works*. London: Lawrence and Wishart.

Marx, Karl, and Frederick Engels. 1976. *The German Ideology*. Moscow: Progress Publishers.

McLennan, Gregor. 1982. "E. P. Thompson and the Discipline of Historical Context." In *Making Histories*, ed. Richard Johnson, Gregor McLennan, Bill Schwarz, and David Sutton. Minneapolis: University of Minnesota Press.

McNay, Lois. 1992. *Foucault and Feminism: Power, Gender, and the Self*. Oxford: Polity.

Milkman, Ruth. 1987. *Gender at Work*. Urbana: University of Illinois Press.

Mill, Mary Beth. 1999. "Migrant Labor Takes a Holiday." *Critique of Anthropology* 19.1: 31–51.

Moore, Henrietta L. 1994. *A Passion for Difference: Essays in Anthropology and Gender*. Cambridge: Polity.

——, ed. 1996. *The Future of Anthropological Knowledge*. London: Routledge.

Nash, June, and Helen Safa, eds. 1976. *Sex and Class in Latin America*. New York: Praeger.

Nash, June, and Maria Patricia Fernandez-Kelly, eds. 1983. *Women, Men, and the International Division of Labor*. Albany: State University of New York Press.

Nee, Victor, and David Stark, eds. 1989. *Remaking the Economic Institutions of Socialism: China and Eastern Europe*. Stanford: Standford University Press.

Oi, C. Jean. 1989. *State and Peasant in Contemporary China: The Political Economy of Village Government*. Berkeley: University of California Press.

——. 1995. "The Role of the Local State in China's Transitional Economy." *China Quarterly* 144: 1132–49.

——. 1999. *Rural China Takes Off: The Institutional Foundations of Economic Reform*. Berkeley: University of California Press.

Oi, Jean, and Andrew G. Walder. 1999. *Property Rights and Economic Reform in China*. Stanford: Stanford University Press.

Ong, Aihwa. 1987. *Spirits of Resistance and Capitalist Discipline: Factory Women in Malaysia*. Albany: State University of New York Press.

——. 1991. "The Gender and Labor Politics of Postmodernity." *Annual Reviews in Anthropology* 20: 279–309.

Ong, Aihwa, and Donald M. Nonini, eds. 1997. *Ungrounded Empires: The Cultural Politics of Modern Chinese Transnationalism*. London: Routledge.

Perry, Elizabeth J. 1993. *Shanghai on Strike: The Politics of Chinese Labor*. Stanford: Stanford University Press.

——. 1994. "Trends in the Study of Chinese Politics: State-Society Relations." *China Quarterly* 139: 704–13.

——, ed. 1995. *Putting Class in Its Place: Workers' Identities in East Asia*. Berkeley: Institute of East Asian Studies, University of California.

———. 2002. *Challenging the Mandate of Heaven: Social Protest and State Power in China.* Armonk, N.Y.: M. E. Sharpe.

Perry, Elizabeth J., and Christine Wong, eds. 1985. *The Political Economy of Reform in Post-Mao China.* Cambridge: Council on East Asian Studies, Harvard University.

Pollert, Anna. 1981. *Girls, Wives, Factory Lives.* London: Macmillan.

Poster, Mark, ed. 1975. *Jean Baudrillard: Selected Writings.* Cambridge: Polity.

Pruitt, Ida. 1967. *A Daughter of Han: The Autobiograpy of a Chinese Working Woman.* New Haven: Yale University Press.

Pun, Ngai. 1999. "Becoming *Dagongmei*: The Politics of Identity and Difference in Reform China." *China Journal* 42 (July): 1–19.

———. 2001. "Cultural Construction of Labor Politics: Gender, Kinship, and Ethnicity in a Shenzhen Workplace." In *The Chinese Triangle of Mainland China, Taiwan, and Hong Kong: Comparative Institutional Analyses*, ed. Alvin Y. So, Nan Lin, and Dudley Poston. Westport, Conn.: Greenwood.

———. 2000. "Opening a Minor Genre of Resistance in Reform China: Scream, Dream, and Transgression in a Workplace." *positions* 8.2 (fall): 531–55.

Rabinow, Paul. 1986. "Representations Are Social Facts: Modernity and Postmodernity in Anthropology." In *Writing Culture: The Poetics and Politics of Ethnography*, ed. James Clifford and George Marcus. Berkeley: University of California Press.

Rawski, Evelyn Sakakida. 1972. *Agricultural Change and the Peasant Economy of South China.* Cambridge: Harvard University Press.

Riskin, Carl, Zhao Renwei, and Li Shi, eds. 2001. *China's Retreat from Equality.* Armonk, N.Y.: M. E. Sharpe.

Rofel, Lisa. 1989. "Hegemony and Productivity: Workers in Post-Mao China." In *Marxism and the Chinese Experience*, ed. Arif Dirlik and Maurice Meisner. Armonk, N.Y.: M. E. Sharpe.

———. 1992. "Rethinking Modernity: Space and Factory Discipline in China." *Cultural Anthropology* 7: 93–114.

———. 1999. *Other Modernities: Gendered Yearnings in China after Socialism.* Berkeley: University of California Press.

Rosen, Ellen Israel. 1987. *Bitter Choices: Blue-Collar Women In and Out of Work.* Chicago: University of Chicago Press.

Rothstein, Frances Abrahamer, and Michael L. Blim. 1992. *Anthropology and the Global Factory.* New York: Bergin and Garvey.

Salaff, Janet W. 1981. *Working Daughters of Hong Kong: Filial Piety or Power in the Family?* Cambridge: Cambridge University Press.

Sargeson, Sally. 1999. *Reworking China's Proletariat.* New York: St. Martin's Press.

Sassen, Saskia. 1988. *The Mobility of Labor and Capital.* New York: Cambridge University Press.

Scarry, Elaine. 1985. *The Body in Pain.* New York: Oxford University Press.

Schein, Louisa. 2001. "Urbanity, Cosmopolitanism, Consumption." In *China Urban*, ed. Nancy Chen, Constance D. Clark, Suzanne Z. Gottschang, and Lyn Jeffery. Durham: Duke University Press.

Schram, Stuart R. 1969. *The Political Thought of Mao Tse Tung*. New York: Frederick A. Praeger.

Scott, James C. 1985. *Weapons of the Weak: Everyday Forms of Peasant Resistance*. New Haven: Yale University Press.

———. 1990. *Domination and the Arts of Resistance*. New Haven: Yale University Press.

Selden, Mark. 1993. *The Political Economy of Chinese Socialism*. Armonk, N.Y.: M. E. Sharpe.

Sennett, Richard, and Jonathan Cobb. 1972. *The Hidden Injuries of Class*. London: Faber and Faber.

Shapiro, Michael, ed. 1984. *Language and Politics*. New York: New York University Press.

Shen, Tan. 2000. "The Relationship between Foreign Enterprises, Local Governments, and Women Migrant Workers in the Pearl River Delta." In *Rural Labor Flows in China*, ed. Loraine West and Zhao Yaohui. Berkeley: University of California Press.

Shenzhen Labor Bureau. 1991. *Shenzhen Tequ Laodong Zhidu Shinian Gaige Licheng* [Ten years of reform of the labor system in the Shenzhen SEZ]. Shenzhen: Haitian Press.

———. 1995a. "Announcement about Applying the Continued Employment of 1995 Temporary Labor, Service Labor Procedure." Shenzhen Labor Bureau, document no. 229.

———. 1995b. "Regulation of Labor Contract of Shenzhen Special Economic Zone." Shenzhen: Shenzhen Labor Bureau.

Shenzhen Statistical Yearbook. 1991–1996; 2001. Shenzhen: Shenzhen Statistical Bureau.

Sheridan, Mary, and Janet W. Salaff, eds. 1984. *Lives: Chinese Working Women*. Bloomington: Indiana University Press.

Shi, Songjiu. 1996. "Strengthen the Management of the Floating Population." *Chinese Sociology and Anthropology* 29.1: 26–52.

Shue, Vivienne. 1988. *The Reach of the State: Sketches of the Chinese Body Politics*. Stanford: Stanford University Press.

Shuttle, Penelope, and Peter Redgrove. 1978. *The Wise Wound: Eve's Curse and Everywoman*. London: Paladin Grafton Books.

Smart, Alan, and Josephine Smart. 1992. "Capitalist Production in a Socialist Society: The Transfer of Manufacturing from Hong Kong to China." In *Anthropology and the Global Factory*, ed. Frances Abrahamer Rothstein and Michael L Blim. New York: Bergin and Garvey.

Smart, Josephine. 1993. "Coercion, Consent, Reciprocity, and Exploitation: Labour Management in Hong Kong Enterprises in China." Paper presented at the Centre of Asian Studies, University of Hong Kong.

Smith, Chris, and Paul Thompson, eds. 1992. *Labour in Transition: The Labour Process in Eastern Europe and China*. London: Routledge.

Solinger, Dorothy J. 1991. *China's Transients and the State: A Form of Civil Society?* Hong Kong: Institute of Asia-Pacific Studies, Chinese University of Hong Kong.

——. 1993. *China's Transition from Socialism: Statist Legacies and Market Reforms, 1980–1990.* Armonk, N.Y.: M. E. Sharpe.

——. 1999. *Contesting Citizenship in Urban China.* Berkeley: University of California Press.

Spencer, Dale. 1980. *Man Made Language.* London: Routledge and Kegan Paul.

Spivak, Gayatri Chakravorty. 1988. "Can the Subaltern Speak?" In *Marxism and the Interpretation of Culture,* ed. Cary Nelson and Lawrence Grossberg. Urbana: University of Illinois Press.

Stacey, Judith. 1983. *Patriarchy and Socialist Revolution in China.* Berkeley: University of California Press.

Stockard, Janice E. 1989. *Daughters of the Canton Delta: Marriage Patterns and Economic Strategies in South China, 1860–1930.* Hong Kong: Hong Kong University Press.

Stichter, Sharon, Jane L. Parpart, ed. 1990. *Women, Employment and the Family in the International Division of Labor.* Philadelphia: Temple University Press.

Strathern, Marilyn. 1988. *The Gender of Gift: Problems with Women and Problems with Society in Melanesia.* Berkeley: University of California Press.

——. 1991. *Partial Connections.* Lanham, Md.: Rowman and Littlefield.

Study Group on Rural Migrant Female Workers, China Academy of Social Science. 2000. *Nongmin Liudong Yu Xing bie* [Rural mobility and gender]. Henan: Zhongyuen nongmin chubinshe.

Sun, Liping. 2001. "Guanyu Nongmingong Wenti De Jidian Jiben Kanfa" [Several basic viewpoints on rural migrant workers issues]. In *Nongmingong Yanjiu Xuanbian* [Selected work on rural migrant workers]. Qinghua: Qinghua daxue dangdai zhongguo yanjiu zhongxin.

Tam, S. M. Maria. 1992. "The Structuration of Chinese Modernization: Women Workers of Shekou Industrial Zone." Ph.D. diss., University of Hawaii.

Taussig, Michael. 1980. *The Devil and Commodity Fetishism in South America.* Chapel Hill: University of North Carolina Press.

Thompson, Edward P. 1963. *The Making of the English Working Class.* London: Penguin.

——. 1967. "Time, Work-Discipline, and Industrial Capitalism." *Past and Present* 38: 56–97.

Topley, Marjorie. 1975. "Marriage Resistance in Rural Kwantung." In *Women in Chinese Society,* ed. Margery Wolf and Roxane Witke. Stanford: Stanford University Press.

Touraine, Alain. 1987. *The Workers' Movement.* Cambridge: Cambridge University Press.

——. 1995. *Critique of Modernity.* Oxford: Blackwell.

Truong, Thanh-Dam. 1990. *Sex, Money, and Morality: Prostitution and Tourism in Southeast Asia.* London: Zed.

Vogel, Ezra F. 1989. *One Step Ahead in China: Guangdong under Reform.* Cambridge: Harvard University Press.

Walder, Andrew G. 1984. "The Remaking of the Chinese Working Class, 1949–1981." *Modern China* 10.1 (January).

———. 1986. *Communist Neo-Traditionalism: Work and Authority in Chinese Industry.* California: University of California Press.

———. 1989. "Factory and Manager in an Era of Reform." *China Quarterly* 118: 242–64.

Walker, Anne E. 1997. *The Menstrual Cycle.* London: Routledge.

Wang Shaoguang. 2000. "The Social and Political Implications of China's WTO Membership." *Journal of Contemporary China* 9.25: 373–405.

Wang Shaoguang, and Hu Angang. 1999. *The Political Economy of Uneven Development: The Case of China.* Armonk, N.Y.: M. E. Sharpe.

Ward, Kathryn, ed. 1990. *Women Workers and Global Restructuring.* Ithaca: Cornell University; ILR Press.

Water, Malcolm, ed. 2000. *Changing Workplace Relations in the Chinese Economy.* London: Macmillan.

Watson, Rubie S., and Patricia Buckley Ebrey, eds. 1991. *Marriage and Inequality in Chinese Society.* Berkeley: University of California Press.

West, Loraine A. and Zhao Yaohui, eds. 2000. *Rural Labor Flows in China.* Berkeley: Institute of East Asian Studies, University of California.

Westwood, Sallie. 1984. *All Day, Every Day: Factory and Family in the Making of Women's Lives.* London: Pluto.

White, Gordon. 1993. *Riding the Tiger: The Politics of Economic Reform in Post-Mao China.* London: Macmillan.

Willis, Paul. 1981. *Learning to Labor.* New York: Columbia University Press.

Wolf, Margery. 1972. *Women and the Family in Rural Taiwan.* Stanford: Stanford University Press.

———. 1985. *Revolution Postponed: Women in Contemporary China.* Stanford: Stanford University Press.

World Bank. 1992. *China: Strategies for Reducing Poverty in the 1990s.* Washington, D.C.: World Bank.

———. 1997. *Sharing Rising Incomes: Disparities in China.* Washington, D.C.: World Bank.

Wu, Harry Xiaoying. 1994. "Rural to Urban Migration in the People's Republic of China." *China Quarterly* 139 (September): 669–98.

Wu, Xianguo. 1996. "Yiwei dagongmei diaoqian deqiande beixiju" [The tragicomedy of the lost and found money of a working girl] *Women Monthly* 49 (April) 56–57.

Xu, Feng. 2000. *Women Migrant Workers in China's Economic Reform.* London: Macmillan.

Yan, Hairong. 2001. "Neo-Liberal Governmentality and Neo-Humanism: Organizing Suzhi/Value Flow through Labour Recruitment Networks." Paper presented at the annual meeting of the Association of Asian Studies, 21–25 March, Chicago.

Yan, Yunxiang. 1997. "McDonald's in Hong Kong: The Localization of America," in James L. Watson, ed. *Golden Arches East: MacDonald's in East Asia.* Stanford: Stanford University Press.

Yang, Mayfair Mei-hui. 1994. *Gifts, Favors, and Banquets: The Art of Social Relationships in China.* Ithaca: Cornell University Press.

——, ed. 1999. *Spaces of Their Own: Women's Public Sphere in Transnational China.* Minneapolis: University of Minnesota Press.

Zhang, Li. 2001a. "Contesting Crime, Order, and Migrant Spaces in Beijing." In *Ethnographies of the Urban in Contemporary China,* ed. Nancy Chen et al. Durham: Duke University Press.

——. 2001b. "Migration and Privatization of Space and Power in Late Socialist China." *American Ethnologist* 28.1: 179–205.

——. 2001c. *Strangers in the City: Reconfigurations of Space, Power, and Social Networks within China's Floating Population.* Stanford: Stanford University Press.

Zhang, Liwen, et al., eds. 1994. "Sex and Morality." *Chinese Sociology and Anthropology* 27.2 (winter): 37–56.

Zhang, Qingwu. 1988. "A Sketch of Our Country's Household Migration Policy." *Zhongguo Renkou Kexue* [Chinese population science] 2: 35–38.

Zhongguo nongcun jiating diaocha zu. [Research Group on Chinese Rural Families], ed. 1993. *Dangdai zhongguo nongcun jiating* [Contemporary Chinese rural families]. Beijing: Books of Social Science.

Zhongguo nüzhigong bu, ed. 1997. *Zhongguo nüzhigong zhuangkuang* [Chinese women workers' situation]. Beijing: Zhonguo gongre chubanshe.

Zhou, Daming. 1996. "Investigation and Analysis of 'Migrant Odd-Job Workers' in Guangzhou." *Chinese Sociology and Anthropology* 28.4: 75–94.

Zhou, Daming, and Zhang Yingqiang. 1996. "Rural Urbanization in Guangdong's Pearl River Delta." *Chinese Sociology and Anthropology* 28.2: 47–102.

Pun Ngai is an assistant professor of social science at
the Hong Kong University of Science and
Technology.

Library of Congress Cataloging-in-Publication Data
Pun Ngai
Made in China : women factory workers in a global
workplace / Pun Ngai.
p. cm.
Developed from the author's thesis (doctoral)—
University of London.
Includes bibliographical references and index.
ISBN 1-932643-18-4 (cloth : alk. paper)
ISBN 1-932643-00-1 (pbk. : alk. paper)
1. Women—Employment—China. 2. Women—
Economic conditions—China. 3. Factory system—
China. 4. Globalization—Economic aspects—China.
I. Title.
HD6200.P86 2005
331.4'87'0951—dc22
2004024769